THE AMERICAN JOURNEY

United States History Through
Letters and Diaries

THE AMERICAN JOURNEY

United States History Through Letters and Diaries

Volume II

Compiled and Edited by

Marsha C. Markman, Jonathan Boe
and Susan Corey

BRANDYWINE PRESS • St. James, New York

ISBN 1-881-089-95-9

1st Printing 1997

Telephone Orders: 1-800-345-1776

Printed in the United States of America

TABLE OF CONTENTS

Part 1
Post–Civil War America

Part 2
An Industrial Society in Peace and War

Part 3
Prosperity, Depression, and War

Part 4
Contemporary America

PREFACE

This book, along with its first volume companion, was inspired by the Freshman Cluster Program at California Lutheran University, which, in this instance, comprised team teaching of freshman English and American history. The reading of diaries and letters, alongside history texts, provided our students with two rarely studied literary genres, a broad historical and cultural perspective and an intimate view of history—one that enhances and enlivens its study.

Because diaries and letters are unique firsthand accounts, they transport the reader to a moment in history through an immediate, eyewitness record of events and reflections. Those moments, sometimes benchmarks in the American past, depict the unfolding of both human experience and the experience of a nation. There is no coloring of autobiography or shaky memories of oral history recorded long after the event.

Selections in this volume cover the period from the middle of the nineteenth century to contemporary times, painting a vivid picture of the United States: its wars (in combat and on the home front), industrialization, women's rights, immigration, technology, civil rights and recent times. They recount the expansion and modernization of the country and reveal a broad spectrum of issues that stretch across generations.

"There is properly no history; only biography," wrote Ralph Waldo Emerson. *The American Journey* rests on this idea. Its focus on diaries and letters provides observations, experiences, and sentiments of both prominent and obscure men and women. These witnesses to history forge a collective testimony to the country's evolution, its diverse and multicultural society, and even to issues disputed in America today.

EDITORIAL COMMENTS

We have endeavored to remain faithful to the diaries and letters excerpted here, in most cases adopting the editorial practices of our sources.

ACKNOWLEDGMENTS

The editors wish to acknowledge the William and Flora Hewlett Foundation for its grant support and California Lutheran University's Pearson Library for its invaluable assistance in obtaining materials for this publication.

Part 1

Post–Civil War America

In the aftermath of the Civil War, each section of the country faced its own problems and challenges. The North, whose cities and factories were untouched by the war, experienced a surge of urban growth. In 1860, two-and-a-half-million Americans lived in cities. By 1880, the figure was six million. Chicago was an extreme example of this pattern. In 1850 only 30,000 people lived there; by 1871 the city was home to 335,000, and was the fastest growing metropolis in the world.

Such rapid growth, combined with a political philosophy that discouraged government regulation, created serious problems, among them crime, disease, polluted water, and unhealthy and unsafe housing. Building codes, for example, usually allowed the cities to be built largely of wood. Fires therefore were a common threat to the lives and property of late nineteenth-century urban dwellers. Jonas Hutchinson's letters describe the most famous of these conflagrations, the Chicago fire of 1871.

Meanwhile, as the cities grew with a new wave of immigration, an earlier generation of immigrants wrestled with the problem of becoming American while trying to maintain cultural ties to their homeland. The letters of Jette Bruns provide an insight into this recurring dilemma.

Before the West could be settled and its resources exploited, the nation had to deal with the native American inhabitants of the land. This usually took the form of confining them to reservations, with war as the alternative if they resisted. The diary of Elizabeth Haas Canfield re-

1

counts her journey through Sioux country and her life in an army post from 1867 to 1868. By 1876 the fragile peace she portrayed had broken down, and John Bourke's diary describes the army's pursuit of the Sioux leader, Crazy Horse, during the summer of that year. A native American perspective is provided by a woman of Arizona's Yavapai tribe, who recalls the subjugation of her people in the late nineteenth century.

In the South, the postwar attempt to establish an equitable system of race relations ended when the North despaired of trying to enforce it. While slavery was gone, racism and discrimination remained and would soon be embodied in segregation laws. The diary of the African-American writer, Charles Chesnutt, tells of the discrimination he encountered in North Carolina in the 1870s and 1880s.

Women had not been included in the civil rights legislation of the Reconstruction Era. Deprived of the vote and of equal rights in general, they organized anew to achieve both. In letters to Susan B. Anthony, women discuss their lives and their hopes for social and political reform.

1.
Elizabeth Haas Canfield
Diary of an Officer's Wife, 1867–1868

In March, 1867, Elizabeth Haas Canfield began a two-month journey up the Missouri River to join her husband, an officer in the U.S. army stationed at Fort Berthold, Dakota Territory. Later that summer she accompanied him by boat to his new assignment at Camp Cooke in Montana Territory, where she stayed until the following summer.

Her diary describes the journey by riverboat into the western territories. It provides an account of the daily life of the officers' families as well as her impressions of the Sioux village near the fort. While Canfield describes the customs and practices of the Sioux in great detail, she also registers her fear at the increase in hostile attacks on the white intruders.

March 27th [*1867*]   The "Deer Lodge" came up today and I am on board and starting on my long journey. I occupy a stateroom with Lieut. Hogans wife. She is going to Ft. Shaw, Montana Territory, where her husband is stationed with a different Battalion of the same regiment to which Mr. Canfield belongs. . . .

/////

April 3rd   Had our first view of a Fort today, Ft. Randall [*west of Yankton, S.D.*] which seems to be on the edge of civilization. . . . The Fort itself is a rude affair. The buildings are placed around a square of ground

Diary of Elizabeth Haas Canfield, April 30,1866 to June 14, 1868. Typescript. Minnesota Historical Society. St. Paul, Minnesota.

called the Parade. One side is occupied by the officers. On each side are quarters for the soldiers and on the fourth side is the Hospital and buildings for clothing and Commissary stores. Outside of all this is a stockade of logs, squared and set very close together, with frequent small loop holes for musketry firing while at opposite corners is a square projection called a Bastion two stories high, the lower containing a swivel gun which could on occasion rake the sides of the fort. The upper room is the lookout where a soldier is stationed all day with a powerful field glass watching for Indians, for we are now in Indian country and they are very hostile. . . .

April 8th   Passed Ft. Pierre today, the country is getting wilder and the current swifter as we ascend the river.

April 13th   This is a worse country than I ever dreamed of. Nothing but hills of dry sand, with little streaks of shriveled grass in the hollows and on the river bottoms. We saw several larger droves of Antelopes today. I suppose several hundred in all, and just before night a large gray wolf came down to the river bank to see us pass. We saw three Indians yesterday but nothing like a human today. . . .

/////

April 25th   . . . Wild Indians are all around us. We do not often see them but we know they are near, for this morning about daylight as our boat was just starting from where it had been tied to the bank all night . . . the Pilot was shot at his post in the Pilot house. As he was shot with arrows no one knew it until he was found. . . .

May 10th   Saw a very imposing sight today. A large herd of Buffalo, several, probably eight or ten thousand, swam the river just ahead of the boat. The boat stopped until they had passed. One of the deck hands lassoed a half grown calf and we had fresh meat for dinner. It was very nice with a wild flavor.

/////

May 20th   . . . I left the boat and am at home with my dear husband. . . . There are two women here, one is our cook and the other is our laundress, both are soldiers wives. There is only one company of soldiers here.

May 22nd (Fort Berthold, Dakotah Territory, 1867)   I spent sometime in the lookout today. The location of the Fort on a bluff on the river bank is very fine. . . . The country is very rough but would be rather nice if there were more signs of civilization. What interests me most is the Indian village of about two thousand inhabitants. It is made up of the remnants of three tribes and they are supposed to be friendly having asked the protection of the soldiers.

Each tribe has its own chief. They are White Shield, Black Moon and Nehetah. There are a few white men there. French fur traders who have been a long time out here and have Indian wives. There is also a Catholic Priest here, Father De Smit, who has been with the Indians on the plains and in the mountains as a missionary for twenty-five years. . . . Looking down on the village there are no streets nor plans in its arrangement. Looks as if the tepees had been dropped from a height and landed anywhere they happened to. They are built by driving a row of poles in the ground in a circle, then drawing the tops almost together, leaving a small opening for the escape of smoke. Brush is piled over the poles, then covered with dirt, except in one place which is left open with a buffalo skin hung for a door. All the light is from the smoke hole in the center. The three remnants of tribes are Mandamus, Arickarees and Groventors (big bellies). [*Mandan, Arikara and Hidatsa, sometimes called Gros Ventres; all tribes of the Sioux.*]

May 23rd . . . We went out to see the way the Indians dispose of their dead. They sew or tie the bodies up in Buffalo skins and place them

In this Sioux encampment, from an engraving by Carl Bodmer, ca. 1834, a scaffold burial at the right and another at center background are plainly visible. *(Courtesy, National Archives)*

on a platform perhaps ten feet above the ground where they remain until the platform falls down, which in this dry climate is a long time, then the bones are left on the ground where they fall. The dead are thus disposed of because of the number of dogs and wild beasts. We saw a good number of men and boys amusing themselves in various ways, such as racing, horseracing and playing ball. But the women do not seem to have any amusements, we saw two of them preparing a buffalo robe for use. . . . The traders get them very cheap, often giving a string of beads or a bright colored handkerchief for a robe.

May 25th Went down to the river bottom to see the squaws planting corn. They had, with hoes and much labor, dug up a patch of ground and making a hole here and there, dropped in the corn, but instead of covering it with the hoe, the squaw stood over the hill and bent down and covered it with both hands. . . .

This Fort is built on the banks of the river and has bastions, stockade and in addition has outside of all a deep moat or ditch. It is dry but would make entrance more difficult in case of attack.

May 30th I was awakened last night by a great screeching, groaning and a series of, to me, distressing sounds, together with a great barking of dogs. My husband assured me I must not be alarmed. It is, he said, only a young warrior serenading or making love to his chosen one, the custom is for the young man to come late at night and tie some ponies in front of her tepee, then spend an hour or two on the roof reciting his own prowess as a warrior and praising the charms of his lady love. If the father of the girl thinks the number of ponies enough he takes them and thus signifies his approval. If not, the lover will the next night bring one more and continues to do so until the father is satisfied. . . .

June 3rd The three chiefs came in today to hold a "Pow Wow" with the officers. It was held in the mess room, with the officers interpreting and myself as guest. . . . Coffee was served, the Peace pipe was lighted and passed in perfect silence from one to another and then as solemnly passed back to the first one. Then the talk began. The interpreter acting for both Indians and officers. . . .

June 5th Today with my husband as guide I made a trip through the Indian village which consists of teepees which have been placed wherever the owner fancied without regard to streets or alleys. . . . We went into a tepee where a white man with his squaw and family of children lived.

There was a fire in the middle of the tepee under the smoke hole and around the edge were piles of skins, buffalo, deer, and bear and so on, which served as lounging places by day and beds at night. . . . This home contained not a single article of furniture so when they start out to hunt or dry berries for winter it will be very easy to pack their buffalo skin tepees, a few robes, a gun and kettle onto a rude conveyance made of two long poles fastened to their ponies. . . .

The women and children go with a hunting party. The men shoot the game and the women clean and cut the meat into strips and hang them on poles to dry then clean the skins. The women do all the work. . . .

/////

June 15th   A tribe of 100 Yankton Sioux came in to day to trade dried meat and skins for corn. The chief "Fooldog" paid the officers an official visit. He was wonderfully decorated for the occasion. . . .

/////

June 26th   My husband is ordered to Camp Cooke Montana Territory, so we are packing our trunks to be ready to go on the first boat going up stream.

/////

July 13th   We passed Fort Peck today. [*South of Glascow, Montana*] It is only a fur trading post but is strongly fortified. When the Indians "the Crows" come into trade the gates are closed and all business is conducted through a small opening in the wall which can be closed at a moments notice.

/////

Sept. 5th (at Fort Cooke, Montana Territory)   Some of the officers went hunting today. They gave us a quarter of venison. Yesterday we had a great excitement at the Fort, the Indians came down to with-in a quarter of a mile and drove off our beef cattle, and some horses, killing one man. A company of soldiers was sent after them but returned late at night empty handed, not being able to follow them through such rough country. . . .

/////

Oct. 1st   . . . Last night the drum beat an alarm. Our saw mill was destroyed by fire. We suspect the Indians. They came around the Fort and as they seem friendly a few are allowed to come inside. I think the Col. wants to impress them with the fact that we have men enough to make it uncomfortable for any force they might bring. One day as I sat working a pair of slippers with bright wool yarn, what seemed to be a cloud passed. I looked up to find two squaws with their faces against the window pane. I held it up for them to see. They laughed and chatted to each other.

/////

May 5th [*1868*]   We have had great excitement today. About 3 P.M. Indians in great numbers were seen coming over the hills south of the Fort. The alarm was sounded and soon every man [was] at his post at a loop hole. Our swivel gun in the bastian was manned. . . . The officers and ladies watched the coming of the Indians from the Sally-port. . . . We saw they were painted and mounted for war, having no women or children with them. They circled round three sides of the Fort (the river being the fourth). The commanding officer took ten men and rode out to parley but was met by a volley of arrows and returned in hot haste. As soon as they were inside, the Sally-port was closed. The Indians were so near that both Artillery and Infantry fire was opened on them which scattered them in short order. They made for the mountains rapidly as possible. We do not know their losses as each man is tied to his pony which will carry him away.

When we ladies saw what might happen, we . . . decided if the Fort could not be held that we preferred to be shot by our own officers rather than be taken captive. . . . But while it would have been done if necessary we are still spared to tell about the attack of the Fort by three thousand Indians. . . .

/////

May 25th   . . . I have packed our household goods and left them in our rooms and shall go to Iowa soon. We have not seen any Indians but the eternal vigilance seems to be the price of safety but it is hard on the nerves. Yet I shall come back next spring if Mr. Canfield [*her husband*] does not resign.

Questions for Discussion

1. What was the purpose of stationing U.S. soldiers in DakotaTerritory?
2. What various aspects of tribal culture are described in this diary? What led to the increase in hostile attacks by the Sioux? How would you compare Canfield's descriptions of the native Americans with John Bourke's account?
3. Although the Indian village of two thousand is near the Fort, Ms. Canfield remarks that the country "would be rather nice if there were more signs of civilization." How do you suppose she would define "civilization"? What assumptions does she make about the native people?

2.
Lieutenant John Bourke
Diary of the War Against the Sioux, 1876

The Sioux, or Lakota, were the most powerful tribe on the northern plains. In 1868 one of their leaders, Red Cloud, had signed a treaty that agreed to the establishment of a reservation extending from the Missouri River west to the Black Hills of South Dakota. Title to the land further to the west, the Powder River country of Wyoming, was left deliberately vague, though the Sioux were clearly allowed hunting rights there. Some of the Sioux, including those led by Crazy Horse and Sitting Bull, refused to be bound by the treaty and live on the reservation, remaining instead in the Powder River country.

The uneasy peace was disrupted by several developments— poor conditions on the reservation, the plan of the Northern Pacific Railroad to build a line through the Powder River country, and the discovery of gold in the Black Hills. Widely publicized by Colonel George Armstrong Custer, the finding of gold led to the invasion of the Black Hills by increasing numbers of white trespassers. The government first tried to buy the land from the Sioux. When that was unsuccessful, it turned to force.

All Sioux were told to return to the reservation by February 1, 1876, an order that would have been impossible to comply with even had the Sioux wished it. By March the problem was turned over to the army, and on June 25th Custer's 7th Cavalry met its famous defeat on the Little Big Horn.

United States Military Academy Library, West Point, New York.

Lieutenant John Bourke had enlisted in the army at the age of sixteen and had served in the Civil War. Later he attended West Point, graduating in 1869. Assigned to the 3rd Cavalry, he remained with that unit until his death in 1896, just short of his 50th birthday. As the diary excerpts begin in July, Bourke is with the 3rd Cavalry under General Crook well to the south of the Little Big Horn. The diary tells of the army's search for the Sioux, who had separated their forces after the battle with Custer and gone to their hunting grounds. Crook chases Crazy Horse east toward the Black Hills in an increasingly frustrating and difficult pursuit. Newspaper reporters and a photographer accompanied the soldiers. The photograph accompanying this selection was taken during the expedition.

July 2. . . . The grandeur of the scenery encountered on this day's march is worthy of portraiture by abler pens than mine, nor would I assume the task were we not the first Americans to penetrate to the arcana of its beauties. We first passed across one or two openings in the forest, of considerable area, and to all appearance suitable for the growth of the cereals. Then the canyon suddenly became very restricted in breadth and the pathway rugged. Our sturdy mules climbed over fallen timbers, slipped down granite boulders, threaded their way with firm steps across the swift rushing stream, which coursed down the bed of the canyon, or forced a path between dense pine, juniper and fir timber with almost impenetrable undergrowth. . . .

/////

July 9. Lieut. Sibley returned early this morning. Reported that between 12 and 1 o'clock on the 7th, while going through a ravine in the foothills, he was attacked by a party he estimated at from 300 to 400 strong. . . . The whole country was covered with them. None of our men were killed or wounded, but three horses and one mule were, the latter slightly. . . .

July 10. [*Couriers*] Louis Richaud and Ben Arnold came into our bivouac at daylight. They brought most important telegrams and correspondence from General Sheridan. . . . General Sheridan sent to General Crook an outline of the press accounts of the terrible disaster lately befallen Custer's command . . . news which made every lip quiver and every cheek blanch with terror and dismay. Grief, revenge, sorrow and fear stalked among us. . . .

/////

July 12. . . . The story was now assured; Custer had, with imprudent rashness, pushed ahead into the thickest of the enemy, seeking for a glory not to be eclipsed, or even shared by his superiors and comrades. His fate was most horrible, above all, when we regard the involution of others' lives in the same deadly conflict. . . .

July 13. . . . Snake (Shoshonee) Indians[1] devote every evening an hour or two of their time to running their horses through the evolutions incident to active skirmishing. They deck themselves out in feather war hats and all the paraphernalia of war, the general effect being very impressive and exciting. To see these wild Indians rush in mad career to the shock of battle, makes a soldier think how irresistible we should be in war, were we provided with a contingent of 10,000 cavalry. . . . We have much to learn from the savage in the matter of cavalry training: the trouble is, our prejudices of education are so deeply rooted, common sense and observation have no permission to assert themselves. . . .

/////

July 19. . . . The quantity of fish in these streams is something startling. A man this morning caught more than one hundred (trout) in a very brief space of time. . . .

/////

July 27. . . . I have spoken of the drilling of the troops: I must not forget that our Shoshonees were fully as attentive to drill as our own: Daily, under Washakie, and Tom Cosgrove, they formed in their camp and moved out in column of twos, going through all the evolution of a company of cavalry. . . . As they moved out in column of twos, riding their frisky war ponies, which had been plentifully bedaubed with mud and paint for the occasion, and their persons hideous in all the accessories of paint, war bonnets, jingling bells, and gleaming lances, these young Shoshonee warriors, chanting their battle song, were well calculated to chill the blood and blanche the cheek of Corporal Muldoon, who so lately had been tramping the bogs of his beloved Ballingford, or Private Switzerkase, whose mouth just watered for the beer of Bavaria.

/////

August 2. Night quite cold. We witnessed today, what, by a stretch of courtesy, was called a game of baseball, between the officers of the Infantry and Cavalry. Quite a number managed to hit the ball, and one or two catches were made. . . . I'll say no more about the game for the

---

[1]The Shoshone were serving as army scouts.

championship of the Expedition, except that the shades of night had closed around the contestants before the Infantry had made a run, so the umpires decided in favor of the Cavalry, who had made two or three. . . .

August 3. . . . William Cody, alias "Buffalo Bill," was in command of the (7) seven scouts attached to Merritt's column. Cody is a gentlemanly man, of pleasing address and quiet bearing. He is a good shot, fine rider and a fair scout. In the last mentioned capacity he plays a very insignificant part in association with our Indians: this is not said to his disparagement at all, because they know almost every foot of this vast country, to which he is a stranger. Cody has good pluck and is a hard worker. The most objectionable feature about him is his long hair—he wears it flowing down his shoulders in a very theatrical sort of way; to sum him up, he is one of the best frontiersmen we have. I give his good points as well as bad. . . .

/////

August 7. . . . On approaching the Rosebud [*a river in eastern Montana*], General Crook and his Hqrs. had again left the main column far in the rear; we had with us the scouts and the Shoshonee Indians, enough to keep off a large force of the enemy, but not enough to withstand such an assault as could have been made by the multitude of savages whose trail we discovered on the banks of the stream.

The trail was well beaten and as fully defined as any wagon road; the manure of the ponies was so dry that our Indians concluded that the hostiles must have left this vicinity about ten or twelve days ago.

/////

August 15. 22 miles to Powder River: latter part of march in "badlands," and in a miserable country, with no vegetation except cactus. . . . In this dismal region, the rattlesnake found a congenial abiding place. The head of the column scared a great many of them basking in the sun. The young Shoshonees had great fun lancing them to death. Surrounding some monstrous fellow, and keeping their agile ponies far enough away to avoid the reptile's spring, they would thrust at him with their sharp-pointed lances, until he was a writhing mass of ribbon, and, at the same time they would at each lunge, exclaim "Gott dammee you! Gott dammee you!," which was all the English they seemed to have mastered. . . .

/////

[On August 10, Generals Crook and Terry briefly joined forces before separating again on August 26th.]

August 22. . . . Drizzling showers all day. In General Terry's column, which I visited today, there has been prevalent an insane idea that the hostile Indians, under Crazy Horse and Sitting Bull, have crossed the Yellowstone near the mouth of Porcupine creek and then moved over the divide and down the stream called "Dry Fork of the Missouri." . . . Why should the Indians go across the Missouri? They are not retreating. The balance of success remains in their hands. . . . If the trail had turned north, we might have reason for assuming that they had some intention of crossing the Big Muddy, but it persistently keeps East, and, if anything, has a Southern tendency. There is only one thing certain about an Indian trail, as I remarked to a party of Terry's officers, and that is that you are at one end of it, and they at the other.

August 23. . . . This night we had a frightful tempest of thunder, lightning, wind and cold rain. . . . For its scenic effects, it would have been a fine study upon canvas; but a man, lying in three or four inches of rain-water, with the pitiless clouds pouring down a perfect Niagara of Water upon him and his half-dead comrades, is not much of an admirer of the fine arts.

August 26. . . . The whole expanse of country within sight has been burned off by the hostile Indians; this will oblige us either to lengthen, or shorten, our marches, dependent upon where and when each day we may discover pasturage for our animals. . . .

/////

August 29. . . . Moved today ten (10) miles to Beaver Creek. . . . The reason for our short march was that the trail began to split, showing that the hostiles knew we were in pursuit and were employing every artifice to bewilder us. . . .

/////

September 4. . . . The conviction is forcing itself upon our minds that we cannot avoid the alternative of starvation or killing and eating our mules and horses.

September 5. . . . There is a feeling of uncertainty—almost of awe—settling down upon us. We have great confidence in Crook, but cannot shake hold of a presentiment of dread as to the possible consequences of our bold plunge, without rations across an utterly unknown zone of such great width as that lying between us and the Black Hills. Frank Grouard says he knows nothing of the country, this side of the Little Missouri River. . . .

/////

September 8. . . . Horse meat had now become our stable food; as one of our mess pithily remarked, "The steaks we munch have a horse or a mule shoe at one end of them.". . .

September 9. . . . We met a courier, riding back from Capt. Mills, with the information he had captured a village of over (25) twenty-five lodges, with all the plunder contained, and some two hundred horses. Most of the Indians had escaped, and Mills was fearful they might return with reinforcements and sweep down upon him before General Crook could arrive with the main body. . . . A small party of the hostiles had taken refuge in a ravine near the village, and were hemmed in by our soldiers. . . .

A cavalry guidon of silk, nearly new, and torn from the staff, an overcoat once the property of an Army officer . . . were the links of circumstantial evidence upon which we rested the conclusion that the inmates of these tipis had assisted in the butchery of Custer and his gallant comrades, on the Little Big Horn, in June last. . . .

The next task was to dislodge those holding the little gulch, fifty or sixty yards outside the line of lodges. . . .

"Buffalo Chips" (White), a sort of guide and scout following the command, a poor, harmless, good-natured liar, who played the role of "Sancho Panza" to Buffalo Bill's "Don Quixote," was the first on our side to die, shot through the heart. His dying exclamation of "Oh Lord! Oh Lord! They've got me now boys!" was blood-curdling. . . .

I don't know how it happened, but Captain Munson and myself, found ourselves in the ravine on one side, while, similarly, Big Bat and another guide, Carey, occupied the other. Alongside, was a "pile"—the term is the only accurate one I know of—of squaws, and little papooses covered with dirt and blood and screaming in a perfect agony of terror. The oaths and yells of the surging soldiers, pressing in behind us, made the scene truly infernal. Just in front, three or four dead bodies lay stretched, weltering in their own gore. . . . So, when, in response to Bat's encouraging call of "Washte-helo" ("all right", or "very good"), the women and children came up to us. It did not take much time to get them out, following down the bends of the ravine to a place of safety, and in communication with General Crook, who came over to them and spoke pleasantly. . . . The women said their village was commanded by (2) two chiefs, "Roman Nose," and "American Horse," or "Iron Shield" the latter still in the ravine. General Crook bade one of them go back and say he would treat kindly all who surrendered; the squaw complied and went back to the edge of the ravine. There, holding a parley, as the result bringing back a young warrior, named "Charging Bear," after-

After the battle at the Little Big Horn in 1876: an Indian lodge with a flag from Colonel Custer's calvary. *(Courtesy, National Archives)*

wards a corporal in General Crook's Company of Indian scouts—about twenty years [*old*]. To him, General Crook repeated the assurances already given the squaws, and this time the young man went back, accompanied by Big Bat, whose presence, unarmed, convinced "American Horse" that General Crook's promises were not written in sand. The interest felt about this moment was almost painful in its intensity; for the first time, almost, in the history of American Indian warfare, hostile savages were about to lay down their arms on the open field. "American Horse," supported on one side by Big Bat, on the other, by one of his warriors, approached the little nucleus of officers clustered about General Crook. The reception accorded the captives was gentle, and the wounded ones made the recipients of necessary attentions. Out of this little nook (28) twenty-eight Sioux, little and great, dead and alive, were taken. The corpses were suffered to lie where they fell, a lesson in significance not lost upon their comrades. . . .

To fully analyze and discuss the situation was not at this moment granted us, for the sharp cracking of rifles and carbines roused to a new danger in the onslaught of Crazy Horse, who with a large band, was making upon our line of pickets. The Sioux, thinking that Mills was alone, and not believing General Crook was within striking distance, advanced, very determinedly to avenge their disaster and disgrace of the morning. . . .

> *[The attack led by Crazy Horse was driven off, and American Horse died of his wounds before morning. The minor victory by the United States Army described here was a sign of things to come for the Sioux. Crazy Horse's village was destroyed in 1877 and its leader captured and soon killed. Sitting Bull escaped to Canada but was forced to return in 1881. The Sioux Wars were over.]*

Questions for Discussion

1. What is Bourke's attitude toward the Sioux? What is his attitude toward the army's Indian allies?
2. How do Bourke's views of native Americans compare to those of Elizabeth Canfield?
3. How would you describe the nature of warfare on the plains?
4. What is important about the selection other than the military history?

3.
Jonas Hutchinson
Letters from the Chicago Fire, 1871

The Chicago fire of 1871 was the most famous of the fires that plagued American cities during the last decades of the nineteenth century. On the evening of October 8, the O'Leary cowbarn on the city's west side caught fire, and soon the conflagration was out of control. Between October 8 and 10 the fire devastated three-and-a-third square miles of the city. Three hundred people died and 90,000 were left homeless.

A common element in eyewitness accounts is the reference to the high winds that drove the fire. These winds were in fact convection whirls, generated by the fire itself, which helped carry the destruction throughout the city.

In the letters below, Jonas Hutchinson, a Chicago lawyer, describes the fire to his mother in New Hampshire.

Chicago, Oct. 9

Dear Mother,

This has been an eventful day. Last night about 9 1/2 o'clock a fire broke out here & from that time to this it has raged fearfully. *We are in ruins.* All the business portion of the city has fallen a prey to the fiery fiend. Our magnificent streets for acres & acres lined with elegant structures are a heap of sightless rubbish. It cannot be described. One needs to see the wreck to appreciate it & then he cannot believe that

---

Jonas Hutchinson, Letters, The Chicago Historical Society.

such havoc could be wrought in so short a time. Had you been with me all night & all day seeing this hell of fire doing its awful mission then you could realize how these ruins came. What a sight: a sea of fire, the heavens all ablaze, the air filled with burning embers, the wind blowing fiercely & tossing fire brands in all directions, thousands upon thousands of people rushing frantically about, burned out of shelter, without food, the rich of yesterday poor today, destruction everywhere—is it not awful? It makes me sick. One could but exclaim: "My God, when will it end!"

The end is not yet. Terribly is the fire now burning, though 'tis five miles from where I write so I am in no danger, though our family dare not go to bed. They are camped on the floor. 'Tis midnight and I am keeping watch. Everything is gone—all our public buildings & massive blocks, all the hotels except one & that a minor one, the courthouse & records, post office & United States courthouse—all, all are gone. This is too true. I wish it were other[*wise*].

The fire extended over acres of ground & it left nothing intact. Our banks are all included in this heartrending catastrophe. I had a few hundred dollars in the Merchants & this is lost. I am discouraged & what to do I know not. My office burned about three o'clock this morning. I barely got out a few papers & just escaped with my life. I had to run for dear life. $5000 worth of books besides furniture fed the flames & as I went out, not to enter again, leaving all that valuable stuff to be devoured, I could but cry. Mr. Roberts, whose library & building this was, & who is my dearest friend here, & with whom I am connected in business, loses all & is tonight a sad poor man. I had many things in the office. They all went—I saved nothing. Mrs. Thomas with [*whom*] I board loses nearly everything. Our house tonight is like the house of death.

The whole city is in grief. Insurance companies can pay nothing.[1] Two Blocks that I had charge of as to renting & collecting rents & for which I received $500 yearly are among the things of the past. My office is gone. I am stripped and you may conclude that I am about vanquished. I cannot see any way to get along here. Thirty years of prosperity cannot restore us. It looks as though I must leave here & what to do I know not—possibly I may come home. All newspaper offices are destroyed. When we get papers I'll send them. I am going to try & sleep a little if possible now.

Thy boy,
Jonas.

---

[1]Insurance companies did pay about 50% of the covered amount.

Randolph Street after the fire. *(Courtesy, National Archives)*

Ed Lovejoy was in for it too. This morning I was strolling along the street & someone caught hold of me. I looked [*and*] I saw Ed sitting on a couple of drawers filled with pictures. "Well," said I, "Ed, you are gone up, too." "Yes," says he, "this is all that's left." The jail doors were thrown open & the prisoners rushed into the streets & took to their heels. The jail was under the courthouse which burnt. Probably many lives were lost yet I can learn nothing definite as yet.

Jonas.

P.S. We have no gas or water. We have to bail water from [*the*] lake & use candles. Bridges burnt.

Chicago, Oct. 10, '71
     Midnight

Dear Mother,
     Last night I wrote you. Tonight I am sitting up and I must tell you more about our great calamity. Ere this reaches you the telegraph & my former letter will give you a faint idea of this sad affliction. Nothing that may come to you can overstate the facts. Two hundred millions of property has been destroyed, 300 acres have been swept by the besom

of destruction.[2] 100,000 people are homeless and the greater portion of them paupers. Only one house stands in the entire North Division and one also in the South Division.

As far as the fire reached the city is thronged with desperadoes who are plundering & trying to set new fires. The police are vigilant. Thousands of special police are on duty. Every block has its patrolmen and instructions are explicit to each officer to shoot any man who acts suspicious and will not answer when spoken [to] the second time. Several were shot & others hung to lamp posts last night under these instructions. The origin of the fire is not known. 40 poor people perished on the prairie last night. Schoolhouses & churches are used to house the destitute. 50 carloads of cooked provisions are on the road from St. Louis & the same from Cincinnati. Genl. Sherman[3] I am informed is here with 5000 troops to protect the citizens. The roughs are improving the time to sack & pillage. The city is in darkness, no gas. 50,000 army tents are being pitched to house the poor.

The like of this sight since Sodom & Gomorrha has never met human vision. No pen can tell what a ruin this is. Frank Peabody, Mark Knowlton, Ed Lovejoy, George Lovejoy, Wright's Stable, Dave Bradley (Lizzie's husband), Willard Bacon, Charlie Briles, Charlie Towne—all of these are known to some of the family, and all burned out. Imagine all of Boston, its business blocks all in ruin & 100,000 of its people homeless, and you will then get an idea of our condition. The railroads are carrying free such of the poor as will go into the country.

The fire extended 5 miles north & south and 2/3 of the way east & west & mind you, it missed nothing in its march. No buildings stand half-demolished & nearly every brick & stone wall has tumbled to the ground. The courthouse & post office walls mostly stand though entirely gutted. Here & there a tall jagged piece of wall limps its form above the chaotic mass of brick & stone. These ghastly obelisks are the only signboards to tell the stroller among the ruins where he is. In groping among the ruins one has to ask where such a street *was* in order to get his bearings. The debris is still smouldering. You can't see far so 'tis easy to get astray. I don't know what I shall do.

Jonas

[Despite Jonas Hutchinson's belief that "thirty years of prosperity cannot restore us," by 1875 few traces of the fire were to be

---

[2]The correct figure was about 2,100 acres.
[3]In fact, it was General Phil Sheridan.

found, and Chicago's rapid growth had resumed. By 1890 the population of the city would approach one million inhabitants.]

Questions for Discussion

1. What were the effects of the fire on the people of Chicago? How did they react?
2. What does the reading tell you about life in nineteenth-century cities?

4.
Charles W. Chesnutt

Journals of an African-American Writer and Teacher, 1877–1882

Author of such works as The Conjure Woman *and* The Marrow of Tradition, *Charles Chesnutt was a major figure in African-American writing in the late nineteenth and early twentieth centuries. Born in Ohio in 1858, he moved with his family to Fayetteville, North Carolina (their original home), after the Civil War, where he remained through the years covered by the journals. Chesnutt was a prize graduate of the Howard School, a free public grade school for blacks and, at age sixteen, became an assistant teacher at the Peabody School in Charlotte, teaching in country schools during the summers. He kept journals from 1874 to 1882, between his sixteenth and twenty-fourth years, while he was teaching elementary school and later while serving as principal of the State Colored Normal School. These years also marked the onset of the Jim Crow era, a period of systematic segregation of African Americans in the South after Reconstruction. The following excerpts depict the local social conditions that often frustrated the aspirations of this talented black man.*

Charles W. Chesnutt, "Second Journal" and "Third Journal," *The Journals of Charles W. Chesnutt*. Richard H. Brodhead, ed. Durham, NC: Duke University Press, pp. 134–72. Copyright 1993. Reprinted with permission.

Charles W. Chesnutt.
(Courtesy, National Archives)

March 30th [*1880*] . . . A few days ago, I was talking to Mr. Haigh [*the Fayetteville bookseller*] about Mr. Harris's[1] health. The conversation then turned on his family; and finally on the colored families who left Fayetteville before the war—in the fifties.

"Those," said he, "were our best colored people. It was a loss to the town when they left."

"Yes, but they couldn't live here. Things were getting too warm for them. You had taken away their suffrage; the laws were becoming more and more severe toward free colored people; and they felt that their only safety lay in emigration to a freer clime. They didn't know how soon they themselves would be made slaves. They had been deprived of every safe-guard of liberty. If one were smitten in the face by a cowardly ruffian, he could not retaliate. He could be swindled of his property, defrauded of his earnings, and could not testify in court of law to the justice of his cause. With such a gloomy prospect is it strange that he

---

[1]Robert Harris, a Fayetteville-born free black, had been Chesnutt's teacher at Fayetteville's Howard School.

should leave? As for my part I can't see how intelligent colored people can live in the South even now."—

And I went on to state my reasons why;—the existing prejudice—the impossibility of a rise in the social scale, etc.

Mr. H[*aigh*] thought that these grades of society were the best preservatives of society. . . . For he said, he thought that this fretting about one's condition was fighting against God—God placed men as they are. . . . He spoke with dread of the state of affairs if the social barriers were broken down. I replied that society even in this case, would regulate itself. . . . I argued that the ignorant do not feel at home among the intelligent, and would therefore shun their company, as they do already. But he said things "never, never, never would be changed," and that the only way for a man who doesn't like it to do, is to go away where things are different. . . .

/////

May 29, 1880 . . . I think I must write a book. I am almost afraid to undertake a book so early and with so little experience in composition. But it has been my cherished dream, and I feel an influence that I cannot resist calling me to the task. . . . If I do write, I shall write for a purpose, a high, holy purpose, and this will inspire me to greater effort. The object of my writings would be not so much the elevation of colored people as the elevation of the whites,—for I consider the unjust spirit of caste which is so insidious as to pervade a whole nation, and so powerful as to subject a whole race and all connected with it to scorn and social ostracism—I consider this a barrier to the moral progress of the American people; and I would be one of the first to head a determined, organized crusade against it. Not a fierce indiscriminate onslaught; but a moral revolution which must be brought about in a different manner. . . . The iron hand of power set the slave free from personal bondage, and by admitting him to all the rights of citizenship—the ballot, education—is fast freeing him from the greater bondage of ignorance. But the subtle almost indefinable feeling of repulsion toward the negro, which is common to most Americans—and easily enough accounted for—, cannot be stormed and taken by assault; the garrison will not capitulate; so their position must be mined, and we will find ourselves in their midst before they think it.

This work is of a twofold character. The negro's part is to prepare himself for social recognition and equality; and it is the province of literature to open the way for him to get it—to accustom the public mind to the idea. . . .

June 25th . . . I must take my Journal for my confidant and write in it things that I cannot well tell to other people. . . . Mr. Neufeld [*a* *recent German immigrant*] told me yesterday that after I had spoken to him a few days ago, Mr. Kyle [*mayor of Fayetteville*] . . . asked him if he intended to give me instruction [*in German*]. Mr. N. answe[re]d that he did not know, and Mr. K advised him not, lest he should lose some of his pupils. Dr. Haigh . . . took up the cudgels in my defence, and thought the Professor ought to take me if he could. Mr. Harris told me yesterday, that Dr. Haigh[2] mentioned my case to him a few days ago, and said he could sympathize with me. . . . He recognized my ability and accomplishments, and felt that my lot was a hard one, to be cut off from all intercourse with cultivated society, and from almost every source of improvement. . . .

June 28. Professor Neufeld has consented to give me instruction in French and German—three lessons a week. . . .

/////

Jan 21st. 1881. I had a conversation with Robert Hill last night, about Southern affairs. He is a very intelligent man, uses good English, and understands what he talks about. He was once a slave, and was badly treated. . . .

He related a conversation he had with Jno. McLaughlin—a poor white man, and a clerk in Williams's store.

"Bob," said McLaughlin, "what kind of fellow is this Chesnutt[?"]

"Well, sir, he's a . . . perfect gentleman in every respect; I don't know his superior."

"Why! he's a nigger, ain't he?"

"He's classed with the colored people, but—['"]

"Well, what kind of an education has he?"

"He's not a college bred man, but he has been a hard student all his life. You can't ask him a question he cannot answer."

"He's this short-hand writer," musingly.

"Yes, sir."

"Does he think he's as good as a white man[?]"

"Every bit of it, sir.". . .

Hill then went on to argue about the equality of intelligence and so on, but McL. wound up with this declaration, which embodies the opinion of the South on the "Negro Question."

"Well, he's a nigger; and with me a nigger is a nigger, and nothing in the world can make him anything else but a nigger." Which reminds me of the sentiment expressed by an old poor white beggar, who was at

---

[2]Dr. T. H. Haigh was a white physician who was Chesnutt's family doctor and chairman of the Board of Managers of the State Colored Normal School when Chesnutt was principal.

the time eating scraps in a colored man's kitchen[.] "Well, for his part, let other people think as they please, he always did like niggers as long as they kept in their place, and he wasn't ashamed to say so either." . . .

/////

May 4, 1881. —*Wednesday Night.* . . . Several things have happened lately which lead me to think that the colored man [*is*] moving upward very fast. The Prohibition movement has the effect of partly breaking down the color line, and will bring the white and colored people nearer together, to their mutual benefit. Some of the white teachers in the Graded School came down to visit our school a few weeks ago, and one of them gave us quite a puff in the "Examiner.". . .

The "Colored Presbytery of Yadkin" have been in session here for nearly a week. I invited them down to visit our school, and yesterday they made a *"reconnaissance* in force," and seemed to be very well pleased. . . . A more intelligent body of colored men have never met in our town before.

I have received a sample copy of "Rumor[,]"[3] a New York paper. . . . It echoes the popular clamor against the Garfield Administration for its scanty recognition of the claims of the colored office-seekers. *Tempora mutantur* [*"times change"*]! If the Democrats adopt an equally fair . . . platform, and bid higher for our support, why shouldn't they get it? I'm a Republican on principle, but if the nigger is one-fourth of the party he ought to have one-tenth of the offices. . . .[4]

/////

Thursday, Aug 4, 81. Election day. The question of Prohibition or free whiskey will be decided to-day. We had a large and enthusiastic Prohibition meeting at the Market House last night. The antis had their row at Liberty Point. I made a rather poor speech; Scurlock and Slocumb very good ones. Our campaign has brought out a number of quiet men to the front. . . .

/////

---

[3]*The Rumor,* first published in 1880, identified itself as "A Representative Colored American Paper."
[4]Black support for the Republican Party became somewhat unsettled after 1876, when Republican administrations began to court Democrats' votes in the reenfranchised South. The issue of federal appointments was a major subject of black political complaint.

March 7, [18]82.   . . . I hear colored men speak of their "white friends". I have no white friends. I could not degrade the sacred name of "Friendship" by associating it with any man who feels himself too good to sit at table with me, or to sleep at the same hotel. True friendship can only exist between men who have something in common, between equals in something, if not in everything; and where there is respect as well as admiration. I hope yet to have a friend. If not in this world, then in some distant future eon, when men are emancipated from the grossness of the flesh, and mind can seek out mind; then shall I find some kindred spirit, who will sympathize with all that is purest and best in mine, and we will cement a friendship that shall endure throughout the ages.

I get more and more tired of the South. I pine for civilization, and "equality." I sometimes hesitate about deciding to go [*north*], because I am engaged in a good work, and have been doing, I fondly hope, some little good. But many reasons urge me the other way; and I think I could serve my race better in some more congenial occupation. And I shudder to think of exposing my children to the social and intellectual proscription to which I have been a victim. . . .

Questions for Discussion

1. What conditions led so many African Americans to leave the South after the Civil War? What does Chesnutt think about the South during this period?
2. What were some forms of racial discrimination that Chesnutt experienced? Why do you think Mr. Kyle advised Mr. Neufeld *not* to give German instruction to Chesnutt?
3. How does Chesnutt see himself in his social world? How does he assess race relations in the South in the 1880s? How representative of his contemporaries is Chesnutt, given that in 1880 the rate for black illiteracy in North Carolina stood at 75 percent?

5.
Henriette (Jette) Geisberg Bruns
Letters of a German Immigrant Woman, 1868–1894

Henriette (Jette) Geisberg was born in 1813 in Oelde, West-phalia, Germany, to a large, close-knit Catholic family devoted to reading and music. At age eighteen she married Dr. Bernhard Bruns, a physician, and, in 1836, emigrated with him and their first child to the settlement of Westphalia in Missouri. Between 1827 and her death in 1899, Jette wrote over 270 letters to her family in Germany, primarily to her brother, Heinrich, detailing her daily experiences in America. The following excerpts are from her later years after her four surviving children were grown (she lost seven children in America). Left with many debts after the death of her husband in 1864, she made ends meet by running a boarding house and renting rooms to German legislators. Her letters reveal concern that her American-born children and grandchildren thrive and continue to maintain ties to their German heritage. They also reveal a woman who, despite her courage and strong character, experienced deep feelings of loss related to her emigration.

Reprinted from *Hold Dear, As Always: Jette, A German Immigrant Life in Letters*. Edited by Adolf E. Schroeder and Carl Schulz-Geisberg, by permission of the University of Missouri Press and Carla Schulz-Geisberg. Copyright © 1988 by the Curators of the University of Missouri.

St. Louis
29 November 1868

Dear Heinrich:

. . . Certainly, since Bruns [*Jette's husband*] is dead, I cannot attain much pleasure from life, and therefore I try to find pleasure in the well-being of my children, and this gives me great satisfaction. If only all grow up decently. It seems to me I will have to keep them together there and must not continue to think that I should be back [*in Germany*] united with you. I have constantly longed for you during all these long years. How grateful I was and am still to my dear husband that he took me back to my home country [*in 1856*]. That satisfied me as far as could be expected. My children must not have to endure this. With the quick and easy travel conditions now I wish we were rich so that the distance did not matter. . . .

Well, let us seek to spend our lives in some good manner! Let the children look for a decent position in the world, and then my task will be finished. . . . As always with love, your sister, Jette.

P.S. Our nephew is not doing so well with his German, although he speaks it here constantly. Therefore for the time being I send in his behalf his grateful acknowledgment. . . .[1]

Jefferson City
6 February 1879

Dear Auguste:

. . . My daughters had insisted that Mother would have to spend the holidays with them for a change, and so I obediently packed my *Lebkuchen* and *Pfeffernüsse* [*traditional German Christmas cookies*] and departed in spite of snow and ice. . . . Christmas evening was peaceful and enjoyable for all. The young people were happy and enjoyed themselves while they were feasting, talking, and trying the new games until late into the night. One thing struck me: Decker's [*late husband of daughter, Effie*] sister's daughter and our grandchild, both Jennies, decorated the tree and put the presents in order—so there we are, another generation. . . .

At present the legislature is in session again, and therefore there are many strangers here. . . . The lieutenant governor is a German, Brock-

---

[1]Although the generation of the Bruns family born in America spoke German in their homes, they did not write the language easily, even though most of them had German instruction.

meyer, and in addition a fellow countryman, from near Minden [*Prussia*]. We have known him a long time. . . .

Farewell, dear Auguste, kiss your children and Heinrich for me, and you will have to tell them about me, just as I tell my children about you. Hold dear, as always, your Jette. . . .

Jefferson City
11 November 1879

Dear Heinrich:

. . . Now we are not very far from the Christmas holidays and the end of the year. I wish you good fortune from the bottom of my heart for both holidays. . . . The younger generation enjoys what is given to them. Effie [*Jette's widowed daughter*] particularly was haunted early in life by hard blows of fate. I probably reported earlier that since her youngest one was in school she had accepted a teaching position. Even though no great income, this was still something constant and always a little contribution to the household, although it did result in a great deal of work and commotion for her before and after school. Now, however, they are contemplating abolishing the German language in the public schools in St. Louis,[2] and the German teachers were dismissed, Effie among them. Now she studies for the English exam. . . . Tillie [*daughter, Ottilie*], in addition to her work, still has three classes in German, which she took over for Effie so that her sister would have more free time for studying. . . .

And now I have written a lot. How many things we could talk about if one could delve more into detail with daily things! Writing is getting difficult for me because I am living in foreign circles. But gradually the family circle is enlarged. . . .

Jefferson City
28 May 1881

Dear Auguste:

For several months I had been impatiently waiting and worrying about a letter from home. . . . Everything is interesting to me, and

---

[2]German language instruction was introduced in the St. Louis public schools in September 1864 as an "experiment," and during the next decade spread through nearly the entire system, reaching forty-seven percent of the elementary school enrollment. In 1878 strong objections, particularly from the Irish, threatened the continuance of German instruction, and a petition to add Gaelic to the curriculum was presented. The German community countered with a petition signed by forty thousand people, and the school board upheld the established system.

sorrow and joy probably touch me more than if I were back in the hometown. . . .·

For a few weeks we have had new help, a girl fresh from Silesia, who now has some very serious difficulties. She is, however, good-natured, clean, and a good learner. And so it is only a matter of patience. We are now all obliged to speak high German. Otherwise it is unfortunately mixed a lot, especially with the young people, who speak English among themselves. . . .

[In March 1882 Jette and daughter Tillie traveled to Germany where they stayed in Münster through September.]

Münster
21 April 1882

Dear Wilhelm: [*Jette's son, Wilhelm Bruns*]

. . . People are living together in such crowded conditions, but they are comfortably situated. They do not have as much and as fine fresh air as we have. I also see many people who are much poorer or who are doing rough work, and they are, of course, clothed much more poorly and wear wooden shoes and work much harder. . . . We in America have to work much harder and don't have as much free time by any means. All in all, everything has become quite foreign to me here. . . .

Jefferson City
12 December 1882

Dear Heinrich:

. . . I miss you so often. . . . This last trip [*to Germany*] affects me much more seriously than the first visit with my husband. Here I alone am the older one, while with you that was different. It is a harsh homesickness, which I have to fight against. I wonder whether I can regain a joy for living on [*Jette is now sixty-nine years old*]. . . . In political affairs there are all kinds of confused things. Our state is going highly Democratic. And then this temperance[3] business. . . .

Jefferson City
12 May 1883

Dear Auguste:

. . . The clover is over a foot high, so the thought very easily occurs that if one goes through it, one might step on some kind of snake, which

---

[3]German-Americans were generally opposed to temperance efforts, which jeopardized businesses and traditional social practices.

would be hurt and could bite. After all, all around us is still a wilderness where such animals could flee and not be disturbed by anything. . . .

[*Jefferson City*]
21 March 1887

. . . In St. Louis the Sunday Law will be enacted. This will result in some rebellion! Here we have become accustomed to this for years. For the time being the sale of drinks is still permitted, although the restaurants will have to pay very high taxes. However, there is a great deal of temperance education, and it could happen that no beer or wine may be had. Curious. . . .

[In 1891 Jette traveled to visit her sons Louis and Wilhelm who had settled in Washington State.]

Seattle
c. 1891

Dear Auguste:

Here is the view of the city where Louis lives with his family. He would not take it very kindly if he knew that part of his letter goes along, especially since he is very weak in German; but in spite of that, he keeps it up just for me. He always threatens that he will study it more and then will instruct his wife in the language. But he has made derisive remarks concerning her style several times, so that Emily will write only in English. . . .

Jefferson City
20 September 1891

Dear Heinrich:

. . . If I were twenty years younger, I would not have objected to staying in Seattle. The youthful, strong striving, the healthy breeze of the sea air, all appealed to me very much. . . . To be sure, thousands of building lots are for sale. The Japanese are very well suited for clearing the land, and they ask forty dollars per acre. In the city the Swedes keep the prices down. . . . The operation of the mines is in full swing again, and the big harvest of hops has begun. For this purpose hundreds of Indians with canoes came to work. . . . A few work in the big sawmill at Port Blakely. There are still more Chinese, some Swedes, as well as Americans. The latter, however, have a higher status. . . . Seattle also now has a German daily newspaper, which Louis sends me so that I can keep up with the local news. . . .

Jefferson City
1 September 1894

Dear Heinrich:

I received your letter of August, and at this time I shall reply to your remark concerning the "American Protection Association."[4] To be sure, a secret alliance against foreigners and particularly the Catholics exists here. I read about that in the *Forum*, an excellent journal by an absolutely neutral author who responded to the appeal of Catholic priests. He says that the above-mentioned association developed first in Clinton, Iowa, and is supposed to have a membership of two million members, and it could become serious, although right-thinking Protestants are unanimously against it. . . .

In general to this day the majority of immigrants have not left their home without some stain, and it is not amazing that we, the older immigrants, feel the same as the Americans and consider new immigrants with some distrust. It is also a great misfortune that so many families who do not at all belong there remain hung up in the cities instead of pursuing their former professions as farmers. And here they could easily obtain property in a rich, wholesome area. . . .

Questions for Discussion

1. What aspects of German cultural identity have been maintained in Jette Bruns' Missouri community? Are there signs that these ties to traditional culture may be loosening in the second generation? What role does language preservation seem to play in Jette's sense of identity?

2. Where do you find signs of Jette Bruns' ambivalence about life in America, or her identity as an American? For example, what does she mean by the comment that she is still living "in foreign circles," or by referring to her surroundings as "wilderness"?

3. What do these letters suggest about the emotional cost of immigration for first-generation adult immigrants who maintained strong ties with their homeland?

---

[4]The American Protection Association was founded at Clinton, Iowa, in 1887 by Henry F. Bowers for the purpose of reviving the Know-Nothing Party's campaign against what was perceived as the increasing power of Roman Catholicism in schools and other public institutions. Its growth increased with the panic of 1893, causing native-born Americans to fear economic rivalry from immigrants and their American-born children. By 1896 the organization claimed over two-and-a-half million members.

6.
A Yavapai Woman

Massacre and Forced Acculturation of American Indians of the Southwest, 1860s–1902

Because of the oral traditions of American Indians, written diaries and letters are not a prominent part of their heritage. Autobiography, however, is a highly developed genre within the oral tradition. An oral history, such as this one, provides a record as close as possible to the immediate experience. The following account by an eighty-five-year-old woman of the Yavapai tribe was recorded as part of the Doris Duke Native American Oral History Project. It is remarkable in that the woman was able to retell, in great detail, experiences from long before her birth, handed down by her father and mother. Her facility attests to the value of oral story-telling in her tribal tradition.

The Yavapai people were a peaceful, isolated, hunter-gathering tribe of some 2,000 members, whose way of life was destroyed as the army and mining interests moved into northern Arizona in the 1860s. This woman's story records the painful displacements she and her people experienced during the set-tling of the American West. By 1870, over half of the Yavapai

The Arizona State Museum, University of Arizona, Tucson.

had been killed; the remaining tribal members were placed on the San Carlos Reservation. The following excerpts, recorded in 1967, describe the massacres of the 1860s, the surrender of Geronimo, and experiences with the Indian school.

Massacre

There was an Indian reservation, a place called San Carlos, and there's where I was then, when I was young. I was born over there, too. Just across the lake. They call it Coolidge Dam now. They were not always there, my tribe. They had the central part of Arizona for their territory. . . . They were under the Spaniards then, but when the United States bought it then, of course, we come in with the United States people. They didn't want to have us live in this state owning the central part of Arizona, so he sent U.S. soldiers. . . .

The western Yavapai, the northern Yavapai, the southern southernest Yavapai, there were three divisions, dialect languages, although it's the same language, well, they started with the western. They promised us they are going to issue them food, clothing, and about maybe two or three in the afternoon, they did give them out some unbleached muslin, and some flour and beans, and then they start shooting at them. And my daddy was a young boy then. He said he run around this way in the bushes, and went way around, and he hid back of the soldiers' camp, and he stayed there. Just before they stopped, he went in and began to chop wood with a soldier's axe, you know. . . . He was chopping wood, and the people were west of the soldiers' camp, so . . . he said that he saw with his own eyes that his mother was killed and his aunt, his mother's sister. They were both killed. That's when he run around. Around, way around, and children, men and women, just everywhere, he said. And then, they moved on to a next place. . . . After they killed many of the western Yavapai, they almost wiped them out, just piled high, so they call it today, Skull Valley. . . . They had no mercy, they act like they're not human beings, and so they just slaughtered them, and it was piled so high, they had to call it, no shame, nothing, no . . . no feeling sorrow, they call it Skull Valley, and it's Skull Valley today. . . . And then they move on to Camp Verde, and the storm was mad. It just rain sleet of ice across the air, and everybody got sick, even the soldiers, and the Indians, of course, didn't have much clothing on. And they tried to get the northern Yavapai, they can't get them because too many woods, you know, cedar trees, just thick, and of course, that grows right close to the ground, and they hide under that, you know, but they heard that they were coming . . . anyhow, they got some, and they slaughtered the cattle. . . . The wind stop them. Looked like it was mad, too, but it stopped in time for them to get dry up a little bit, and then it began to be spring. . . . The Indians said that's what they needed, the sunshine, so they got all right, and that was in '72. Eighteen-seventy-two. . . .

Surrender of Geronimo

They got a little bit stronger, and they said, we are to move them over to San Carlos. That's where Coolidge Dam is now. To meet with Geronimo,[1] other soldiers were there, they're getting him, but they couldn't get him, he's fighting furiously, and they couldn't get him. But anyhow, they took these Yavapais over there. They tried to get the southernest Yavapai . . . but southern Yavapais said, they're not going to take us and starve us to death. We're just going to kill ourselves, so there's a ravine, come from the north, very deep, at Superior mine . . . and so they went over there with their children, and they just drop in themselves and died there, many of them just kill themselves. They said, they're not going to starve us to death, so many of them have thrown themselves in that deep creek, they said, canyon, and died. So they just weeped and weeped. . . . And then they went back to San Carlos, and they told the officers what happened. . . .

And then they turn around and, the soldiers said, we can't get Geronimo, you got to help us, so they ask these Yavapai men. . . . So they joined them. And just in a few days, U.S. from Washington said, we want them to surrender, instead of killing them anymore. They heard that they killed most of the Indians, and they don't want to kill them anymore. . . . So the first battle . . . it happened that they took one of our young men and taught him their language, and he was speaking fluently of Geronimo's language, and so they ask him to interpret what the white man says to them. That they must surrender. . . . You can't run away, he said. We have soldiers on the north of you. We have soldiers on the west, and on the south, and right here on the east. You cannot get away, not one of you. So this Yavapai, learned the Apache language, told it. There was a nice little hill, they say. . . . Little hill and kind of flat and one tree on it, and he climb up there and stood up there and told them what this high officer said, that a word from Washington, the great father, what he has said to them. . . . He said, yes, you are all about wiped

---

[1]Geronimo was chief of the southern Chiricahua band of Apache Indians. In 1876, when the U.S. government put the Apaches on the White Mountain reservation in Arizona, he led his followers into Mexico and camped in the Sierra Madre Mountains. For over ten years, he led his warriors on raids into the U.S. in the area around Tucson, Arizona. In September, 1886, he surrendered to Gen. Nelson A. Miles.

A young Yuma mother and her baby. The Yavapai are a branch of the Yuma.
(Courtesy, National Archives)

out. I think you better surrender. We don't want to kill you. . . . If we did, we're going to have tears in our eyes to do it. You know we are Yavapais, we don't belong to your tribe, but we, we feel bad to do that. . . . So quiet for almost an hour, say just like death, and then Geronimo got up. They were way down there. He got up and talked in his language, and then this Yavapai, a young man, interpret, and another one interpret in English. . . . And so it took, oh, almost half a day. . . . Geronimo didn't want to give up. He'd rather die, he said than to live on. How would you gonna treat me, I don't know. . . . You might starve me to death, he said, and he cried they said.

I think he's right, Yavapai's right. All right. They went peacefully, he said. And he cried just loud, they said. Everybody hear him, and then at last they said all right, we'll surrender. . . . And crying, everybody's crying. . . . Even the horses neigh. . . . So they parted, soldiers got in, drove them to the train and loaded them and took them. That's the last we seen, my daddy said. He was a scout then. . . .

Return to the Reservation

And then they sent us back to old San Carlos, where Coolidge Dam is. That's the way it had been with us people, he said. They never try to say, you can have your land back. . . . You can go back where you used to live and have things to eat, your natural food, they never even say that to us. . . . They keep them over there at old San Carlos. The grass was gone, the food that grow natural was gone, there's no wood, and yet they never say. They give us ration, that's gone too. Scarce all the time. . . . We almost go naked, he said, but they manage to have little piece of goods, you know, for the women and children. And that's the way they got us to become white people. . . . I don't know how you will be, but we went through hard hardships. Lose all our people, our best relatives and people. . . . It's up to you, told the young people.

The Indian School Experience

And then this word came, there's a school they built at old San Carlos. Said that compulsory law, you have to go to school whether you have just one child or not, you have to send it. It happened that I was the only child they had, because he was scouting, you see, he didn't stay home. And they cried, mother and grandmother just cried their heart out, but said she have to go. She ran away and took me and lived in the mountains, but they hunted her up like animal. . . . We come back way midnight and to eat. . . . And then she carry me back and forth in the mountain, where Coolidge Dam is, where those mountain is, that's where we sleep at night. And then we overslept one morning and the scouts were there with my daddy standing there crying . . . and that's how he got me, and the white soldiers and the Indian soldiers, they surrounded us, said, the captain said you can't get away. If you want to be killed, he said, we'd kill everyone of you, he said. . . .

. . . And then, in a year's time, I was sent to the school. I was still nursing they said, you know, some are like that, they run around, but they stop and go nurse, that's the way I was they said. And so, mama told one of the big girls, my relative, she said, you take care of her because she's that way and she's gonna cry and miss me and everything, she said, and I had to go to the school, see, so I went to school, and I stayed, but I did pretty good, said, I never wake up at night. And then in a few days . . . this superintendent come from Grand Junction, Colorado, came and got, maybe, forty, fifty, I think fifty-two, they said. He took 'em over there to go to school because a governor in that state, Colorado, said he'd like to have an Indian school there, too, so they had one. . . .

In the fall I had to go over there. Oh, that's the time they cried like everything, too. They camp around the building all night long. You hear crying, mamas crying, crying, and early in the morning, they wake us up to go to breakfast, then, we come back, they told us to go in the wagon right here, and so they make us climb the wagon, get in, and here my mama was, right over there. Just as soon as I sit down, she grabbed me, pull me out and take me out, and put her arm around me and said, no, you can't take her. You've got to kill me, she said, and you cannot take my only one, and she sit down, tried to hide me like, you know, between her legs. . . . The teachers were around us, so they got the white one and they hold me, and I didn't cry they said, but mama won't let them take me, and she cried, but . . . my daddy tried to come and hold her, and she fight him. . . . So these white men have to hold her, and then take me and put me in the wagon. They go, went, go quick, so she couldn't get onto me, and they held her until she cross a big river there. . . . The other mothers did not do that, see, like the Apaches, like Geronimos, they did not do it. They just let it go because they have big families, you know, but with them, they only had me that's why. . . . And that's how I went away to get my education. And it was in 1890, and I never come home until 1902.

. . . We were to go for five years, and some three years, but some did come back, but, see, I didn't want to. I forgot my language. I just forget it altogether when I come back here in 1902. And I had to learn it all over, but it didn't take me long. They were glad, these superintendents, because they wanted me to be a teacher here at Ft. McDowell. . . . I didn't want to come back. Isn't that awful? And so I cried all the way over here,

I think. I didn't want to come back, but my teacher. . . . She said, you ought to be ashamed. . . . They are your people, she said. We are not your people, you just went to school with us, she said. . . .

Religion

I wasn't a religious woman. I don't know anything about that. When we went to school, the government said, don't teach them the Bible because they wouldn't understand. There are too many churches, but give them hymn books, let them sing, so I don't know nothing about the Bible, but I do know, from my Indian, about the Great Spirit. They teach just this: thou shalt not steal. That's what the mother tells the daughter, and the father the son. That covers everything, you know that. . . . Don't steal somebody's wife or husband or horse or blanket or shoes or what. . . .

My daddy became a Christian . . . and he just worry to death . . . because I wouldn't join no church. Just he and my little boy, three years old, join the Presbyterian church. I help with that, I interpreted, and I teach the Sunday school children, all that, but it didn't strike me, but I do believe. The Indians say the Great Spirit, I believe that. . . .

Questions for Discussion

1. What can you learn about Yavapai culture from this account? In your opinion, which experiences contributed to the demise of that culture, or to the destruction of self-identity? What did the woman mean by the phrase, "That's the way they got us to become white people"?
2. What forms of resistance did these native people employ against the attacks on their families and way of life? Try to imagine yourself in such a situation. How do you think you would respond?
3. What were the negative or positive parts of this woman's school life? In your experience, has school ever created barriers between children and their families? What might be the advantages or disadvantages today of separate schools for native American children?

7.
Mrs. A. Beaumont, Jane E. Sobers, Mrs. H. Griswold, Alzina Rathbun, Mrs. Mary Travis, Live Pryor, Mrs. Callor, Mrs. L.M.R. Pool

Letters to Susan B. Anthony on Suffrage and Equal Rights for Women, 1880

In the 1860s, woman suffrage advocates suffered a deep split over the wording of the Fourteenth and Fifteenth Amendments and the issue of black male suffrage. Susan B. Anthony and Elizabeth Cady Stanton broke with Republican abolitionists to found the National Woman Suffrage Association, which refused to support the Fifteenth Amendment unless it enfranchised women. Fearing that simultaneous consideration of woman suffrage would jeopardize black male suffrage, the Republican abolitionists supported a state-by-state campaign for woman suffrage, whereas Anthony and Stanton chose to work at the national level for an all-inclusive suffrage amendment. In order to gather support for their cause, the two women reached across class lines to new groups of women, who had not previously been involved in the movement. The following letters from 1880 offer a sample of the support they received from women around the country, who took the opportunity to tell their stories and describe their social and family conditions.

Chicago Historical Society, National Woman Suffrage Association Correspondence.

The typewriter (ca. 1900). Typing became a woman's job. Both she and the machine were called typewriters. *(Courtesy, National Archives)*

I believe that women should be emancipated from the accursed bondage that has kept them down for hundreds of years; laws invented by rascally men in the dark ages; knowing the women were too smart for them if they only had a chance to show what they were capable of. But now I hope the time is coming when the women can put their foot down heavy on any man that dares to trample on their rights. Women must arise in all their strength to let men know that she is his equal in all that is great and good. If Bergh in N.Y. City, can be paid to punish men for their cruelty to dumb brutes, I go for a law that will give women the power to go throughout the land to search out the poor and oppressed women, and in every case where a man ill treats his wife, I want him carried off to the Insane Asylum in Indiana or some other infernal place. I am over 76 years old; have lived in different places; have seen man's cruelty to women many times; just because they delight to show their power over them. It must be stopped. I should be glad to say something on that great occasion and hear others; but I am a poor woman and a widow; and could not get money to come to save my life so sent my name and children's.

Mrs. A Beaumont, Illinois City,
Illinois

i have a disire to vote from ms Jane E. Sobers free holder and tax payer when will we have our Rights and Justice in this world. i do not know some times what to think of some of the woman of our city they are a sleep they want to be roused up in Some way i for one have Bin Struggling hard with this world Scince 1874 all Lone By my Self. i have to be man and woman boath i have to be at the helamn and look out for the Brakers i am now 48 years old. have Bin the mother of 9 children and still struggling for my freedom. Are we to have the chinia man to governs us and the colard man it Looks as it was fast approaching.

i feel proud that we had some noble woman to help unnBar the Prison Doors for the Poor Down trodden honst hard working woman of this countery. i have Suffered inJustice from the Law of this my native city. wronged and Robbed of what Did by Rights Belong to me. So good Bye you have my hand and my hart. i only wish i had to power to help you though But I hope the day will come soon. . . .

Jane E. Sobers, Philadelphia,
Pennsylvania

Withholding from feminine humanity every natural right from infancy to death, is man's natural propensity. It is so natural that it requires more than ordinary courage in one to favor equal rights legally or morally.

So much has the world been accustomed to subjecting females (human) to all sort of penances that even female children are forced to forego nearly every pleasure encouraged in the MALE sex. Bah! My blood has been brought to boiling heat while reading the contemptable pusilanimious proceedings of the late great Methodist Conference. Even now my cheek burns with contempt and disgust for the foolish virgins who unsuspectingly support them.

Believe me, I cannot use and plead for my *every* natural right. But am bitter enough if it comes to that, to fight manfully for our liberty. I would, were it in my power make a destroying Angel of my self, and go from house to house and should I personally receive the treatment that I daily receive in common with other female human beings, *destroy* the man or woman who would utter against equal and unqualified rights and privileges. Words fail to convey the bitter hatred I have for the foul demagogues who would take from me the freedom they claim for themselves.

Mrs. H. Griswold, Leavenworth,
Kansas

I cannot be at the meeting although it is my greatest desire to be there. I am an old lady not able to make the journey. And what a sadness it brings over me when I look back when I was young and had to stay at home and work while my Brothers was away to school never had time nor means to educate my self. I have worked many a week for two dollars while my brothers got 2 or more a day and can this awful curse ever be wiped from our free country as they call it. What a sham is freedom. My mother, good old lady living yet most one hundred and never wrote her name in her life she said that boys must be educated so they could go out in the world smart men well they are what the world call smart judges and statesmen while I old lady not capable to do anything for my poor down troden sisters. I am so thankful there is so many capable to do something strike your best blows go to all their great conventions let them know you mean freedom if we never get it keep them stirred up that is some satisfaction if nothing more all this scribbling does not amount to much of course but I have given you my mind on the subject now you can laugh over my composition it will do that much good any way you will find my name in the list from Shellsburg Iowa was not able to write when I put it there poor show for a town of 600 inhabitants we had to work hard to get that many.

Alzina Rathbun, Shellsburg,
Iowa

Do I wish to vote? do the farm-house slaves of the north want to vote? This is a question involving a two sided problem. What has the Womens-rights movement done for us? Just this, if nothing more, raised the wages of women and girls, and opened places in shops and stores where girls may earn more in a month than the farmers wife can command in a year. Well this is good for the girls in some respects but it means death, after a short life of endless toil and care, for the poor Mother at home. Help cannot be had in the farm house, for love nor money. Our young people are all rushing to Town. . . .

Dear Sister. . . . I would not tie any woman down to this life of unpaid toil, but justice means justice to all; and it is an undeniable fact that the condition of the farmers and their poor drudging wives, is every year becoming more intolerable; we are robbed and crowded to the wall on every side, our crops [is] taken for whatever the middlemen are of a mind to give us, and we are obliged to give them whatever they have the force to ask for their goods or go without, and this all means so much more self-denial and suffering. So much toil, and I would like to be Robertspere—or the heads-man just one year or till the head of every murderer, and every sin-licensing states-man had rolled down from the guillotine. This slow murder and usurpation calls for just such a bloody, unmitigated remedy.

Mrs. Mary Travis, Fore's Bend,
Minnesota

. . . Your Call for all woman of These United States to sign a petition or postal Card to be sent to you, from Your Mass Meeting to be sent to the Republican President Convention asking them to extend to us Woman some recognition of our rights. We are your Sister though Colored still we feel in our Bosom and want of Faternal love from our White sister of the Country. Our White men of this State of Virginia, who rule us with a rod of iron, and show themselves on every occasion the same Crule Task Master, as ever, had introduce on the Statute books right to wipp woman for any poor Discretion, that she might be guilt of. During the early part of february a poor week colored Woman who was in the Extremes wants, stole a Over skirt Value fifty Cent, for which the presiding Magistrate Named J. J. Gruchfield, Did order the poor crea-ture 72 lashes to be well laid on. 36 lashes at the time the Other 36 in a week time and the man or, brute, went himself and saw the whipping was executed. Captain Scott a Col Man became indignant went to the jail to see the poor Creature, was refused admission at first but succeed at Last. O My God, what a sight he then saw. the poor Woman Breast was cut wide open by the lash, her poor back cut to pieces I call some woman together went to the Governor and stated the Case. he forbid the further lashing of the poor woman because the Dr. Beal said she could not live to receive further whipping. Yet the woman still have to remain in jail 12 months for stealing one over skirt Value fifty Cent and have since then been enable to enroll quite a number of Woman to gather form a Club. Our Object is to petition Lecture and to do all things which shall so soffen the heart of Mankind that they will see and must grant and respect our rights. Would and pray that the Mass Meeting may endorse or demand of the Republican Convention to be Held in Chicago the rights of Woman to put an Amendment to the Constitution a Cumpulsory Education of Every state of this Union.

Pardon me for this long letter i must feel let my feeling go out, so to you Dear Madam have i address you on Behalf of your Down Trodden Colored Sisters of Virginia.

Live Pryor, Richmond Virginia
President, Ladies Enterprise Club

[P.S.] If you have any prayers or book that is of no use to you or society would feel grateful to receive them as we wish to form a library.

Although only a working woman, I have by hard work and close economy accumulated a small property that I find I have the privilege to pay taxes for, but have not right to vote for men that tax me. I also find that I am taxed for said property as much again as what many men are that have political influence. Last year I appealed against the enormous tax the assessor put on my property. But could get no resolution because I have no political influence. . . .

Mrs. Callor, Jersey City,
New York

I always come to the same conclusion, namely that our rotten marriage institution is the main obstacle in the way of womans freedom, and just as long as our girls are taught to barter the use of their body for a living, must woman remain the degraded thing she is. Of course the Ballot is the great lever to lift her into self esteem and independence. I am more than glad to see the women getting so in dead earnest in the matter.

Mrs. L.M.R. Pool, Vermillion,
Ohio

I thank God, for giving you the *moral courage* to insist, and persist, under such difficulties and discouragements, as you for so many years have, that woman should have some of the rights she for so many centuries has unjustly been deprived of; and may your life be spared, until you see *all women* in possession of the first great right, Suffrage!

With deepest Love and Gratitude, I am Yours.
[*Name Illegible*], Cleveland

P.S. I saw the notice of this call several days ago and intended to have answered immediately, but many things prevented, for I am a married woman and not free, by any means, from the cares that relationship brings: and, 56 years old. I have added this explanation, as this Monday morning, I find my hands almost too stiff to write.

May God speed this note, so one more name may be added to your list. My whole soul goes out to you with great *hopes* and *wishes*.

Questions for Discussion

1. How do these women feel about their lives and about general conditions for women? What broader issues related to the status of women are evoked by the woman suffrage issue?
2. What various injustices are cited by these writers?
3. Why does Mrs. Travis feel ambivalent towards the woman's rights movement?

Part 2

An Industrial Society in Peace and War

During the first two decades of the twentieth century came the triumph of industrialism as the dominant force in American life. By 1920 most Americans lived in urban areas rather than on farms, and they worked principally in factories or in commerce rather than in agriculture. The diaries of Martha Farnsworth and Hamlin Garland reflect the wonder Americans felt as industrial technology wrought major changes in their lives.

The letters of Jewish immigrants to the newspaper column, "A Bintel Brief," give insight into the conditions of those who labored in the factories, while the letter from Victor Myllymaki and the diary of H. Minderman recount two examples of labor protests and attempts to suppress them.

The workers who filled the factories came both from Europe and the rural United States. While earlier European immigrants came largely from the north and west of Europe, the "new immigrants" of the late nineteenth and early twentieth centuries were more likely to be from the south and east. They were also more likely to be Catholic and Jewish rather than Protestant, and often faced prejudice as well as harsh economic conditions. The letters included in "A Bintel Brief" reflect the difficult process of adjustment many faced. With the approach of World War I, many African Americans from the southern United States moved north, repelled by conditions at home and attracted by the prospect of factory jobs. Their letters describe the process of migration and something about their new lives in the North.

Women too became part of the new urban, industrial labor force, though they were largely limited to positions that offered little either in wages or in prestige. Nevertheless, professional opportunities were slowly becoming available. By 1900, for example, over a dozen medical schools admitted women. Life for a professional woman, however, remained difficult. Mabel Ulrich's diary poignantly reflects the challenges a woman doctor faced in both her career and her marriage.

World War I confirmed the place of the United States as an industrial and military great power. For many who fought in it, the war was a life-changing event. The diary of Guy Emerson Bowerman illustrates how one soldier's attitudes were transformed as a result of his experiences. On the home front citizens patriotically sacrificed peacetime luxuries but also suffered from the suppression of unpopular opinions, as illustrated in letters from Carrie Chapman Catt and Alice Hamilton.

8.
Victor Myllymaki
Letter of a Finnish-American Miner and the Mesabi Strike, 1907

Myllymaki was a Finnish-American in Eveleth, Minnesota, caught up in the Mesabi Iron Mines Strike of 1907, a time when many workers across the United States were organizing to demand an eight-hour day and wages that would allow them to feed their families adequately. With their tradition of socialism, the Finnish immigrants in northern Minnesota were particularly active in demanding labor equality. Myllymaki's letter home describes the effect of the strike on workers.

Eveleth, Minnesota
August 5, 1907

Dear Brother:

I just returned from the post office and got your letter. I decided to answer it right away conveying my heartfelt thanks for it. I have kept in good health which is what I hope for you there in my homeland. Now I'll describe a bit what the conditions are like over here. There is a great strike going on. There are many of us out of work. I don't know how long the strike will last. It's only been 2 ½ weeks since it started and this isn't a very pleasant time at all. There are a 100 stooges with guns paid

"America Letters" Microfilm Collection, Immigration History Research Center, University of Minnesota, original microfilm held by Turku University, Finland.

by the mining companies harassing the workers just like some animals. A worker can't peacefully walk down the street anymore. People are jailed everyday. They say this America is the land of the free but that's a lie. A week ago Finnish socialists in Michigan had a large summer festival and they used some old flags in the festival procession just like the custom is in Finland. About 100 of them began the march to the festival site. But the local police and their accomplices met them, took their flags away and beat up 13 marchers and threw them in jail, from where they were later taken to the hospital.

You wrote that Kalle would like to come here. I'll sure send him a ticket, but not now. I myself might have to leave here if this strike lasts very long. The workers have decided to strike for a year if their demands aren't met. They are asking for $3.00 a day and an eight-hour day. If we win the strike, I'll send Kalle a ticket right away.

Greetings to everyone in my homeland.

Your brother,
Victor Myllymaki

Questions for Discussion

1. What kinds of pressures did the mining company apply to discourage strikers and break the strike? What changes have been instituted since 1907 to improve labor-management relations and minimize the occasions for labor strikes?

2. What labor strikes in the recent past are you aware of? What were the reasons for those strikes?

9.
H. Minderman
Diary of an
IWW Free Speech Fight,
1910–1911

*The years between 1901 and the American entry into World
War I in 1917 are often referred to by historians as the Progressive Era, a time of widespread reform of the political and
economic systems. Moderate reform energies were channeled
into the major political parties as well as Theodore Roosevelt's
Progressive Party of 1912. Among labor unions, the American
Federation of Labor (AFL) showed the same moderate impulse,
organizing skilled craft workers and demanding economic
benefits rather than fundamental change.*

*At the same time, however, interest in more radical reform
was also growing. In 1912 Eugene V. Debs, the Socialist Party
candidate for President, received the party's all-time high of
nearly a million votes. Among labor organizations, the Industrial Workers of the World, usually known as the IWW or the
"Wobblies," took a more radical tack than the AFL. The Wobblies called for an end to the capitalist system, and attempted
to organize unskilled, often immigrant, workers such as miners,
timbermen, and farm laborers. Not surprisingly, Wobblies were
often the targets of political repression. Their protests were
sometimes marked with violence, and several Wobbly leaders
were lynched. Organized in 1905, the IWW, as an effective
movement, was over by 1924.*

United States Commission on Industrial Relations. National Archives, Washington, D.C. C.M.E., 12-7-14, Serial No. 819.

The Wobblies have earned a place in American folklore. They had courage and idealism, and even a sense of humor. ("Hallelujah, I'm a Bum" became the Wobbly anthem.) Their songs were among their most effective recruiting devices, and at least one of them, "Solidarity Forever," is sung on union picket lines to this day.

The Wobbly free speech fights grew out of attempts by local authorities to suppress the organization by arresting their speakers. In response, the Wobblies would flock to a town where a free speech fight was on and get themselves arrested in such numbers that the system could not handle them. The diary below describes this process in Fresno, California in 1910 and 1911. The selection begins with the IWW men, having been released from jail once, deciding to get themselves rearrested by making more political speeches. Of H. Minderman nothing is known other than his brief description of himself in the diary: "one of the boys who went through the whole fight."

1910

November 27th. Little made a speech and told what the master-class has done in the Goldfield and Cripple Creek Country.[1] Pointed out the necessity of organization and as example took the police. He told them that the law in California is that every State, County or City official shall work not more than eight hours a day, but that the police in Fresno work ten hours a day. . . .

November 28th. We send three men out to get arrested in order to make a test case.

November 29th. Everybody except committee goes out to speak on the street, twenty-three men altogether. We did this to prevent the men being isolated in the cells and their spirit being broken in the start of the fight. Two men clubbed in jail.

/////

December 4th. Five came in and we got a small piece of bread for our breakfast. Some think they are shortening our rations and others think that they were short on bread this morning and that it is better to wait until we know if they are shortening our food before taking action.

/////

---

[1]Frank Little was a Wobbly organizer who would be lynched in Montana in 1917. The reference is to an IWW miner's strike in Colorado.

An IWW strike. *(Courtesy, National Archives)*

December 6th. Battleships[2] are made in the black-hold and got the watercure. This is the first time the night jailer has given someone the watercure in eight years and the men in the black-hold are raising hell, too. At 11:00 o'clock A.M. Lefferts is taken out of the cell and brought into the bull-pen. He had not eaten or drank anything for four days and was soaking wet.

/////

December 10th. We got notice that the police had organized a mob with the help of the fire department, Pinkertons, and thugs and had mobbed our speaker,—after this the mob had gone to our camp and burned down the tent and took away everything they could carry. The mob was about five hundred strong. After this the mob came to the jail and wanted to mob us. The jailor and a trustee, in for murder, and who had helped the thugs in clubbing two men in jail, thought the mob was an I.W.W. mob and they closed the safety doors and hid themselves in a safe place in jail. Murdock got six months.

---

[2]A "battleship" was a protest method in which the prisoners would lock arms and huddle in the center of a room and jump up and down together. It could have the effect in old buildings of severely rocking the structure.

/////

December 19th. White of the free speech committee visited us and wanted our vote on the following proposition,—All prisoners shall be liberated and leave town. We notify headquarters that the fight is over and that they send no more men to Fresno. That the City Council shall make an ordinance against street speaking and we obey this and test the ordinance in the courts. We refuse this by a unanimous vote. . . . [*In other words, the jailed Wobblies refused a compromise that would have freed them.*]

/////

December 23rd. We got water and bread diet. The big majority refuse to take the bread. We decided to go on a hunger strike because no food at all was better and healthier than water and bread. The experience in Spokane had shown that the boys who had not eaten at all, got back their health and of the boys who took and ate the bread, two died and some became invalids. For supper we sing the red flag and other songs and that brought some spectators to the jail. Five speeches were made through the windows, explaining what was going on in the jail. Every time the spectators leave, we start to raise hell again. . . . The sheriff orders the speakers to stop this, but we ordered him to go ahead. Then we got the watercure. With our mattresses we prevent the jailor from driving our speaker from the window. There are two sewerholes in the bull-pen and the water flows into them as fast as they put it in. This lasts for two hours—then the fire department came. They started with twenty pounds pressure and the pressure is getting stronger until it is one hundred and fifty pounds. The stream bored a hole through our mattresses in one minute. It knocked the men down on the floor and they had to stand against the wall in order not to get drowned. Every time the stream struck a man his body was paralyzed where the stream struck. Schulz got the stream on his head and he was lifted from the floor and then dropped down. The top of his hat was torn off and his eye badly hurt. It is a wonder that nobody was killed. Another man got a sore ear and many got black eyes. The fire engine was in operation for one hour. After they quit, the water was one foot deep but soon the sewer got stopped up and we were refused a wire to fix this. After this the sheriff told us that he was sorry that he had done this, but that he was ready to do it again and that we were to get our full rations again in the morning. We get fifteen dry blankets for eighty-one men.

/////

December 27th.   Five men came in. We learn that the papers had printed that we had insulted women in the jail and that was the cause the fire department gave us the watercure.

/////

1911
January 1st.   Some of the boys lose their courage; there is talk of giving up the fight, because the fight is lost. The same cowardly arguments are used in the first round, hiding their real thought behind a lot of nonsense. Got news that last night again a mob was before the jail.

January 2nd.   Nobody comes in and the future of the fight looks dark. Murdock puts up a good bluff in the way of a speech and that brought back the spirit of the discouraged ones. After he finished his speech, he got a slime cough for an hour and a half and it was necessary to call a doctor. The doctor got him in good shape in ten minutes.

At 10:00 o'clock P.M. the night jailor came in the bull-pen and said that this was his last night and he wished us good luck.

January 3rd.   Only the men who are sentenced can get clothing from the sheriff. Four men were arrested for giving out leaflets. In the evening the new jailor forbade us to sing, but the boys did as they liked and sang a little bit louder. . . .

/////

January 7th.   . . . The health inspectors inspect the jail and the bull-pen. They declare there is room for fifteen men in the bull-pen but there are eighty-five. Five men came in. Got telegram that Chief Sullivan of Spokane is killed which made some of the boys happy,—too bad.

/////

January 11th.   Little had a conversation with the health inspector and he told Little that he was on our side in the fight.

/////

January 16th.   The jailer cut the store business out. Two volunteers who came in on the 9th and 16th of December, plead guilty. Trouble over our sour bread. After supper we get a letter from Haslewood, and he stated that the locals are against this fight and the locals are right to do so and that the best for us to do was to make a compromise. (It looks as though everything is lost.) In the evening at our propaganda meeting Filigno and others made good speeches and statements about the way of fighting and cause and effect in fighting and that drove the clouds away.

/////

January 31st. Three cases are dismissed and the men liberated one minute before supper. The Socialist Party condemns the actions of the authorities in Fresno against the I.W.W. . . .

February 1st. Two cases are dismissed and two men have rheumatism and can't leave their beds. The first stone for the rock pile is delivered. Little got a trial in Selma and got free. Jury was out four minutes.

/////

February 7th. The Health Inspector interviewed us through the bars. He is out of his job and gave us tobacco, and stated that we would win this fight if we stuck to it. Six came in and one case dismissed because the man had sold out papers and had not spoken on the street. The sheriff complains that we have a chance to smuggle something into the jail from the store. He said that we must give the money to him with our order for tobacco etc. and that he will buy the things we want himself. We instruct our committee to tell him that he can appoint a store where we shall buy and that our committee on the outside will pay the store and not the sheriff. In case the sheriff refuses this they shall tell him that we do not believe in discrimination and that we will not behave as we are doing at present. This motion was carried by a vote of 33 to 23.

February 8th. The city demanded that the sheriff starve us out of jail. The Mayor offered Murdock his liberty, if we went back to Seattle. (Murdock had been sentenced to six months.) He refuses this. Three came in.

/////

February 19th. The prosecuting attorney had a conference with our committee and offered that if we plead guilty that we would not get more than forty days; that he would do all he could to liberate the men who are sentenced and that we can speak on the county ground in the park. At our meeting we instructed our committee to ignore the proposition. Ten men taken out of the bull-pen and put in another part of the jail.

/////

February 21st. Two men came in and eight were for trial. We are now one hundred and fifteen men strong in jail.

February 22nd. . . . The sheriff notified the police that the jail is over-full and that he would refuse to take men in the jail for breaking the city ordinance. The chief said that in that case he would arrest our men on another charge.

/////

February 25th.   . . . A committee from the Chamber of Commerce interviewed our committee about the fight and what our demands were.

February 27th.   The sheriff offered us a compromise that he says he can make stick. This compromise is all that we are demanding, with the exception of one street of minor value to us. We notified him that we are in favor for this if we got it in more definite form. We got all of the men in the jail and bull-pen to decide on this proposition. We got news that the public is mobbing our speaker again. The time for three of the men is out.

February 28th.   Ten men taken out to clean the streets by the courthouse, but they refuse to do this. They were brought back to the bull-pen and in order that the city could not put us on bread and water, the sheriff put all sentenced men on the rock pile. The amount of rock crushed per day and per man is one fourth cubic foot. The citizens committee gave us the statement that we can get what the sheriff had just put before us if we promised to leave the city and to make no more inflammatory speeches. We refused this and instructed our committee to strike out the clause referring to leaving town and inflammatory speeches. . . .

March 1st.   The sheriff notifies us this afternoon that our terms had been accepted by the city.

/////

March 3rd.   This is the last day of the diary. There is only to be added that within three days all of the I.W.W. men in Fresno jail were released and that when they left the jail they took most of the rock pile with them. They had made it up into souvenirs of the Free Speech Fight. These souvenirs they distributed among their different locals and their friends. We might also add that from this time on the police did not intercept their meetings, neither did they molest members of the organization. They even quit arresting men for petty offenses such as vagrancy, disturbing the peace, etc.

Questions for Discussion

1. What do you learn from the diary about Wobbly principles and beliefs? How do they behave themselves in jail?
2. What explains the Wobbly victory in this encounter with the authorities?

10.
Abraham Cahan
"A Bintel Brief":
Immigrant Letters,
1907–1911

"Dear Abbey" and Ann Landers' columns are not recent phe-
nomena in American journalism. At the turn of the twentieth
century, Jewish immigrants (men, women and even children)
were writing to the editors of the Yiddish newspaper, the Jewish
Daily Forward, *for advice concerning marriage, child rearing,*
education, employment, anti-Semitism, an assortment of so-
cial and political issues, and the various adjustments they faced
in their adopted country. Their published letters in the column,
"A Bintel Brief" (a bundle of letters), provide a profile of life not
unfamiliar to other cultural groups and by those who were
American born as well.

"A Bintel Brief," valued by readers for sixty-five years, was
the brainchild of Abraham Cahan (1860–1951), one of the
founders and editor of the Forward, *which became the leading*
Yiddish newspaper in the United States. Cahan, who was born
in Lithuania and emigrated to the United States in 1882, wrote
in English and Yiddish and is noted for such works as The Rise
of David Levinsky *and* Leaves From My Life. *For the historical*
record it should be noted that some recent scholarship has
discovered that a few of the "letters" were fabricated by the
newspaper.

Isaac Metzker. *A Bintel Brief: Sixty Years of Letters from the Lower East Side*
to the Jewish Daily Forward. New York: Ballantine Books, 1971.

[1907]

Worthy Editor,

Allow me a little space in your newspaper and, I beg you, give me some advice as to what to do.

There are seven people in our family—parents and five children. I am the oldest child, a fourteen-year-old girl. We have been in the country two years and my father, who is a frail man, is the only one working to support the whole family.

I go to school, where I do very well. But since times are hard now and my father earned only five dollars this week, I began to talk about giving up my studies and going to work in order to help my father as much as possible. But my mother didn't even want to hear of it. She wants me to continue my education. She even went out and spent ten dollars on winter clothes for me. But I didn't enjoy the clothes, because I think I am doing the wrong thing. Instead of bringing something into the house, my parents have to spend money on me.

I have a lot of compassion for my parents. My mother is now pregnant, but she still has to take care of the three boarders we have in the house. Mother and Father work very hard and they want to keep me in school.

I am writing to you without their knowledge, and I beg you to tell me how to act. Hoping you can advise me, I remain,

Your reader,
S.

ANSWER:

The advice to the girl is that she should obey her parents and further her education, because in that way she will be able to give them greater satisfaction than if she went out to work.

[1908]

Esteemed Editor,

We were sitting in the shop and working when the boss came over to one of us and said, "You ruined the work: you'll have to pay for it." The worker answered that it wasn't his fault, that he had given out the work in perfect condition. "You're trying to tell me!" The boss got mad and began to shout. "I pay your wages and you answer back, you dog! I should have thrown you out of my shop long ago."

The worker trembled and his face got whiter. When the boss noticed how his face paled, he gestured, spat and walked away. The worker said no more. Tired, and overcome with shame, he turned back to his work and later he exclaimed, "For six years I've been working here like a slave, and he tells me, 'You dog, I'll throw you out!' I wanted to pick up an iron and smash his head in, but I saw before me my wife and five children who want to eat!"

Obviously, the offended man felt he had done wrong in not standing up for his honor as a worker and human being. In the shop, the machines hummed, the irons thumped, and we could see the tears running down his cheeks.

Did this unfortunate man act correctly in remaining silent under the insults of the boss? Is the fact that he has a wife and children the reason for his slavery and refusal to defend himself? I hope you will answer my questions in the "Bintel Brief."

Respectfully,
A.P.

ANSWER

The worker cannot help himself alone. There is no limit to what must be done for a piece of bread. One must bite his lips till they bleed, and keep silent when he is alone. But he must not remain alone. He must not remain silent. He must unite with his fellow workers and fight. To defend their honor as men, the workers must be well organized.

[*1909*]

Dear Editor,

We, the unfortunates who are imprisoned on Ellis Island, beg you to have pity on us and print our letter in your worthy newspaper, so that our brothers in America may know how we suffer here.

The people here are from various countries, most of them are Russian Jews, many of whom can never return to Russia. These Jews are deserters from the Russian army and political escapees, whom the Czar would like to have returned to Russia. Many of the families sold everything they owned to scrape together enough for passage to America. They haven't a cent but they figured that, with the help of their children, sisters, brothers and friends, they could find means of livelihood in America.

You know full well how much the Jewish immigrant suffers till he gets to America. First he has a hard enough time at the borders, then with the agents. After this he goes through a lot till they send him, like baggage, on the train to a port. There he lies around in the immigrant sheds till the ship finally leaves. Then follows the torment on the ship, where every sailor considers a steerage passenger a dog. And when, with God's help, he has endured all this, and he is at last in America, he is given for "dessert" an order that he must show that he possesses twenty-five dollars.

But where can we get it? Who ever heard of such an outrage, treating people so? If we had known before, we would have provided for it somehow back at home. What nonsense this is! We must have the money on arrival, yet a few hours later (when relatives come) it's too late. For this kind of nonsense they ruin so many people and send them back to the place they escaped from.

It is impossible to describe all that is taking place here, but we want to convey at least a little of it. We are packed into a room where there is space for two hundred people, but they have crammed in about a thousand. They don't let us out into the yard for a little fresh air. We lie about on the floor in the spittle and filth. We're wearing the same shirts for three or four weeks, because we don't have our baggage with us.

Everyone goes around dejected and cries and wails. Women with little babies, who have come to their husbands, are being detained. Who can stand this suffering? Men are separated from their wives and children and only when they take us out to eat can they see them. When a man wants to ask his wife something, or when a father wants to see his child, they don't let him. Children get sick, they are taken to a hospital, and it often happens that they never come back.

Because today is a holiday, the Fourth of July, they didn't send anyone back. But Tuesday, the fifth, they begin again to lead us to the "slaughter," that is, to the boat. And God knows how many Jewish lives this will cost, because more than one mind dwells on the thought of jumping into the water when they take him to the boat.

All our hope is that you, Mr. Editor, will not refuse us, and print our letter which is signed by many immigrants. The women have not signed, because they don't let us get to them.

This letter is written by one of the immigrants, a student from Petersburg University, at Castle Garden, July 4, 1909, on the eve of the fast day of *Shivah Asar B'Tamuz [the seventeenth day of the month of Tamuz when Jews fast in memory of Nebuchadnessar's siege and destruction of Jerusalem].*

Alexander Rudnev

One hundred immigrants, aged from eight to fifty-eight, had signed this letter (each one had included his age). To stir up public opinion and the Jewish organizations, the letter was printed on page 1 with an appeal for action to help the unfortunates. To affirm the authenticity of the facts in the letter, the *Forward* stated that in the English press it had been announced that during the previous week six hundred detained immigrants had been sent back. And on the day the letter from the one hundred was printed, they were sending back two hundred and seventy people.

The *Forward* has previously printed many protests against the unjust treatment of the immigrants confined on Ellis Island, also against the fact that masses were being sent back, and the *Forward* was not silent on this letter.

[*1910*]

Dear Editor,

Since I do not want my conscience to bother me, I ask you to decide whether a married woman has the right to go to school two evenings a week. My husband thinks I have no right to do this.

I admit that I cannot be satisfied to be just a wife and mother. I am still young and I want to learn and enjoy life. My children and my house are not neglected, but I go to evening high school twice a week. My husband is not pleased and when I come home at night and ring the bell, he lets me stand outside a long time intentionally, and doesn't hurry to open the door.

Now he has announced a new decision. Because I send out the laundry to be done, it seems to him that I have too much time for myself, even enough to go to school. So from now on he will count out every penny for anything I have to buy for the house, so I will not be able to send out the laundry any more. And when I have to do the work myself there won't be any time left for such "foolishness" as going to school. I told him that I'm willing to do my own washing but that I would still be able to find time for study.

When I am alone with my thoughts, I feel I may not be right. Perhaps I should not go to school. I want to say that my husband is an intelligent man and he wanted to marry a woman who was educated. The fact that he is intelligent makes me more annoyed with him. He is in favor of the emancipation of women, yet in real life he acts contrary to his beliefs.

Awaiting your opinion on this, I remain,

Your reader,
The Discontented Wife

ANSWER

Since this man is intelligent and an adherent of the women's emancipation movement, he is scolded severely in the answer for wanting to keep his wife so enslaved. Also the opinion is expressed that the wife absolutely has the right to go to school two evenings a week.

Dear Editor,

I am an operator on ladies' waists for the past four years and I earn good wages. I work steady but haven't saved money, because I have a sick wife. I had to put her in the hospital where she lay for four weeks, and then I had to bring her home.

Just after I brought her home, the General Strike began and I could see that I was in trouble. I had to go to the union to beg them not to let me down in my situation. I just asked for some money to have a little soup for my sick wife, but they answered that there wasn't any money. I struggled along with my wife for four weeks, and when I saw that I might lose her I had to go back to work at the shop where we were striking. Now my conscience bothers me because I am a scab.

I am working now, I bring home fifteen, sometimes sixteen dollars a week. But I am not happy, because I was a scab and left the union. I want to state here that I was always a good union man.

Dear Editor, how can I now go back in the union and salve my conscience? I am ready to swear that I will remain a loyal union man forever.

Your reader,
F.H.

ANSWER

Neither the operator nor the union is guilty. During the strike, thousands upon thousands of workers complained that they were in need, but at the beginning of the strike there really was no money.

It is now the duty of the union to investigate the case, and if it is shown that circumstances were as the operator describes, they will certainly forgive him and he can again become a good union man.

[1911]

Dear Editor,

I am a newsboy, fourteen years old, and I sell the *Forverts* [*Forward*] in the streets till late into the night. I come to you to ask your advice.

I was born in Russia and was twelve years old when I came to America with my dear mother. My sister, who was in the country before us, brought us over.

My sister worked and supported us. She didn't allow me to go to work but sent me to school. I went to school for two years and didn't miss a day, but then came the terrible fire at the Triangle shop,[1] where

---

[1]The Triangle Shirtwaist Factory fire of 1911 killed 146 people.

she worked, and I lost my dear sister. My mother and I suffer terribly from the misfortune. I had to help my mother and after school hours I go out and sell newspapers.

I have to go to school three more years, and after that I want to go to college. But my mother doesn't want me to go to school because she thinks I should go to work. I tell her I will work days and study at night but she won't hear of it.

Since I read the *Forverts* to my mother every night and read your answers in the "Bintel Brief," I beg you to answer me and say a few words to her.

Your Reader,
The Newsboy

ANSWER

The answer to this letter is directed to the boy's mother, whose daughter was one of the shopworkers who perished in the Triangle fire. The unfortunate woman is comforted in the answer, and she is told that she must not hinder her son's nighttime studies but must help him reach his goal. And an appeal is made to good people who are in a position to do something for the boy to come forward and help him further his education.

Dear Editor,

I plead with you to open your illustrious newspaper and take in my "Bintel Brief" in which I write about my great suffering.

A long gloomy year, three hundred and sixty-five days, have gone by since I left my home and am alone on the lonely road of life. Oh, my poor dear parents, how saddened they were at my leaving. The leave-taking, their seeing me on my way, was like a silent funeral.

There was no shaking of the alms box, there was no grave digging and no sawing of boards, but I, myself, put on the white shirt that was wet with my mother's tears, took my pillow, and climbed into the wagon. Accompanying me was a quiet choked wail from my parents and friends.

The wheels of the wagon rolled farther and farther away. My mother and father wept for their son, then turned with heavy hearts to the empty house. They did not sit shive [*seven days of mourning*] even though they had lost a child.

I came to America and became a painter. My great love for Hebrew, and Russian, all of my other knowledge was smeared with paint. During the year that I have been here I have had some good periods, but I am not happy, because I have no interest in anything. My homesickness and loneliness darken my life.

Ah, home, my beloved home. My heart is heavy for my parents whom I left behind. I want to run back, but I am powerless. I am a coward, because I know that I have to serve under "Fonie" [*the Czar*] for three years. I am lonely in my homesickness and I beg you to be my counsel as to how to act.

Respectfully,
V.A.

ANSWER

The answer states that almost all immigrants yearn deeply for dear ones and home at first. They are compared with plants that are transplanted to new ground. At first it seems that they are withering, but in time most of them revive and take root in the new earth.

The advice to this young man is that he must not consider going home, but try to take root here. He should try to overcome all these emotions and strive to make something of himself.

Questions for Discussion

1. What were some of the problems faced by these immigrants? In what ways were they similar or different from other cultural groups?
2. How do the problems addressed in these letters compare with those of immigrants at other periods in United States history? Would the answers be different from those given here?

11.
Mabel S. Ulrich

Changing Roles in Marriage and Professional Life, 1904–1932

Mabel Ulrich studied medicine along with her husband, both of whom planned joint careers and shared responsibilities in the home. Traditional views about a woman's role, especially in medicine, however, relegated her to secondary professional roles and to being the primary homemaker in the family. Ulrich records, with humor and determination, her struggle to gain acceptance equal to that of male physicians and her work for the rights of women in medical school.

April 4, 1904. S. and I have decided to get married next year when we get through medicine. Of course we shall be fearfully poor at first, but as long as we are both going to work we shall make twice as much money as we could alone. . . . I told him I didn't know a thing about housekeeping, and he said why should I? That he could see no more reason for a woman's liking cooking and dishwashing than for a man's liking them. That since our education had been precisely similar, we are starting out exactly even, therefore there would be no justice at all in my having to do all the "dirty work"—although of course we both agree with Tolstoy that *all* manual work is honorable. So we have decided that one week I shall take over all the duties connected with the running of our house and the next week he will. Of course we are going to have an office together and be partners in every sense of the word. I was so happy I couldn't speak. Then after a long time we talked about our children. We are going to divide up the care of the children exactly as we divide the housework.

Sept. 23, 1905. It is no go. We have given up the 50-50 housekeeping plan. We tried for a month but by the end of one week I knew. S. is a fearful mess as a housekeeper. . . . And then of course he is busy and I am not. I have to laugh when I think how scared I was before we were married lest I might be the more successful at the start! Would he mind? I even asked him that, and he swore he would be proud. Well, you are perfectly safe, my dear S.! I have sat in that damned office for three months without a real call. Of course there are the hospital and dispensary, but I haven't made a cent. Today a woman came to the house and asked for the lady doctor. I was at the hospital but S. was in. Would she see him? Well—her little boy had broken his leg and she wanted the "lady" because she would be cheaper. When assured that the price would be the same she was delighted that after all she could have "a real doctor."

June 5, 1907. Twenty-five today—a quarter of a century old. A doctor, a wife, and a mother—yet I don't seem to have learned anything. Am just as mixed up as ever. Tried staying awake last night to see if I could size things up a bit. But it was no use. Got as far as—Let me see, what do I honestly think of this state called marriage? Decided that I love my husband—that my daughter is undoubtedly an incipient genius and a beauty to boot—then remembered that I forgot to tell Alma that S. wants his bacon crisper, and that all S.'s buttons are off his pajamas, that I must send in the next payment on the washing machine, that we simply must have Dr. and Mrs. S. to dinner one night this week—that I must find out what the greedy Miss L. is eating to keep her blood sugar up, that I was to give an anaesthetic at eight A.M. Then it was morning.

/////

January 16, 1910. S. could stand and watch me cut off a leg or make the most brilliant of diagnoses and remain unmoved—but let him catch me in the kitchen with an apron on, or sewing on a button, and he is dissolved in loving admiration. This I have endured with a "twisted smile" for two years. But tonight—We had planned to go to the medical meeting to hear Dr. Williams from Johns Hopkins. Then P. suddenly shot a temperature, and I couldn't leave. She had fallen asleep, and I was in the library with a basket of mending when he came home. "It was a great talk," he began, all excitement, while he took off his coat.

Then he saw one of his socks on my hand. Instantly the most fatuous my-little-wife expression came over his face. "So that's why you didn't go to the meeting," he said tenderly, and started to pat my hair. Something snapped. I jumped up and threw the entire basket in his face and rushed from the room. Well, I have apologized—and he has been the sport he always is.

After all he can't help it. A man, it seems, may be intellectually in complete sympathy with a woman's aims. But only about ten per cent of him is his intellect—the other ninety his emotions. And S.'s emotional pattern was set by his mother when he was a baby. It can't be so easy being the husband of a "modern" woman. She is everything his mother wasn't—and nothing she was.

/////

Aug. 7, 1911. Have walked out on my job. Nobody can ever make me believe again that a husband and wife can work together in a small laboratory. From the beginning S. would never accept a single finding of mine without corroborating it. His air of skepticism made me wild. And his determination to be patient! It got so that whenever he walked into the lab with that ironic, tolerant curve to his lips, I'd drop a test-tube. I did good work though, and in his heart S. knows it. Apparently a husband just can't accept his wife as an equal in his own pet field. . . .

Verily, I am no technician. But oh *what* a woman I should be if an able young man would consecrate his life to me as secretaries and technicians do to their men employers.

Yet I can't rid myself of a sense of guilt and failure. My Victorian hangover at work.

Well, we have celebrated our professional dissolution with cocktails. After the second, S. was laughing heartily at the whole thing. S. laughs a lot more than he did. Do I imagine it, or do I laugh less?

Nov. 20, 1914. Have had a thrilling week at . . . [?] University lecturing to the women students. Got me some gorgeous clothes for the occasion and have disquieting suspicion that they were responsible for much of the week's undoubted success. But not all. Submitted my plans for an organized health service to President M. He took it up with his Board and they have asked me to install the department and run it for them. And with a real salary—one big enough almost to support the family while S. gets started again in a new place. For of course we shall have to move. Will S. be willing? I haven't told him yet. But he must. It's my big chance.

Nov. 23, 1914. Have had a long talk with S. He is a grand sport. . . . I told him about the new job. He was silent for a long time. So long that although I tried not to, I knew exactly what he was thinking about; the terribly hard pull it had been to get started, his hospital and teaching affiliations, the break, the beginning at the bottom again. At last he said, "You wouldn't hesitate a minute if I were the one who wanted to make a move." We both knew that. "All right then—we go!" And he squared his shoulders and smiled.

And so to bed.

November 25, 1914   Have just written President M. to say I cannot leave. No, I'm not being noble—I'm not making any sacrifice—for I just can't face it. S. loves his work here too much. What if he should be years getting under way again? I couldn't endure his unhappiness—and neither could he, and neither could the children. He would make the gesture beautifully, but soon his subconscious would start in hating me.

Have done a lot of thinking in the last twenty-four hours. Granted that unquestionably if our positions were reversed we should move at once. But the reason that this is not a fair argument is that under those circumstances I should not *care* half as much as he does. Here comes a big admission from me. *I don't believe a woman's work is ever so important to her as a man's is to him.* Why? Well, first she knows that in the long run, no one's work—except that of a rare genius—has any unique significance except to the person who does it. Men never know this until they are old, whereas most women are born knowing it. Then to women happiness depends more upon intimate human relations than upon any amount of "success." But success is veritably the breath of life in the nostrils of a man. Why not? Both men and women demand it of him, and who cares a damn for a woman's "success"?

Occasionally her mother. . . .

April 19, 1915   A Red Letter Day! Went over to our own University to present my college health plan to President S. He was a joy and seems even enthusiastically interested. We discussed the plan in detail and I believe it is going through. It was a great help to be able to say that the important . . . [?] U. had wanted me to try it out there! I am soaring.

April 25, 1915   Prof. W. telephoned this morning that she thought my health plans were doomed because the President had heard I smoked cigarettes. I laughed and said she was crazy, but I rushed over to the campus just the same. And will you believe it, dear Diary, she was right! For the sake of my children's children let me put that conversation down as it transpired. This then, dear grandchildren, is how your grandmother and a president of a great university conversed in the Year of Our Lord 1915:

Your Grandmother, trying to smile quizzically: I have been told that you have given up having me install my plan for health work because I smoke cigarettes.

President of a Great University, archly: But you do, don't you?

Y.G., attempting puzzled amazement: Yes, certainly, but what has that to do with it? Surely you do not think smoking a question of morals?

P. of G.U., hastily registering broadmindedness: I don't of course. But others know this about you too, and it is an undoubted fact that in the minds of most people a woman who smokes is—ah—confidently associated with—er—far more serious faults.

Y.G., frightened but gentle: Do you honestly believe my plan to have value?

P. of G.U., indulgently: I do.

Y.G. still gently: Do you know any other person as well or better qualified to put it through?

P. of G.U., nervously: No, I don't, but—

Y.G., triumphantly: Well, then! You wouldn't deny this valuable opportunity to the students, merely because I smoke in my own house. I don't smoke in public, you know.

P. of G.U., looking at his finger nails and becoming more and more presidential: You have gained the reputation. We have very few women on our faculty, and they must be above suspicion. Our regents demand this. It is even said that you have been known to serve cocktails. (This he added with real reproach. I laughed. I couldn't help it. A mistake.)

Y.G.: Don't you ever drink anything, President S.?

P. of G.U., again impressively broadminded: I used to enjoy a glass of wine with my dinner when I lived in New York, but since I have been President I have given up alcohol in any form. As an example to—

Y.G., interrupting hopefully: Yes, of course. Well, then, you go right to the Regents and say, "Even as I used to drink wine and have given it up, so this woman used to smoke cigarettes and has given it up." For I will give it up—even if it does seem silly. Oh, President S., I do so want to try this out. I'll do it without any pay—I—

P. of G.U., his presidential hand upraised: It won't do. (A long silence.)

Y.G. All because I'm a woman?

P. of G.U., solemnly: Yes, but I want you to know how sorry I am.

Y.G., dreamily as she gathers up gloves: When my mother was a girl it was thought "fast" to use powder—possibly immoral to rouge.

Exit, leaving P. of G.U. booming a benediction.

So that, my dear grandchildren, although you will scarcely believe it in 1940—is exactly that!

Sept. 29, 1917 S. dazzling in a spick-and-span uniform has "gone to the War." For a few days I thought I was going. But President Wilson won't have us both . . . what kind of a world would it be if women went to war and men stayed to keep the home fires burning? I wonder. . . .

/////

*[In 1918 Ulrich was named Director of the educational depart-
ment of her state's Board of Health. Later that year she notes
her appointment as Health Director for the Red Cross; and in
January 1919 she records her appointment to the Board of
Charities with the city's hospital and health departments in her
charge, a political appointment shared with six men, a position
that she held for the next five years.]*

Feb. 1, 1919   Up betimes, to order meals, write school excuse note,
explain washing-machine to new laundress, and down to the Courthouse for 8.30. First Board meeting. All seven of us eye each other and
try to take each other's measure. . . . All six men, however, unite in
eyeing me with a certain wariness and a this-damned-Woman's-vote
expression. . . . Was suddenly reminded of the way strange dogs, hair
erect, but tails wagging, sniff each other before they commit themselves.

It's going to be great fun!

/////

March 10, 1922   Now that Health Department and Hospital have
been reorganized, there remains just one thing more I've set my heart
on. We have got to make women graduates of the State Medical eligible
for internship at the City Hospital. Had anticipated no trouble. After all
it meant only that they be permitted to take a competitive examination.
Today introduced subject for discussion. Was immediately opposed by
every member! "If we let them take the examinations we will have only
women in our hospital," said G. "The girls are always at the head of the
class." Nobody but me thought that was funny. They all nodded their
sympathy with G.

But this is not the end!

April 11, 1922   Eureka! From this year on girls may compete for
internship and two at least may hope to win! After all it wasn't so
difficult. Preliminary tactics consisted of sowing fear in hearts of members. One woman from each women's organization of note was asked
merely to call up each Board member, mention her name, and ask him
how he intended to vote on the subject. That was all. Then this morning
we saw to it that the Board room was packed with women. Each carried
a pencil and pad *very* ostensibly, and very obviously intended for the
record of votes. The prettiest and cleverest of the girl medics made an
excellent speech, but it was hardly necessary. I asked that the vote be

taken by name. The ladies busily scratched on their pads. There was only one dissenting voice.

Thus ended the only occasion when pressure has seemed indicated. Usually the method is much simpler. If I want anything very much, I introduce the idea to a member, persuade him tactfully that the proposition in reality has sprung from his own brain—and let him do the rest. Not forgetting of course to encourage, admire, and applaud at frequent intervals. This policy of indirection, so contrary to lofty standards, was adopted after I found that my direct suggestions were met invariably by a suspicion six-male strong.

/////

June 17, 1924 Home this morning after a week in New York. R. had in mind grand national job for me with salary of $10,000. But even L. couldn't swing it, and it fell through. Reason—the big salary. "They say," explained R. back from laboring for me in Washington, "they simply cannot afford to give a woman a job with that salary. You will find out, if you haven't already—that few men object to women holding jobs which pay up to $5000. But try beyond that! There's not a chance in a thousand."

And now? Steady! The important thing is not to feel beaten. Now is the time for all middle-aged (Yes, say it) women to come to the aid of their party. Woman's Club work? Charity? Volunteer lunch committees where fussy God-earnest gentlemen and graying ladies read reports and pass resolutions? No, I am through with that. Can a professional return happily to the amateur class? I doubt it.

Have decided to take the summer off and think it over!

Jan. 2, 1932 While looking for an old letter this morning I found this diary hidden away in the bottom desk drawer. It has lain there eight years. I started to burn it, then began reading and ended by calling L. and reading it to her. L., now twenty and "majoring" in psychology, took it in with a sort of indulgent gravity. . . .

L: You rebellious girls of the nineties were a sort of cross between Joan of Arc and the Pioneer Mother, weren't you? And as stuffed with causes as a Strassburg goose. Settlements, Suffrage, Economic Independence! I can't help envying you a cause, though. There isn't one we can get excited over.

I: There are lots left, you know. War, Poverty, Injustice are still with us.

L: Yes, of course, but they are so damned complex and impersonal that we are discouraged before we start. . . . Do you think women in medicine are getting a fairer deal than they did, say thirty years ago?

I: No. I can think off-hand of only two medical women who have won fair rewards—fair even for a man. Yet a number of others have done splendid work for which men, often their chiefs, have been given the glory. . . .

L: Well, what's glory anyhow? . . . I've decided to study medicine before I do any more psychology. And Jack's going to Hopkins too. I do think, darling, that we have heaps better chances than you had. So many things about sex have been cleared up, you see. And now women have the vote and everything you all worked for. It's going to be a totally different story.

I wonder.

Questions for Discussion

1. What problems did Ulrich face both as a physician and in her work in public health? What reasons can you cite for those problems?
2. How might you characterize the marital relationship of Ulrich and her husband? Did that relationship change?
3. Does inequality for women still exist? If so, what forms does it take?

12.
Martha Farnsworth and Hamlin Garland
The Birth of Technology, 1902–1932

Martha Farnsworth was born in Iowa in 1867 and moved to Kansas at the age of five, where she lived the rest of her fifty-seven years, first near Winfield, and then in Topeka. An energetic homemaker, active in community and political affairs, she kept a daily record of her life from the age of fourteen.

Hamlin Garland was a writer whose personal and professional life brought him close to a wide range of political and literary personalities. His forty-volume diary (a daily record from 1898 until his death) is a graphic and frank picture of a country at the crossroads of change.

The following diary excerpts—arranged thematically—provide vivid observations and reactions to emerging technology.

The Automobile

August 1, 1902. [*Western Wisconsin*] This day we passed as before in keen enjoyment of the glorious scenery as seen from this exquisite little floating bungalow. About four o'clock we started for Winona in the auto [*a distance of 16 miles*], Easton, Miss Losey, Z. and I. We had one of the wildest, most exciting rides I have ever taken. The day was very

Marlene Springer and Haskell Springer, eds. *Plains Woman: The Diary of Martha Farnsworth, 1882–1922.* Bloomington: Indiana University Press, 1986.

Hamlin Garland. *Hamlin Garland's Diaries.* San Marino: The Huntington Library, 1968.

beautiful and the roads fairly good. We made the trip in about four hours including all stops, which seemed wonderful to me.

This was my first long motor ride and I decided to celebrate it by writing an article descriptive of it. It is predicted that this is the coming mode of travel but at present the farmers resent it for it scares their teams into fits of rearing and plunging.

October 4, 1914 [*Chicago*] Angus came at noon and we got the Darrows and went away down to La Porte for a "pleasure trip." It is not much pleasure for me to be whizzed through a landscape at twenty-five miles an hour. If we could have gone slowly on some cross street and eaten our lunch under some of the beautiful trees we saw, I should have enjoyed it. As it was I got home in a used-up state, eyes aching, weary with 140 miles of dangerous going, and Angus was in worse case, for he had been driving. Darrow was interesting and we had some good talk, only the rush and roar of our speed made speech difficult.

Hamlin Garland

The Telephone

Wed. 1 [*Nov. 1905*]. . . . I walked to town after dinner to pay some bills, do some shopping and leave an order to have a Telephone put in our house. . . .

Mon. 13. A grand day. Men here stringing wires for a Telephone which I don't want but my neighbors want me to get, so as to visit over the Phone.

Wed. 15. Spent most of forenoon at Phone talking to friends and telling them my number. . . .

Thurs. 16. Such grand weather one can hardly stay in house but I've spent whole day, between the Telephone, jollying my friends and writing letters.

Tue. 22 [*Dec. 1914*]. O Its cold these days and snow deep. Ironed this morning, baked three cakes this afternoon and did lots of work . . . and went to bed tired at 10:30. My work has not gone at all well today . . . so that is why I am tired. . . . I have the coal to carry in from the barn, the cow to feed and water noon and night, the chickens also, and the milking to do. Then the Telephone keeps one "Fox trotting" to answer it, often for a "wrong number" or "false" call. . . .

Thur. 30 [*Dec. 1915*]. [*Farnsworth's husband was ill and confined to the house for some weeks*] . . . We are all alone all the time now and being Holiday week, everyone so busy with their plans for the New Year, no one comes in and I can hardly get a letter posted—all our Calls are by Phone and I almost wish I had no phone.

Martha Farnsworth

Silent Movies

Fri. 25 [*May 1906*]. . . . After supper Fred, Freda and I, with the Joneses and Mr. & Mrs. Radcliffe, attended the *Novelty Theatre* to see the "Moving Pictures" of the *San Francisco Earthquake*. The pictures were good, tho' some were dim, but showed the *awfulness* of the wrecked city; *falling buildings, fire* and *discharge* of *dynamite*.

Martha Farnsworth

Electric Lights

Thurs. 30 [*Mar. 1911*]. Edison Co., thro' H.B. Howard, sent men out this afternoon to "wire" our house for Electric-lights. . . .

Martha Farnsworth

The Airplane

Mon. 11 [*Sept. 1911*]. . . . Saw my first *"Aeroplane"* this evening as we sat on the Porch. It had flown from the Fair Grounds to the State House and was on its way back. A very pretty flight.

Martha Farnsworth

An early airplane, 1910. *(Courtesy, National Archives)*

August 14, 1911 I went down to the club where I found everything in confusion but working toward order. Luncheons begin again on Tuesday—tomorrow. At 3:30 as I stood "on the ledge" at the club, I heard a puffing clattering below and then for the first time I saw a heavier than air flying machine rise from the ground so illogically, so unexpectedly that I did not realize it for a moment. Half an hour later seven were in the air together and before the end of the day two had mounted to the clouds and nine more were playing about [*barnstorming*]. *The air is conquered!* I realize it now as never before. And yet, before an hour had passed it all seemed a part of my daily life, as little surprising as kiteflying. I wrote at once for father to come down. I want him to see the miracle.

Hamlin Garland

Wed. 25 [*Dec. 1912*]. . . . Dressed and went to . . . Mr. Clarence Radcliffe's to Christmas dinner. . . . In the midst of dinner we were called out to see Phil Billard [*a well-known barnstormer in Topeka*] in his Aeroplane and he was certainly making a most beautiful flight and very high—*its wonderful*. . . .

Thurs. 24 [*July 1919*]. Another *hot* day. We went out to Washburn this evening to the Flying Field. . . . Three Aeroplanes out there, and some pretty Flying. I'm crazy to take a Fly, but can't afford the price $10.00. . . .

Martha Farnsworth

The Vacuum Cleaner

Sat. 3 [*Feb. 1912*]. Cold, very cold, but I used my new "suction sweeper" this morning from the Daily Capitol and soon warmed up: it's the finest thing *under* the sun, if not "new" and most certainly revolutionizes "house cleaning"; in thirty minutes I had gotten about a bushel of dirt—(more or less, but any way, enough to astonish one) from under the carpets, and wore out the muscles of my back and shoulders and made myself lame in great shape.

Thur. 2 [*Nov. 1916*]. . . . Jonesie cleaned my carpets with her vacuum cleaner, the "Thor" and it certainly cleaned them too. Electricity is wonderful.

Martha Farnsworth

The Victrola

Thur. 2 [*Nov. 1916*]. This afternoon "Jonesie" and I went to town to "shop" a wee bit and pay Bills . . . and we went in to Rohr's to "investigate" the Victrola: Fred wants a "music box." Well I fell com-

The new vacuum cleaner (1910) was more efficient than a broom. *(Courtesy, National Archives)*

pletely in love with the Victrola, like it much better than the Edison and think I shall give my husband one for Christmas. . . .

Tue. 28 . . . I ordered a Victrola today from W.F. Roehr's—$100.00 My!

Thur. 30 . . . Thanksgiving Day! and O, we have so much to be thankful for. . . . We enjoyed Victrola music today . . . we always do without everything in way of pleasure, we work hard and "skimp," with our noses always on the grindstone and can't "lay by" so we decided to get a bit of pleasure by buying a Victrola. . .

Martha Farnsworth

The Radio

January 2, 1926 [*New York*]   There is something rather terrifying in the fact that by pulling a knob one can open the sluiceway for all the cheap music, droning speeches, commonplace singing and dreary wit of the radio stations of the world. I dread to think what the results will be to men who are engaged, as I am, in work which requires solitude and silence. It is not merely the actual voices, tones, and words of this frightful horn but the sense of being open to invasion. The fact that it is always there!

January 30, 1932   Today at noon, I tuned the radio in on the Metropolitan Opera House broadcast of Die Valkyrie and for an hour and a half. Mary Isabel and I sat entranced by the glorious voices which uttered Wagner's elemental music. These voices had a dignity and fervor almost unequalled by any I had ever heard on the stage. The orchestral harmonies came to us with finer effect than we could have obtained while sitting in the orchestra of the opera house. We could hear the faint echoes of the vast building and the rap of the conductor's baton and every lightest note of the violins. All this we heard seated in easy chairs in our own reception room three thousand miles away [*in Los Angeles*].

Adjectives are of no value when such a marvel comes into one's life. The music moved me more strongly than at any other hearing. With no rustling, coughing, whispering to distract me and with no bobbing heads between me and the actors, I was free to lave in the billows of harmony which came rolling with elemental power from the amplifier. We could not have heard it with the same fullness of power in the hall, for here the instruments were subordinated to the voices.

Hamlin Garland

Motion Pictures . . . With Sound

Wed. 24 [*Sept. 1913*] . . . went to Grand Opera House to see Edison *"Talking* Moving pictures" and they were *great.* I canned a crate of blue-plums and one of peaches this morning—worked very hard all day, but enjoyed, immensely, the pictures this evening—not too tired for pleasure.

Martha Farnsworth

February 8, 1927 [*New York*]   Zulime and I felt well enough to go down to Warner's theater [*in New York City*] and hear the vitaphone reproduction of Hardy [*son-in-law, Hardesty Johnson*] and his orchestra. It was all quite marvelous as we had anticipated but it did not give us pleasure. Some of it was almost lifelike but the knowledge that it was not substantial kept us from being really moved. This may be only a necessary first stage of the process. We came later to take them as real bodies rather than as shadows. We are stuffed full of marvels in these later days. Beginning in a quiet age without telephones, automobiles, mechanical pianos, radio and all the rest of it, I am even now at sixty-six overwhelmed with all these devices. If I live ten years more I shall be completely alien to my neighbors who will find all these things necessities.

Hamlin Garland

The Zeppelin

October 13, 1928   The approach of the [*first Atlantic crossing of the Graf*] Zeppelin airship was announced from time to time by wireless all day. Wonders are now commonplace with this age. Nothing really thrills us. We say, "Well, well! I never expected to see this in our time," and straightway forget it or cry out against any further allusion to it. We get bored by radio, airships from Europe, or television within a week and clamor against the news of them. Everything gets to be an "old story" with us even while it is only a few days old. But there is [*no*] use arguing for or against this tendency. It is inevitable. What its effect is to be, what it will do to our life and literature, is too vast a problem for any man's attempt at solution. All we can do is drift with the immeasurable current of what most thinkers call "progress." It is no doubt an old man's weariness but I am tired of the incessant clamor concerning inventions to spread intelligence when there is so little that is worth distribution.

Questions for Discussion

1. What are Farnsworth's and Garland's responses to these modern inventions? Do their responses differ? If so, in what ways? What effects does this technology have on their lives?
2. In what ways has technology changed our lives? Are all of the changes for the better? Do they in any way detract from the quality of life?

13.

Anonymous

Letters from the African-American Migration, 1916–1917

Between 1916 and 1919 at least 500,000 African Americans left the South for the North, primarily for northern cities. This estimate, derived from the census of 1920, may greatly under-state the actual number, since African Americans have tradi-tionally been undercounted in census figures.

There were a number of reasons for the migration. The start of World War I in Europe in 1914 drastically reduced European immigration. While the United States remained out of the war until 1917, the prewar production boom in northern factories increased the demand for labor, and agents went south to recruit black workers. At the same time, conditions for blacks in the South were worsening, as the letters that follow illustrate. The result was a massive internal migration, encouraged by African-American newspapers like the Chicago Defender, *which had a wide southern circulation.*

The following letters are divided into two sections. Initially come letters from the South to newspapers such as the De-fender *and to civil rights organizations such as the Urban League, explaining conditions in the South and inquiring about opportunities in the North. Then personal letters from newly arrived migrants describe the conditions they found. The histo-*

Emmet J. Scott, comp. "Letters of Negro Migrants of 1916–1918," *Journal of Negro History* 4 (July 1919): 290–340 and "Additional Letters of Negro Migrants of 1916–1918," *Journal of Negro History* 4 (October 1919): 412–75.

rian who collected these letters and published them in 1919 did not include the names of the writers, for reasons that will become apparent.

Letters to Newspapers and Organizations in the North

Fort Gaines, Ga., Oct. 9, 1916.

Dear Sir: Replying to your letter dated Oct. 6th the situation here is this: Heavy rains and Boll weevel has caused a loss of about 9,000 bales of cotton which together with seed at the prevailing high prices would have brought $900,000.00 the average crop here being 11,000 bales, but this year's crop was exceptionally fine and abundant and promised a good yeald until the two calamities hit us.

Now the farmer is going to see that his personal losses are minimised as far as possible and this has left the average farm laborer with nothing to start out with to make a crop for next year, nobody wants to carry him till next fall, he might make peanuts and might not, so taking it alround, he wants to migrate to where he can see a chance to get work.

Troy, Ala., Oct. 17, 1916.

Dear Sirs I am enclosing a clipping of a lynching again which speaks for itself. I do wish there could be sufficient presure brought about to have federal investigation of such work. I wrote you a few days ago if you could furnish me with the addresses of some firms or co–opporations that needed common labor. So many of our people here are almost starving.

Newbern, Ala., 4/7/1917

Dear Sir: Doubtless you have learned of the great exodus of our people to the north and west from this and other southern states. I wish to say that we are forced to go when one thinks of a grown man wages is only fifty to seventy five cents per day for all grades of work. He is compelled to go where there is better wages and sociable conditions, believe me. When I say that many places here in this state the only thing that the black man gets is a peck of meal and from three to four lbs. of bacon per week, and he is treated as a slave. As leaders we are powerless for we dare not resent such or to show even the slightest disapproval. Only a few days ago more than 1000 people left here for the north and west. They cannot stay here. The white man is saying that you must not go but they are not doing anything by way of assisting the black man to stay.

African-American migrants arriving in the North. *(Courtesy, National Archives)*

Houston, Texas, April 20, 1917.

Dear Sir: wanted to leave the South and Go an[y] Place where a man will Be any thing Except A Ker I thought would write you for Advise As where would be a Good Place for a Comperedly young man That want to Better his Standing who has a very Promising young Family.

I am 30 years old and have Good Experience in Freight Handler and Can fill Position from Truck to Agt.

would like Chicago or Philadelphia But I dont Care where so long as I Go where a man is a man.

Lutcher, La., May 13, 1917.

Dear Sir: I have been reading the Chicago defender and seeing so many advertisements about the work in the north I thought to write you concerning my condition. I am working hard in the south and can hardly earn a living. I have a wife and one child and can hardly feed them. I thought to write and ask you for some information concerning how to get a pass for myself and family. I dont want to leave my family behind as I cant hardly make a living for them right here with them and I know they would fare hard if I would leave them. If there are any agents in the south there havent been any of them to Lutcher if they would come here they would get at least fifty men. Please sir let me hear from you as quick as possible. Now this is all. Please dont publish my letter, I was out in town today talking to some of the men and they say if they could get passes that 30 or 40 of them would come. But they havent got the money and they dont know how to come. But they are good strong and able working men. If you will instruct me I will instruct the other men how to come as they all want to work. Please dont publish this because we have to whisper this around among our selves because the white folks are angry now because the negroes are going north.

Pensacola, Fla., 5–19–17.

Dear Editor: Would you please let me no what is the price of boarding and rooming of Chicago and where is the best place to get a job before the draft will work. I would rather join the army 1000 times up there than to join it once down here.

Letters from Friends and
Family Members in the North

Chicago, Illinois. [*n.d.*]

My dear Sister: I was agreeably surprised to hear from you and to hear from home. I am well and thankful to say I am doing well. The weather and everything else was a surprise to me when I came. . . . I am quite busy. I work in Swifts packing Co. in the sausage department. My daughter and I work for the same company—We get $1.50 a day and we pack so many sausages we dont have much time to play but it is a matter of a dollar with me and I feel that God made the path and I am walking therein.

Tell your husband work is plentiful here and he wont have to loaf if he want to work.

Pittsburg, Pa., May 11, 1917.

My dear Pastor and wife: It affords me great pleasure to write you this leave me well & O.K. I hope you & sis Hayes are well & no you think I have forgotten you all but I never will how is ever body & how is the church getting along well I am in this great city & you no it cool here right now the trees are just peeping out. fruit trees are now in full bloom but its cool yet we set by big fire over night. I like the money O.K. but I like the South better for my Pleasure this city is too fast for me they give you big money for what you do but they charge you big things for what you get and the people are coming by ca[r] Loads every day its just pack out the people are Begging for some whears to sta.

Dixon, Ill., Sept.–25–17.

Dear Sir: Time affords of writting you people now as we have raised to wages to three dollars a day for ten hours—eleven hrs. a day $3.19. We work two wks day and two wks night—for night work $3.90. This is steady work a year round. We have been running ten years without stopping only for ten days repair. I wish you would write me at once.

Philadelphia, Pa., Oct. 7, 1917.

Dear Sir: I take this method of thanking you for yours early responding and the glorious effect of the treatment. Oh. I do feel so fine. Dr. the treatment reach me almost ready to move I am now housekeeping again I like it so much better than rooming. Well Dr. with the aid of God I am making very good I make $75 per month. I am carrying enough insurance to pay me $20 per week if I am not able to be on duty. I don't have to work hard. dont have to mister every little white boy comes along I havent heard a white man call a colored a nigger you no now—since I been in the state of Pa. I can ride in the electric street and steam cars any where I get a seat. I dont care to mix with white what I mean I am not crazy about being with white folks, but if I have to pay the same fare I have learn to want the same acomidation. and if you are first in a place here shoping you dont have to wait until the white folks get thro tradeing yet amid all this I shall ever love the good old South and I am praying that God may give every well wisher a chance to be a man regardless of his color, and if my going to the front would bring about such conditions I am ready any day—well Dr. I dont want to worry you but read between lines; and maybe you can see a little sense in my weak statement the kids are in school every day I have only two and I guess that all. Dr. when you find time I would be delighted to have a word from the good old home state. Wife join me in sending love you and yours.

I am your friend and patient.

Chicago, Illinois, 11/13/17.
Mr. H——
Hattiesburg, Miss.

Dear M——: Yours received sometime ago and found all well and doing well. hope you and family are well. . . . Whats the news generally around H'burg? I should have been here 20 years ago. I just begin to feel like a man. It's a great deal of pleasure in knowing that you have got some privilege My children are going to the same school with the whites and I dont have to umble to no one. I have registered—Will vote the next election and there isnt any 'yes sir' and 'no sir'—its all yes and no and Sam and Bill.

Florine says hello and would like very much to see you.

All joins me in sending love to you and family. How is times there now? Answer soon, from your friend and bro.

> *[The optimistic view of race relations in the letters above did not tell the whole story. Racial tensions exploded in Chicago in 1919 when an African-American teenager swimming off a beach that whites regarded as their own was frightened by whites, swam a few strokes, and drowned. The violence that followed left nearly 40 dead and over 500 injured. Despite this and other examples of northern racial violence in 1919, and a depression in 1920–1922, few migrants abandoned the northern cities.]*

Questions for Discussion

1. What were conditions like for African Americans in the South before World War I? Why were so many eager to move North?
2. How did southern whites feel about the migration? Why?
3. What reaction did the migrants have to life in the North?

14.
Guy Emerson Bowerman, Jr.
Diary of an Ambulance Driver During World War I, 1917–1918

When the United States declared war on the Central Powers in April 1917, Guy Emerson Bowerman, Jr. was a twenty-year-old student at Yale University. Too young to be drafted, he volunteered out of a sense of patriotic duty and a desire for adventure. Initially he planned to serve in the air corps, but his parents persuaded him instead to join the ambulance corps, believing it to be safer. In fact the ambulance corps proved to be most dangerous, and during the course of the war the French government awarded Bowerman the Croix de Guerre *for his bravery under fire.*

Bowerman's diary is the story of a rite of passage. In 1917 he was a naive young man full of romantic notions of war and unexamined social prejudices. By the end of the war he was a different person. As he wrote when the Armistice was signed, "the old life was gone forever."

1917
June 28. Enlisted at New Haven. Sworn in by Major Stiles, U.S.A. It's a funny feeling when you hold up your right hand to take the oath,

Guy Emerson Bowerman, Jr. *The Compensations of War: The Diary of an Ambulance Driver During the Great War,* ed. Mark C. Carnes. Austin: University of Texas Press, 1983.

89

you swear away your body to your government; lose your identity and become a cog. Well I'm in the thing for better or for worse, soit!

/////

[Bowerman made the following entry after his ship to France was attacked by submarines.]

August 20. . . . There seemed to be a perfect nest of subs and our shells were falling everywhere. . . . I can honestly say that I wasn't afraid. I was excited of course but was perfectly deliberate in everything I did. I hope I'm never more frightened than I was during that hour and a half. Everyone is keen to know how he'll act in a tight place what you fear is that when the test comes you'll show fear. All the fellows behaved admirably and seemed to consider it all a matter of course.

/////

[The rest of the diary was written while Bowerman was in France.]

October 3. . . . Went thru the trenches tonight and after we sit around on the grassy slope talking of home and watching the full red harvest moon come up thru a gap in the beautiful wooded hills across the valley. . . . How useless war is; what a waste of human energy not to mention life and yet I suppose some good will come of it in the matter of government; social conditions; inventions and a closer bond between all peoples. Here are men with three years absolutely lost from their lives and existing under such conditions that should the war end tomorrow it will take 2 yrs more for them to readjust themselves. Surely God wouldn't permit all of this for extermination only. It's hard tho for a ordinary man to reconcile this war and a conception of a gentle God.

/////

October 27 to November 2. This job of waiting for something to do is a wearisome one and we're dead of ennui. . . . Thank Heaven the outfit is a small one and composed of men who are or at least have been gentlemen. I can't imagine how these days would pass in the company of men with whom you had nothing in common. . . .

/////

November 13. Big battle with two Boche [*German*] avions [*airplanes*] by three A.A. [*anti-aircraft*] batteries about 6:45 this evening. It was a wonderful sight to our unaccustomed eyes. . . . The bursting shells

Camouflaged ambulances in France. *(Courtesy, National Archives)*

were beautiful to see—big red blotches of flame way up in the heavens, like a tremendous Fourth of July spectacle. . . .

/////

1918
January 15. . . . The night was so black that we were forced to go on low [*headlights*] most of the way excepting when a star shell or a gun flash lighted up the road for a brief while. By the time I returned the abri [*shelter*] was filled up with French & German wounded so I went down to see the doctors dress the wounds. As I stood in the narrow winding gallery they brought in three wounded, one with his shoulder torn off, another minus half his arm and the third with raw meat and blood where his eye should have been. Being my first close–up of wounded I got rather sick at the stomach and decided I needed some fresh air. My curiosity soon got the better of me and I returned. This time some wounded Germans were brought in looking rather sunked cheeked and old. They are the Landstrummers, men from 35 yrs up who like the French Territorials are used to hold quite [*Bowerman's spelling of "quiet"*] sectors or work on the roads. Two of them impressed me, one

a grey–haired man of about 43, bitterly tired out, wet, covered with mud and the strangest mixed expression of fear and dejection. The other was a lad of about 21 with his fore arm shot away. As the French wounded are cared for first he had to lie on a dirty little bunk built into the side of the abri till his turn came. He bled profusely, his clothes and the mattress upon which he lay were soaked with blood which dripped off the boards to form a red–dish pool on the earthen floor and reflected the light of the wavering candles. Tho he must have suffered intense pain he remained absolutely quite possibly thru fear for they have been told the same stories about French atrocities to German prisoners that we are told are perpetrated by the Boches. I had more pity for the young fellow because every time I looked at the old one I saw Belgian women raped, French peasants shot down and the memory of the little Belgian boy who had showed me his arm with the hand gone at the wrist the night we stopped in Sezanne. . . .

/////

April 4. . . . As to events on the Somme[1] one can only guess and pray for the best. The newspapers say that they are holding a little, but one can place little confidence in newspaper reports. But surely Germany cannot succeed. Why if all else fails God would be with us and [*stop*] these ravages. Just now it is hard to believe Pope's philosophy that "whatever is, is right" and surely "God works in mysterious ways his wonders to perform." When I stop to think of our going to the Somme or of a big offensive here I wish to write here my opinions on duty and death so that if I should be killed the family will not mourn me, death is not a thing to cause unhappiness—

> *[Bowerman cut out what he had written here. As he later explained, this was "due to some natural aversions which a man has to making a will or to talking about death in this war. Death is something one sees constantly and while one hides his fear of it, it is disappointing when you're young and is never mentioned except jokingly. A serious consideration of death is kept secret, I know not why either thru superstition or the effect talking about it has on one's morale."]*

//////

May 12. An air raid last night and tho they only dropped two bombs near the castle they succeeded in killing three civilians and

---

[1]The location of a major German offensive.

injuring two others. Our cars answered the call and did their work so well and quickly that the men were complimented by an English Capt. of M.P.'s The baby killers lived up to their rep for one of those hit was a little girl who died on the way to the hospital. The other two killed were an old man and a middle aged woman. Three generations wiped out! Surely this is every one's war and we Americans can thank God that the war is being fought on this side. . . .

/////

May 28.   . . . going down into a little valley we could see the bombs landing just ahead of us. They make a beautiful sight, huge fountains of sparks and flames. Arriving at the bottom we could not see the car immediately behind us because of the smoke. Driving some five kilometers further and entering a little village we were again subjected to the aerial bombardment. This time the bombs fell all around us and we were saved by the fact that at this point the road had been cut thru a hill and the bombs were all falling some five feet above our heads. . . .

/////

May 30.   . . . big guns, little guns, cavalry, ammunition trains, supply trains and ambulances in flocks streamed by in such an endless line that one imagined the whole French army must be concentrated at this point. It is on such a night as this and during such a time of uncertainty and suspense that this war seems the least bit romantic and as one conceives of it. In the darkness men, guns and trucks appear phanthom like, indistinct beings of another world, even the voices of the men and the creak of wagons & gun [*illegible*] take a different unreal character. But in the broad light of day these things appear the realities that they are and war realities have no romance.

/////

[Bowerman was awarded the Croix de Guerre *for the actions described in the next entry.]*

June 14.   About 4:30 this A.M. the Boches developed a violent dislike for our woods and from the quantity & quality of their shells I do believe they had some evil intention against our persons. . . . Bill's face was an open book in which I read how badly he had been frightened. "Bowie," he said "as soon as you pass under the bridge go like the devil. It's hell on that road they're shelling hell out of it." Comforting words these and my spirits rose accordingly. Borrowing Bill's helmet (I had left my own at M.F.) I hurriedly cranked my car saying a little prayer that I would have the guts to go thru with it. The car started. I yelled for a guide who would show me the way as I had never been over it and didn't care to loiter along looking for the place. As we left . . . we could [*see*] them [*artillery shells*] breaking on both sides of the bridge, sending up big clouds of dust & smoke. I saw them but somehow they didn't seem to register on my brain. I saw them & that was all. The road surely had been & was being shelled. Shell holes, branches & wires littered the road. Despite this I had had from the time I said my prayer the most peculiar feeing almost of abstraction, the shells didn't worry me in the least because something inside me kept saying "you're safe"; "they won't hit you"; "don't be afraid." As we dashed along the road I recall how it seemed that I was merely driving along a country road at home. A most peculiar feeling and I believe I have failed to express just exactly what it was. . . . I had to wait nearly an hour before the wounded came in. Meanwhile the thundering went on about us and by stepping to the door of the cellar one could hear the small 88's (we were 200 yrds from the front) go swish, swish, swish past till you would have sworn that by stepping outside you would be cut in several pieces as by a giant scythe. . . . At the end of the hour a coucheé [*a patient unable to sit up*] and an assis [*a patient able to sit up*] were brought in both having been wounded on the main road. While I fixed up my car some brancardiers [*stretcher bearers*] went down the road a ways to remove a tree which had fallen since we passed there. As soon as they returned we left the poste losing no time on the way. About a kilo and a half from the poste and about 200 yrds from the first bridge another tree had fallen which completely blocked our road. As it was too huge to move it was necessary that I return to Gare Rameé for men & saws. . . . Returned to the poste I yelled to the cellar that I wanted some men & saws. I shall never forget the look of disgust and anger on the faces of those men who were detailed to go with me. . . . Just as we were fairly started with our work a Boche avion flew overhead & spotted us. He opened up his machine for a moment & then flew away. If he shot at us he was a poor marksman, but I decided to run the car off to one side where it would not be so apt to cause another visit by enemy aircraft. Shortly after the avion left a couple of shells landed about 100 yards down the road. Evidently the aviator had reported our being there and the artillery was trying to precipitate a strike. Whatever the purposes of the Boche, he would have been delighted with the result of his firing. Four of us hastily threw ourselves in a ditch behind convenient trees while three jumped into the capacious & rather deep hole left by the trunk of the fallen tree. Recalling the advice to besieged ambulanciers I tried to get a brancardier who lay near me to assist in taking the couchee from the ambulance and placing him in the ditch with us. The idea didn't seem to appeal strongly to my French friend who added, as he refused to move, that the couché was well enough where he was and that for all of him he would remain where he was. Shortly after I called to the men and we started after the tree again. I have sawed some wood in my life but it was play compared to this. Despite the speed (almost frenzy) with which we worked it was a full half hour before the trunk was severed and moved aside sufficiently to allow us to pass. While stopping under the bridge for my assis and guide I thot I heard a shell coming and ducked my head. A Frenchman who saw my movement laughed and said "You're not dead yet" to which truism I answered "No not yet" and off we went. . . .

/////

June 28.   Just one year from today since I held up the old "lunch book[?]" and said "I do." What a change there has been in me and in my life. Wonderful experiences; sad experiences, dangers with all their thrills and uncertain consequences, all these shared with the finest fellows God ever made and commencing true honest to God friendships which shall, I hope endure as long as we all live. "He who has never faced death can never know the joy of living" I don't remember who said that but he spoke trully. Life which is uncertain is doubly sweet, things which formerly were necessities have become luxuries and give more satisfaction and joy than any luxury formerly did. Say what you will and admitting that war is a terrible thing it still has its compensations for those who live. What has the war done for me? This—I have traveled in a "far country"; I have partially learned another language; I have met all manners and breeds of men and have learned true human values. I have learned to take my life as I found it and generally with a smile. I have broadened mentally, am less selfish, have more self confidence, initiative and courage and have developed definite and higher ideas of religion. I have seen men suffer, men die and men offer their lives freely within and outside their line of duty. I have seen a "tough" show a yellow streak and a "sissy" show the "Divine Spark" and I am convinced that there a[re] few cowards in the world. I am living in a time when history is being made and am doing my infinitesimal "bit" to help make it. Here I am living a story such as would have held me enthralled as a boy, and—I think nothing of it! The whole business is unromantic, too close at hand for a man of my capacity to grasp the "heroics" of it. It seems that I have never known any other life but this, there are so very, very many here with me doing the same thing that it is just as if we'd been born again in another world and this war was a perfectly natural mode of life. Thus are we able to adapt ourselves and we may thank God who in his infinite wisdom made us as we are. I wouldn't trade this past year for any five other years of my life. Allah be praised! Vive L'Amerique,

"Vive La France," "Vive L'Angleterre," "Vive L'Italie" and on with the dance! Are we down–hearted? No! No! . . .

/////

July 18. . . . About a half kilometer from Corcy I picked up a Senegalese who had just been wounded. His entire left shoulder had been shot away but the stretchers were filled and I had to put him in front with me. He kept continually falling against me so I put one arm around him and tried to hold him up. Never once did he moan or utter a sound and when I got to Fleury I made them take him out and put him on a stretcher he could never had stood the trip to Boursonne for he would have died of loss of blood since he had only a rough field bandage on his shoulder. I had never supposed that I would like to have my coat stained with a nigger's blood but if I could have eased that fine fellow one jot of pain I would gladly have had my whole uniform wet with it. . . .

/////

July 22. . . . Our shelter was neither bomb proof nor éclat [*shrapnel*] proof but we knew of no "better 'ole" and it does give one comfort to have anything over his head. We were joined shortly by 3 others and then the show started as friend Boche released those bombs. How they did drop—swish–zoom! swish–zoom! each one nearer. I have said before that bursting bombs are beautiful and I wish now to denounce myself as a liar—a monstrous liar. Bursting bombs are the ugliest things on God's green earth and if you doubt me ask any of the five. . . .

/////

October 31. . . . I drove a captain up to an advanced poste a little thatched cottage at the end of a lane. While I was waiting outside I heard a terrible scream from within. I rushed inside but was too late to see the cause of the scream—an amputation without ether of a young Boche's leg. Never in my life have I seen anything which could compare to the pain and anguish in the face and every muscle of the body of that German. As we lifted him into the ambulance his huddled body expressed far better than words his—I know not what—could I describe what I saw there I would be a writer—I only know that I saw something trajic—more than trajic something I cannot put into words.

November 4. . . . One day I ascended into the tower of a chateau (which had recently been a German headquarters) in order to get a view back of the German lines. The tower had been a Boche observatory and some observer had written in charcoal on the plaster these conciliating words. "Pensez toujours au mot 'c'est la guerre' et pour cette raison pardonnez les hotes malvenus." (Think always of the expression 'it's the war' and for this reason pardon your unwelcome guests.) A rather decent expression for a German but somehow I am inclined to think that it was conceived and written simultaneously with the author's realization that the Germans were doomed to defeat. But perhaps I am unjust and the man who signed himself "an soldat Allemande" (a German soldier) was merely a gentle, God fearing person who realized that the Germans were unwelcome guests and not God sent over lords of a benighted race.

/////

November 10.   10 P.M.   LA PAIX EST SIGNEE!!
[*Written in margin:*] They're playing the Marseillaise now. God be praised for His goodness.

All the sky is lighted up with Verey Lights and gun flashes. All the Frenchmen are shouting and shooting and we're so plain damned happy we don't know where we are. All the Section is out.

LA GUERRE EST FINIE!

November 17.   Really the entry for Nov. 10 should end on page 54 [*of Bowerman's original diary*]. The make up of the bottom of that page portrays exactly our, or should I say my? feelings but those few lines were written while the daze had not left me. Then all was supreme gladness, un–adulterated, supreme, estatic joy. Joy, pure joy, but thoughtless joy. The entry under Nov. 10 does not explain why our joy was insane nor why, a little later when the spasm had spent itself, we drew within ourselves and went quietly back to our bunks where some of us laid till almost morning, silent, but wide awake. I remember how Rouget the French sergeant threw up his arms and fell limply into his cot exclaiming "Bon Dieu, it is the end of a bad dream." And so it was but like the awakening from a bad dream we were troubled to assure ourselves that the dream had ended, that now we were awake safe from the hideous thing which pursued us in our slumbers. And I remember how Hank looked up into that clear starlit heaven above us and said quite reverently "Do they mean to say that we won't hear again the hum of a Boche bomber and the shrill noise of a bomb falling" then he shook his head uncomprehendingly. We had heard so many rumors that we thot this but the fabled cry of "wolf." We had hoped so long and passionately for this hour to come and had been so long disappointed that our minds could not grasp the meaning of it when it was here. As I have said before, after our first few months in the war we had so far identified with war that we were as men who have had a lapse of memory. The old life was gone forever and each succeeding day and each succeeding horror drove the peaceful part farther behind us till at last it was gone completely from our ken. Here we were, men made for war, men born to war—men whose life filled from beginning to end with war and we felt secretly in our hearts that there could be no other life. Then to those of us who had been enough in war to lose our peace identity completely were suddenly, precipitately and unwarned flung into another life, a life of peace. We could have been no more awed, no more bewildered than would the men of Mars could they suddenly find themselves on this planet. Then gradually we came to realize what it all meant tho we walked warily like men fearing ambush fearful of having this new found joy snatched from our grasp. Even, when after a week the guns were still quite, though we outwardly were jovial and carefree, certain of seeing home again yet within ourselves we questioned, doubted nor were we ever sure deep down within us till we got our final pay, took off our uniforms and again sat at our family table.

> *[After the war Bowerman married and went to work as a bank teller, eventually becoming a branch manager and later an inspector for the Federal Reserve System. In 1936 he purchased a small exporting company in Los Angeles, which he owned until his death in 1947. The illness that caused his death may have been traceable to inhaling poison gas during the war.]*

Questions for Discussion

1. How do Bowerman's attitudes toward war and the meaning of courage seem to change? What about his attitudes toward his fellow soldiers and toward the Germans?
2. What does Bowerman mean when he writes on November 17, 1918 that "the old life was gone forever"?

15.
Carrie Chapman Catt and Alice Hamilton

Two Letters from the Home Front: World War I, 1918

Carrie Chapman Catt was a leader in the woman suffrage movement in the 1900s and 1910s. She wrote the following letter to her Dutch friend, Aletta Jacobs, describing conditions in the U.S. during the First World War.

Alice Hamilton, a physician and scientist, was a resident of the Hull House[1] Community in Chicago. Her letter to her sister, Margaret, describes a near riot caused by harassment of IWW [Industrial Workers of the World, or "Wobblies"][2] members and Russian immigrants during the First World War. America's entry into the war in 1917 provoked a serious assault on political dissent in this country, heightened later that year by the success of the Bolshevik Revolution in Russia, whose early stages many socialists and radicals had supported.

The Aletta Jacobs Papers. The International Archive for the Women's Movement in the International Information Center and Archive for the Women's Movement, Amsterdam.

The Alice Hamilton Papers. Schlesinger Library. Radcliffe College.

[1]Hull House was one of America's first social settlements, founded in Chicago in 1889 by Jane Addams and Ellen Gates Starr.

[2]See the introduction to the Minderman diary, page 53.

New York, September 4th, 1918

My dear Aletta:—

. . . Our country has been transformed from a land of peace wherein
a soldier was rarely seen and where military affairs were rarely discussed, into a military nation. Soldiers are now seen on every hand.
Long trains of them are continuously passing to and from the training
camps and from the camps to Europe. Everybody is now a part of the
big war machine. It is a strange experience. Many things in this connection would prove of great interest to you were it considered wise to talk
of them freely at this time. Out of respect to the censorship regulations
I will confine my comments to those subjects which are not taboo.

We often talked of the wonderful capacities of the bamboo and the
palm. The war is developing similar capacities in our corn (maize). Long
before the United States entered the war, olive oil chiefly imported from
Spain and Italy, was difficult to secure, and the price was high. We are
now using oil made from cotton seed and from corn. . . . We have such
quantities of fruit and vegetables that they eke out our menus and allow
us to save the flour and sugar and meat which go to the army and to the
Allies. We here in this country have plenty to eat. Prices are going up.
We have our profiteers as every other country seems to have had, but
the government is after them heavy and fast. Wages have gone up also,
perhaps not quite so fast as the cost of food. You spoke about the need
of coal in Holland last winter. The trouble is that there seems not to be
coal enough in the world at this time to keep us all customarily warm.
The Government has tried to make people buy their coal in the summer
so as to avoid the difficulties of last winter. We are now informed that
we should be willing to live in houses of 64 degrees Fahrenheit next
winter in order to save coal, and we are encouraged by the assurance
that this temperature is very much healthier for us than that to which
we are accustomed. I have no doubt there is plenty of truth in that
statement. But you can imagine how many Americans will shiver, if that
regulation is really carried out. The entire country is very obedient to
all requests of the Government for conservation and seems to be very
united in every respect.

Women in large numbers are engaged in doing the things which in
other belligerent countries they have been doing for some time. For
instance they are running many of the elevators in New York City; they
are serving as conductors on street cars, as ticket sellers in the railway
stations, and we have quite a reserve of women police. I do not think
the work of the women in this country in substitution of the work of
men has been as picturesque as in the other countries. Those women
blazed the trail and proved that women could do certain things which

nobody in the world had believed they could do at all. Therefore our women simply slipped into these positions without much public comment.

The general opinion here seems to be that the war will not end for at least a couple of years. There is no doubt in anybody's mind as to how it will end.

Hull-House
June 22nd 1918

Dear Margaret,

. . . When I went for dinner to Salam's, at about nine, I noticed a crowd outside Bowen Hall [*another settlement house in Chicago*] and got uneasy and went over. I found the house packed with Russians, a fine lot of men and women, mostly young, and at the moment in great excitement, on their feet demanding that a man who had been arrested be released. At the end under the gallery was a group of plain clothes men, big heavy-jawed, stupid-looking brutes, and of course my heart sank at the sight. They are the ones that make all the rioting really. . . . While I was trying to find out what had happened—it was all in Russian—she [*Rachel Yarros, a resident of the house*] mounted the platform and told them that nobody had been arrested and quieted them down. Then she came back and told me she had made the police release a man they had dragged out of the gallery for no reason than that they knew him to be an I.W.W. How she did it I don't know, for the police were in an ugly mood. One of them told me that we had no business letting that bunch in, they were all pro-German and I.W.W. and another told me that the whole lot ought to be lined up against a wall and shot. There they stood, big, stupid brutes and I looked at them and looked at the audience of eager-faced, intellectual idealists and thought that it was absolutely in the power of those creatures to pick out any man, drag him off to the station, kicking him all the way, throw him into a cell and refuse him access to his friends or to a lawyer, bring him before a judge as stupid as they and send him for fifteen years to the penitentiary. That is not imaginary, it might have happened any minute, it was what they wanted to have happen. They were agents provocateurs [*there for the purpose of provoking conflict*] and so was the group of reporters who hovered around like vultures waiting for something to happen that they could make headlines of. Of course the audience was excited and turbulent, for about three quarters of them, including the speaker, an old Revolutionist, were Menshiviki, and the rest Bolsheviki who were more noisy than all the others. But there was no harm and I would not have been really uneasy if it had not been for those miserable police.

They sent for reinforcements from Maxwell street and I heard them say there was a patrol wagon on the corner and there were six men outside and about six inside in one group and then others scattered around the room, and they made themselves so prominent and wanted to hustle people and interfere. I never had a more nervous time than those three hours, for it lasted till midnight when the lights went out and at any moment we thought a riot might start. . . .

Questions for Discussion

1. What changes in everyday life at home did the war bring about, according to Catt? What other effects of the war are described in Hamilton's letter?
2. How did this war open working opportunities for women?
3. How would you compare the situation described by Hamilton with other riots or near-riots involving confrontations with law enforcement officers? How might the ethnicity, immigrant status, or language limitations of the people affect such a conflict?

Part 3

Prosperity, Depression, and War

The experience of World War I had been disillusioning for many, and in the postwar era younger people in particular had doubts about the belief in progress that had informed the previous generation. While the idea that a thoroughgoing revolution in morals occurred during the decade is an exaggeration, values and social roles were changing in significant ways.

This was particularly true about the place of women in American society. With the passage in 1920 of the Nineteenth Amendment, women gained the right to vote. During the rest of the decade came a growing assertiveness by the so-called "new woman," who at times demanded equality with men in all areas of life. Some women now smoked and even drank openly (despite Prohibition). More significantly, by 1930 over ten million held jobs. There was also increased sexual freedom, influenced by loose interpretation of the theories of Sigmund Freud and personified by the "flapper," with her short skirt, silk-stockinged legs, and bobbed hair. The diary of Martha Lavell shows the effects of the ideas of the day on a thoughtful young college woman.

African Americans also challenged the status quo during the decade through organizations such as the integrated National Association for the Advancement of Colored People and Marcus Garvey's separatist United Negro Improvement Association. At the same time the Harlem Renaissance promoted pride in African-American cultural achievements. Nevertheless, persistent racism as illustrated by the rise of the

Ku Klux Klan precluded significant gains in civil rights. Alice Dunbar-Nelson's diary recounts a frustrating attempt to gain presidential support for a federal anti-lynching law.

The 1920s had been prosperous for many sectors of the American economy, but not for all. Farm income had been in decline even before the Great Depression struck in 1929, and in some parts of the country the dust storms of the 1930s worsened the already disastrous situation. Resulting from the effects of prolonged drought on a land that had too often been overgrazed and carelessly plowed, the storms blew away the fertile topsoil and left the land barren and desolate. While the effects of the Dust Bowl were greatest in the area from the Oklahoma panhandle to western Kansas, all of the Great Plains states from North Dakota down to Texas were affected. The diary of Ann Marie Low portrays the effects of the dust storms on a North Dakota farm family.

The worldwide depression encouraged the rise of aggressive dictatorships in Germany and Italy. Linda Benitt's letter shows an American family watching with apprehension as Hitler's aggression made a new world war more likely. The war brought increased government spending and a labor shortage to the United States, ending the depression. The American people united behind the nation's military effort and the sacrifices it demanded, as shown in the diary of Dorothy Blake. The labor shortage meant new economic opportunities for women as factory jobs became available and "Rosie the Riveter" became a national heroine. Augusta Clawson's diary provides a picture of the accomplishments of women in war-time factories and of the pressures they faced.

As in World War I, this period again saw violations of civil rights on the home front, most notably in the internment of over 100,000 Japanese resident aliens and Americans of Japanese ancestry. Charles Kikuchi's diary recounts life in one of the internment camps. African Americans continued to face discrimination, although as Harold Ickes's diary shows, government officials, under pressure from civil rights leaders, did take at least a few steps to include African Americans in the employment opportunities the war provided. Meanwhile, on the battlefield, the war exacted a high toll on the combatants. Richard McIntire's diary reveals the cost of the war to those who fought.

The war came to an end in 1945, shortly after the dropping of atomic bombs on Hiroshima and Nagasaki. Phyllis Fisher's diary from the nuclear laboratory at Los Alamos describes life at the top-secret facility, the elation at the success of the bomb, and the sober second thoughts that followed.

16.
Alice Dunbar-Nelson

Anti-Lynching Laws and the Ku Klux Klan: A Meeting with President Warren G. Harding, 1921

Alice Dunbar-Nelson, widow of the poet Paul Laurence Dunbar, was herself a poet and newspaper publisher in Wilmington, Delaware. In 1921 she was part of a delegation of prominent African Americans who met with President Warren Harding in an effort to deliver a petition requesting clemency for sixty-one soldiers from the black 24th U.S. Infantry imprisoned for life following the Houston "race riot" of 1917, at which racial attacks by white citizens provoked the fighting. Nineteen black soldiers were hanged as a result of that event (thirteen without trial), with no whites prosecuted. The delegation's further, and more radical, efforts were to convince Harding to establish federal anti-lynching laws and outlaw the Ku Klux Klan. Those efforts failed, however, with the 1922 defeat in Congress of the Dyer Anti-Lynching Bill. The following entries document the delegation's visit to the White House as recorded by Ms. Dunbar-Nelson.

Alice Dunbar-Nelson. *Give Us Each Day: The Diary of Alice Dunbar-Nelson*. Gloria T. Hull, ed. New York: W.W. Norton, 1984. Reprinted by permission of the Charlotte Sheedy Literary Agency, Inc. Introductory comments culled from Hull's notes.

Friday, September 30 [*1921*] . . . I reached Washington at 4:35 . . . started for the Y [*M.C.A.*] building on 12th street.

Not many present when I got there. Kelly Miller [*Howard University professor*], Mrs. [*Carrie*] Clifferd, [*James Weldon*] Johnson [*Secretary of the N.A.A.C.P. and leader of the delegation*], F.B. Ransom, of Indianapolis, Dr. W.W. Wolfe, of Newark, N.J., R.W. Stewart, also of Newark. Emmett Scott [*former secretary to Booker T. Washington and Howard University; special assistant for Black affairs to the Secretary of War*] came a bit later. . . . John W. Parks came in shortly after, Dr. Sinclair, and a Rev. [*R.H.*] Singleton, from Atlanta. We were well in the swing of things, Johnson read the memorial he had prepared and as the evening papers had published—at least the papers that were carrying the Ku Klux Klan exposures—that we were going to the president to protest the K.K.K., we discussed the advisability of touching on the matter at all. Arguments pro and con flew to and fro. If we did not touch it, it would seem that we were insensible to the dangers of the situation. If we did, it might give the president a loophole to escape from the responsibility of the Houston affair. . . .

I was up with them next day—Wednesday, the 28th, September. Ever memorable day. Almost a year to a day since I had made that equally memorable trip to Marion and seen Warren Gamaliel Harding for the first time. . . .

Found all the delegation, except Scott already at the executive offices, and he soon came in. Our engagement was at 10:20. At 10:10 all of us were in the ante-room. . . . At 10:15, five minutes before our scheduled time, the president's secretary, Mr. Christian, called us. I suppose Harding thought he might as well get the disagreeable task over and be done with it. We toddled in single file, Johnson introducing us each in turn to the president who repeated our names, giving us a quick practiced handshake, and bending towards each one, with that charmingly intimate manner he has, which is disarming, though you know it is a gracious pose.

We ranged ourselves in a semi-circle around the room, and Johnson began his reading. He was plainly nervous, and had trouble keeping his glasses on . . . and he had to hold his glasses to his eyes. The president remained standing, partly facing Johnson, three quarters away from us. I watched his face closely. It was heavily impassive, as you would expect it to be.

When Johnson began to read his memorial, the president's lips were slightly parted. Gradually they began to draw together, so slowly that it was almost imperceptible. The rest of his face remained immobile. When Johnson came to that sentence, "The eyes of the colored people will be focussed upon whatever action you may choose to take," he winced perceptibly, and his lips closed in a firm line. Pleasure was the last emotion that was in his breast at that time.

Shelby Davidson [*a member of the delegation*] . . . now stepped forward, when Johnson had finished, and presented his package, which the president took in his hands, and placed on the edge of the desk. "A formidable document," he said, and even this attempt at lightness and jocularity did not lighten his face or manner, which continued heavy, cold and depressing.

I thought at the minute of what Johnson had said on the evening before, when he had once had audience with President Wilson, how after their allotted time was out, Wilson sat chatting pleasantly with them, about his "old black mammy" in the south. Someone snorted and said, "Well, Harding won't brag about his mammy, that's sure."

The president began to speak; he did not think the executive (delightful impersonality) had final word in the matter. He was in the south at the time of the trial, and had naturally heard a great deal about it (southern viewpoint, of course). There would have to be investigations. We had presented the petition, but that was not all. As if we were mere sentimentalists; he was the practical one. He would look into the matter as soon as possible. We understood, of course, that other things might have to take precedence, but he would assure us it would be looked into. Bang! went the door of hope. We had indeed shot an arrow into the air, but it had fallen into slippery waters, and not to earth.

Johnson continued, he could not refrain. . . . There was indeed a trace of animation in his [*the president's*] manner at once, but whether the animation of impatience or of interest, it is difficult for me to say. "Oh, I do not think," he began slowly, "I believe," more quickly, then he turned towards the semi-circle patiently standing on the thick carpet, "No, I won't say that," with a swift shake of his head, "I won't say that, but I do not believe the Ku Klux Klan is aimed at your people." More, he continued to the effect that the older organization was so constituted, but again he said, "I may be mistaken, but I do not believe it is aimed at your people."

I have been wondering what it was that the president would not say, and it has just come to me that perhaps the sentence that almost slipped out was that "if you people would cease agitating the attack upon the Ku Klux Klan, it would be more speedily wiped out of existence." I wonder if some such thought was not on his mind?

He terminated the interview, and we filed out slowly. . . . One slight dark man hovered in the little communicating passageway. Evidently a secret service man. Mrs. [*Mary B*] Talbert [*former president of the National Association for Colored Women's Clubs*] said they did not even think enough of us to have plenty of secret service men to protect the president. They know "niggers wouldn't have sense enough to attempt to assassinate the president.". . .

[A federal anti-lynching law was never passed.]

Questions for Discussion

1. What problems did the delegates face in their quest for abolition of the Ku Klux Klan and federal anti-lynching laws?
2. How would you characterize President Harding's response to the delegation?
3. What other groups might Harding have had in mind in addition to blacks as Klan targets?

17.
Martha Lavell

Diary of a College Woman, 1926–1929

Martha Lavell was a thoughtful young woman who entered Mills College as a freshman in 1926. The next year she transferred to the University of Minnesota, closer to home. Her "Book of Thoughts" shows the influence of the times as well as her reflections on them.

1926

September 26. . . . College life is so different from a home life. But we do have loads of fun. Sunday night, while Alice and I were studying, we heard the awfullest noise in the hall and rushed out to investigate. Beryl Pear (since elected Hall pres.) was trying to play a violin, and she didn't know much about it. Another girl had a cello, and a third a tin horn. I joined in with my harmonica and you would have thought some one was being murdered. But it was so much fun. I love to make noise, but I don't have a chance very often. . . .

October 17. Mother sent me a bridge case yesterday, rose leather, with two packs of cards and a score pad. So, of course, we played bridge last night. We had a grand time, played until about nine, and then went up on the hill for some ice cream. I didn't get to bed until eleven.

/////

The Sophia Smith Collection, Smith College, Northampton, Massachusetts.

Martha Lavell. *(Courtesy, National Archives)*

November 7.   Last night was the Hall dance, but several of us couldn't go since we couldn't get blind dates. However we formed the Old Maids' Club and had one grand scandalized meeting about what the young people were coming to. We went up on the hill to have some ice cream and decided it was our duty to reform the boys and girls. Just think, they bobbed their hair (the girls I mean) and wore stockings that could be seen through! Shocking!

/////

1927

December.   . . . Civilization has been all wrong through all these ages. Of course, it is evolving from something worse to something better all the time, but I sometimes wonder, why did it start out the way it did? Why didn't men and women live on an equal basis, in the first place? I'm glad I'm living in this age; people are beginning to wake up. There was a time when I thought woman suffrage was "insufferable," and when I was very indignant at seeing a man sitting down in a streetcar with a woman standing. I've changed my mind in the last year. I don't know how it happened.

I don't think I have much pity in me; I hate lots of people; I get mad very easily, though only inside, but I must live my life on a square basis. I am beginning to see the other side of the question. It isn't just that women want their rights; it's that they want men to have theirs, after all these years. I figure a man has just as much right to a seat as I have. He shouldn't have to spend his money on a woman when she spends none on him. He shouldn't have to earn the family's living any more than she. But neither should she have to bring the children up any more than he. I think God made us to go hand in hand through life together, sharing burdens and joys equally. And how many thousands of years it has taken us to realize it! We're not there yet; there are many people in this world who haven't learned how to *think*.

I must share my ideas and ponderings, if only with a notebook. Perhaps someday I shall find someone who will understand.

/////

1928

January 8. . . . [*Cousin Ann*] got to talking about musicians the other day; said it was sissified for a man to write music or paint pictures. Aunt Marguerite thought so too so I kept silent. Sometimes it does no good whatever to argue. But oh, how can they think that only women can appreciate beauty? If I felt that I never will find the man who will love the wind and clouds and sunset as much as I do, I'd think that life isn't worth living. . . .

Ginny [*Martha Lavell's sister*] gets so worried over the youth of today. She says everyone at school puts on lipstick and rouge and smokes and "pets" and everything. She thinks flappers are terrible. She was horrified at my ideas that the modern youth is better than it ever was. I'm an enthusiastic champion of modern ideas. At last we have reached the conclusion that though there will be girls and boys who are coarse enough to smoke, drink and pet, still we can be modern without copying them. She seems to be satisfied with that, though she does refuse to read a story in which a woman smokes.

Jane [*a friend*] and I used to wonder if there are any boys in this world who wouldn't insist on a girl's petting, real boys, that is, not saps. Goodness knows, I've known plenty of nice old-fashioned boys who wouldn't think of petting, but the kind I'd like to know is an up-to-date one with advanced ideas. I consider myself a free-thinker, a reactionist and a radical. I'm a one-man person, of which there are few today. And the reason that I'm a one-man person is that I believe that's what Nature intended us to be. I'm not that because I'm old-fashioned or because I believe in modesty and purity for women. I do believe that Nature intended "free love," but also at the same time the "one-mate" idea. There, is that old-fashioned?

If I ever get married, it won't be by a minister. Of course, there'd have to be a representative of the law present, but I wouldn't have even that if I could have my way. In my mind, a marriage is made by two people when they declare their love for each other, and that's all there is to it. . . .

/////

April 2. . . . I was reading something Dorothy Dix [*a social reformer*] wrote yesterday. She said that the girl who is merely average gets along best in this world. That may be so, but aren't there superior men to like the superior women? She spoke as if men don't like the superior girl, superior in wisdom, beauty, accomplishments, intelligence and the like. But heavens, it seems to me that there must be men that are above average in the same way, and that they would be interested in only people like them. Also Miss Dix said that a girl should not be a good talker, but a good listener and that she should know just a little less than her husband so that he can feel his superiority. That's all wrong. How are we going to have absolute equality in this world if men are to feel superior to women? Surely there must be men who feel the same way. . . .

/////

July 7. . . . I'd give anything if I could wear trousers. It's perfectly terrible to have to sit with one's knees together for fear someone might see up, and to be in constant danger of having one's skirt blow up to one's waist. Darn. Why can't we women be treated the same as men? My children are not going to be brought up with a single distinction between boys and girls. I realize the fact that there has to be some difference. Girls might wear silk trousers and such. And why should they have longer hair than men?

If I were a man, it seems to me that women wouldn't seem human to me. They'd seem so unnatural and *stilted*. . . .

Mother says I'll never find a man who will have all the same ideas as I have. I suppose that's logical but I don't quite see why it is. My ideas seem to me right, so how could anyone who has a brain, have different ones? It's all a mixup, and I suppose my ideas aren't right, but they seem so now. . . .

/////

November 6. A great step forward to the equality of men and women has been taken by the men of this University. They have formed a club whose purpose is to further the custom of the woman's paying for herself on all dates. I was beginning to think that I would have to forget my vow of January 18 [*not to let a boy pay for a date*], until I should find a man with the same idea. Jane Secrest wrote in great protest that such a stand would outrage a man's vanity. However such doesn't seem to be the case with the Dutch Date Club. I'm so tickled over it!

/////

1929

October 22.   I wish I knew of something I could do to promote the cause of peace. I myself believe that pacts, world courts and disarmament will do little; that it is only by educating the children to be peace-minded that we will make any progress. The 100 percent Americanism, the anthem singing, the scorn for all other nations, the flag worship which are being drilled into the coming generation will lead inevitably to another war.

October 24.   . . . I was very pleased the other day in French class (18th century) when the prof. quoted Pierre Boyle as saying that atheists are no more immoral than theists and that Christians make virtues of what were sins to Jesus, i.e., war. Whereupon, Mr. Sirich launched out on a wholesale condemnation of the attitude of the ministers toward the last War. Quite apparent that he's an agnostic and a pacifist. Oh, I'm getting a big kick out of French this year.

We're studying sex differences in Psych. just now. At first I didn't think I'd like Mr. Paterson as a prof. (he's not at all like Mr. Bird). However the other day he said he believed that all sex differences could be attributed to differential training, and I am completely won over. Any man who recognizes no inherent difference between the sexes receives my vehement blessing.

> [*After some years working as an editor, Martha Lavell turned to a career in social work and social research. In 1976 she was one of the founders of the Women's Rights Centennial Committee which commemorated the 1876 Declaration of Women's Rights.*]

Questions for Discussion

1. What are Martha Lavell's attitudes toward the social trends of her day?
2. How do her views compare with those of Mabel Ulrich and the women who wrote to Susan B. Anthony?
3. What do you think of her views on equality of the sexes?

18.
Ann Marie Low
A Dust Bowl Diary, 1934–1937

Ann Marie Low lived in southeastern North Dakota, where the dust storms were at their height in 1934. That year Ann Marie was twenty-two years old and in her last semester at Jamestown College, not far from her family's ranch, where she was studying to become a teacher.

February 19, 1934 — Monday.   Practice teaching is fun. The only trouble is the school is so far downtown I can't run fast enough to avoid being late for American Lit, which is bad in a lecture course. . . .

[Late April, 1934] Professor Travis says my practice teaching supervisor gave me a high recommendation. That is nice. But nothing is much help for us inexperienced girls looking for jobs. My applications to schools having vacancies all come back "No vacancies," meaning they have hired someone else.

April 25, 1934 — Wednesday.   Last weekend was the worst dust storm we ever had. We've been having quite a bit of blowing dirt every year since the drouth started, not only here, but all over the Great Plains. Many days this spring the air is just full of dirt coming, literally, for hundreds of miles. It sifts into everything. After we wash the dishes and put them away, so much dust sifts into the cupboards we must wash them again before the next meal. Clothes in the closets are covered with dust.

Ann Marie Low. *Dust Bowl Diary*. Lincoln: University of Nebraska Press, 1984.

Ann Marie Low. *(Courtesy, National Archives)*

Last weekend no one was taking an automobile out for fear of ruining the motor. I rode Roany to Frank's place to return a gear. To find my way I had to ride right beside the fence, scarcely able to see from one fence post to the next.

Newspapers say the deaths of many babies and old people are attributed to breathing in so much dirt.

May 7, 1934 — Monday.   The dirt is still blowing. Last weekend Bud [*Ann Marie's brother*] and I helped with the cattle and had fun gathering weeds. Weeds give us greens for salad long before anything in the garden is ready. We use dandelions, lamb's quarter, and sheep sorrel. I like sheep sorrel best. Also, the leaves of sheep sorrel, pounded and boiled down to a paste, make a good salve.

Still no job. I'm trying to persuade Dad I should apply for rural school #3 out here where we went to school. I don't see a chance of getting a job in a high school when so many experienced teachers are out of work.

He argues that the pay is only $60.00 a month out here, while even in a grade school in town I might get $75.00. Extra expenses in town would probably eat up that extra $15.00. Miss Eston, the practice teaching supervisor, told me her salary has been cut to $75.00 after all the years she has been teaching in Jamestown. She wants to get married.

School boards will not hire married women teachers in these hard times because they have husbands to support them. . . .

Dad argues the patrons always stir up so much trouble for a teacher at #3 some teachers have quit in mid-term. The teacher is also the janitor, so the hours are long.

I figure I can handle the work, kids, and patrons. My argument is that by teaching here I can work for my room and board at home, would not need new clothes, and so could send most of my pay to Ethel [*Ann Marie's sister*] and Bud.

In April, Ethel had quit college, saying she did not feel well.

May 21, 1934 — Monday. . . . Saturday Dad, Bud, and I planted an acre of potatoes. There was so much dirt in the air I couldn't see Bud only a few feet in front of me. Even the air in the house was just a haze. In the evening the wind died down, and Cap came to take me to the movie. We joked about how hard it is to get cleaned up enough to go anywhere.

The newspapers report that on May 10 there was such a strong wind the experts in Chicago estimated 12,000,000 tons of Plains soil was dumped on that city. By the next day the sun was obscured in Washington, D.C., and ships 300 miles out at sea reported dust settling on their decks.

Sunday the dust wasn't so bad. Dad and I drove cattle to the Big Pasture. Then I churned butter and baked a ham, bread, and cookies for the men. . . .

May 30, 1934 — Wednesday. Ethel got along fine [*after having been hospitalized for appendicitis*], so Mama left her at the hospital and came to Jamestown by train Friday. Dad took us both home.

The mess was incredible! Dirt had blown into the house all week and lay inches deep on everything. Every towel and curtain was just black. There wasn't a clean dish or cooking utensil. . . .

Mama was very tired. After she had fixed starter for bread, I insisted she go to bed and I'd do all the dishes.

It took until 10 o'clock to wash all the dirty dishes. That's not wiping them—just washing them. The cupboards had to be washed out to have a clean place to put them.

Saturday was a busy day. Before starting breakfast I had to sweep and wash all the dirt off the kitchen and dining room floors, wash the stove, pancake griddle, and dining room table and chairs. . . .

Mama couldn't make bread until I carried water to wash the bread mixer. I couldn't churn until the churn was washed and scalded. We just couldn't do anything until something was washed first. Every room had to have dirt almost shoveled out of it before we could wash floors and furniture.

We had no time to wash clothes, but it was necessary. I had to wash out the boiler, wash tubs, and the washing machine before we could use them. Then every towel, curtain, piece of bedding, and garment had to be taken outdoors to have as much dust as possible shaken out before washing. The cistern is dry, so I had to carry all the water we needed from the well.

That evening Cap came to take me to the movie, as usual. Ixnay. I'm sorry I snapped at Cap. It isn't his fault, or anyone's fault, but I was tired and cross. Life in what the newspapers call "the Dust Bowl" is becoming a gritty nightmare.

[Late June, 1934] . . . This country doesn't look pretty any more; it is too barren. I'm herding the milk cows on what is left of the grain fields. We replanted the corn and garden. Dad has the best well in this vicinity. If it holds out, we can carry water to the garden. If it doesn't rain, the corn is out of luck. . . .

July 6, 1934 — Friday. I am still herding cows, and it is awfully hot. Where they have eaten every weed and blade of grain, Bud is plowing so the ground will be softened to absorb rain (if it comes). He is very fed up and anxious to get away to school and fit himself for a job.

Poor Bud. He has worked so hard and saved so hard. He has done without nice clothes and never went to a dance or movie oftener than about once a year because he was saving every penny for college. He hoped his livestock would pay his way for four years. The price was so low he didn't sell any last year. This year they are worth less, and he absolutely must sell them because there is not enough feed for them and no money to buy feed. All the stock he has won't pay his way through one year of college. . . .

July 9, 1934 — Monday. Saturday night Cap and I went to the movie, Claudette Colbert in *The Torch Singer*. Afterward he bought ice cream cones and we sat in the car in front of the store eating them. He brought up the subject of marriage. I reminded him that he promised if I would go out with him occasionally, he would not mention marriage. I also pointed out the impossibility. He has to run the farm until Sonny is old enough and then will have nothing to start out on his own. I have to work until Ethel gets through college and can help Bud, at least two years. If she doesn't help Bud, we are looking at four years. Though I didn't mention it, in four years Cap will be thirty-six years old. Forget it.

He insisted he wants to get married now. Then I turned shrewish and said I'd seen him leave a dance last year with Joan. If he wants a wife, she would doubtless marry him.

He said he did take her home from a dance once, but there is absolutely nothing between him and Joan and I know it—I am all he wants and I know it.

"Let's not quarrel," I murmured. "Things will work out somehow."

He leaned back against the car seat, saying somberly, "Oh, how I wish it would rain."

The light from the store window was on his face. He is really a handsome man, with a John Barrymore profile and thick wavy auburn hair. Suddenly I seemed to see what his face will be someday—a tombstone on which is written the epitaph of dead dreams. I shivered.

"Oh, Sweetheart, you are cold and have no wrap. I'll take you home."

I didn't tell him I wasn't shivering from cold.

/////

July 18, 1934 — Wednesday. It is 104° in the shade. The grain fields are all eaten up, so I'm herding the cows along the ditches of the roads. The garden is burned up. We don't dare carry water to it because the well is going dry and we need all the water there is for us and the livestock. The river is dry. We have fenced a lane from the Big Pasture to the lake so the beef cattle will have access to water.

August 1, 1934 — Wednesday. . . . The drouth and dust storms are something fierce. As far as one can see are brown pastures and fields which, in the wind, just rise up and fill the air with dirt. It tortures animals and humans, makes housekeeping an everlasting drudgery, and ruins machinery.

The crops are long since ruined. In the spring wheat section of the U.S., a crop of 12 million bushels is expected instead of the usual 170 million. We have had such drouth for five years all subsoil moisture is gone. Fifteen feet down the ground is dry as dust. Trees are dying by the thousands. Cattle and horses are dying, some from starvation and some from dirt they eat on the grass.

The government is buying cattle, paying $20.00 a head for cows and $4.00 for calves, and not buying enough to do much good.

[Early September, 1934] . . . Our bountiful and interfering government sometimes creates awful messes. When this region was opened to homesteaders, the government and railroads encouraged people to come in here for an almost free 160 acres. The broken lives and broken hearts that caused was criminal. People back East had no idea a 160-acre tract here does not make a viable farm.

Grandpa realized that. He started out with 480 acres and planned to get more. The drouth of the 1880's cost him his preemption and tree claim. The fire forced him to mortgage the remaining 160 acres. It was a man-killing struggle, but his family managed to hang on until the prosperous times after 1900.

Then during the war the government cried out for all the wheat it could get. People came in here, bought small farms on mortgages, and planted wheat on land which should never have been plowed. After the war, prices dropped drastically. These people have never been able to pay their mortgages. The government has never done a thing to protect them against the terrible gouging of the wheat and cattle markets and of the railroads.

Now another prolonged drouth has struck at a time the whole country is suffering a severe depression. Men like Dad and the Holmes brothers, who have been here a long time, who have plenty of land and no mortgages, have a chance to hang on until better times come again. Better times will come. Meanwhile the man on a mortgaged 160 acres is out of luck.

Since 1920, the newspapers say, 43,000 farmers in North Dakota have lost their land through mortgage foreclosures. . . .

School takes up much of my time. It is cold for September, so I have to be there by 7:30 in the morning to fire the old stove and get the room warm enough for the kids. There are 22 classes a day and all janitor work, which takes anywhere from 5:15 until 6:00. I walk the mile and a half to school because there is no place to keep Roany during the day.

Some of the girls I graduated with don't have it that easy. Leona is really out in the sticks and has to ride horseback four miles to school. Grace has far more pupils than I do and gets only $50.00 a month.

/////

October 31, 1934 — Wednesday. . . . Dora [*one of Ann Marie's students*] is going like a house afire with her crocheting. She has just string to work with. If I ever get a few pennies ahead, I'll buy her some crochet thread. Right now there are no pennies to spare. Ethel's college expenses have taken all my money except what I gave Dad to pay taxes. Out of the next check I want to pay $30.00 for a $1,000.00 life insurance premium. Then if anything happens to me the folks will have the money to plant me and help Bud and Ethel to the extent I could if alive. That can be spared from the next check because poultry money will be coming in. In December I need to save a few dollars for Christmas presents, Christmas treats for my pupils, and a couple dollars for bus fare to Medora. Yep, it will be a while before I can afford crochet thread for Dora.

/////

[*The dust storms in North Dakota lessened after 1934, but the depression continued, and the family was forced to sell their ranch. The following entry is the last one in the diary.*]

June 4, 1937 . . . I feel trapped in the same round all over again. Ethel never contributed a cent last year, so all I could spare, including almost all my last pay check, went to Mama and Bud. I have scarcely enough money for bus fare home—to just an everlasting round of work in a Stony Brook country that has been ruined.

This is a round that will go on forever. At least it will go on until my youth is gone. *Somehow, I've got to get out!!*

[*In 1937 Ann Marie married Seth Low, a government biologist, and a few years later moved away from North Dakota. She did not return for a visit until 1983, and never lived there again.*]

Questions for Discussion

1. What do you learn from the diary about the social effects of the depression and the dust bowl?
2. What effect does the situation in North Dakota have on Ann Marie Low personally?

19.
Harold L. Ickes
Politics and Civil Rights, 1940–1941

Harold Ickes served as U.S. Secretary of the Interior under President Franklin D. Roosevelt and later under Harry Truman, until he resigned following a dispute. A man noted for his integrity and incisive convictions, Ickes was an outspoken champion for social reform. The following entries reveal his efforts to change the status of African Americans in the 1940s and the political and social climate in which that struggle took place.

September 15, 1940 . . . The President told [*Henry*] Stimson [*Secretary of War*] that he was in favor of announcing that with respect to the Negroes who are conscripted, our policy will be to put them into various units in proportion to their ratio in the general population, which is about ten per cent. Negro leaders are very much concerned because they anticipate that conscripted men of their race will all be turned into labor regiments. The President is opposed to this and said so. There is some doubt whether they can qualify as first-class aviators, but the President wants them to be given a chance in this branch of the service, and on ground aviation work they are to have their full ten percent proportion. . . .

/////

Harold Ickes. *The Secret Diary of Harold L. Ickes. Volume III: The Lowering Clouds, 1939–1941*. New York: Simon and Schuster, 1955. Reprinted by permission

Harold L. Ickes. *(Courtesy, National Archives)*

May 17, 1941 . . . Walter White, secretary of the National Association for the Advancement of Colored People, was in at noon. . . .

White is very much disturbed over the refusal of industry in general to take on Negro workers in defense industries. When we are supposed to be making our maximum efforts, here are ten per cent of our people who are not even considered for defense jobs while, at the same time, the color line is pretty rigidly drawn in the Army. I do not see what enthusiasm the Negroes could be expected to show in helping us defend ourselves from Hitler. Of course Hitler has drawn the color line openly and boldly, notwithstanding which I doubt if the Negroes would fare much worse under him than under us. Of course this is an exaggeration because, despite all, they have been making great advances, especially during this Administration.[1] . . .

[*White*] asked [the *president of a large food company*] what his great corporation had done for the Negroes. Specifically, did he give employment to Negroes? This took him aback. He thought for a minute. He said that he had never paid much attention to that matter and then he remembered that a Negro was employed in the chemical section of the

---

[1]Reference is made to the New Deal which did not exclude blacks.

company. White queried: "As a chemist or as a porter?" He said that he did not know but that he would find out and if it were as a chemist, he would telephone the next day. White never heard from him further. . .

/////

July 5, 1941 . . . Last Sunday tickets to play golf were sold to one or two Negroes and it looked for a while as if there would be a race riot. However, our park police were summoned, and although some bad feeling was incited, there was no physical demonstration. On Thursday morning we were advised that Negroes would appear and apply for tickets that would permit them to play Thursday afternoon.

We went into a huddle but I could see no reason why Negroes should not be permitted to play on the golf course. Players go around by twosomes or foursomes and they don't come into as close contact with each other as they do on the streets and in common conveyances. They are taxpayers, they are citizens, and they have a right to play golf on public courses on the same basis as whites. To be sure, we have maintained a golf course for Negroes in Washington, but the cold fact is that we haven't kept it up and it is not surprising that Negroes do not care to play on it. I said that so far as their playing on municipal courses was concerned, nature would have to take its course. If there are physical disturbances, we will have to send in the police but we will not incite to violence by having police there suggesting, by their mere presence, that there may be violence. . . .

July 20, 1941 . . . on Friday, Dr. Brown and his wife went over to [*the East Potomac golf*] course to play golf. They were followed by a jeering, booing group of whites. When I learned of this I called Demaray and told him to have enough police there to protect the Negro players and to lose no time in making arrests of those who were conducting themselves in an improper manner. . . .

Questions for Discussion

1. What does Ickes's diary tell you about government policies and attitudes toward Negroes during 1940–41? What are his attitudes and efforts toward equal rights?
2. In what ways did African Americans resist discrimination? Were their efforts successful? Can you point to specific entries for support?

20.
Linda Benitt
Letter from a Minnesota Farm: Pre-war Tensions, 1938

Linda Benitt and her husband, William, farmed near Hastings, Minnesota. In the following letter she expresses her concerns for the future, as events in Europe seem to point toward war.

Sept. 28, 1938

I have driven over with William to an electric show of the R.E.A. [*Rural Electrification Administration*] in Dakota Co., and, while he contracts the people he has come to see, I seize the chance to write to you. It seems as tho all our thoughts and hearts these days are absorbed by the European crisis. When I am at home or candling in the poultry house I have the radio going steadily, and thus keep in close touch with each new development as far as it happens. Chamberlain's speech yesterday addressed to the world at large was the most moving one I have ever heard, truly as good a speech as Lincoln's Gettysburg address. Tomorrow Hitler, Mussolini, Daladin & Chamberlain meet in Munich.[1] What will come of it? By the time this letter reaches you we should know whether it is peace or war in the immediate future. And war in Europe

---

William A. Benitt and Family Papers, Minnesota History Center, St. Paul, Minnesota. Box 1.

[1]Neville Chamberlain was Prime Minister of Great Britain in 1938. The meeting with Hitler in Munich ended with an agreement that forced Czechoslovakia to give up part of its territory to Nazi Germany. Although Britain and France hoped that this policy of appeasement would lead to peace, in retrospect the Munich Agreement was a tragic mistake that led to Hitler's invasion of Poland and the beginning of World War II.

Linda Benitt, 1938. *(Courtesy, National Archives)*

means war for us, too. Let us not delude ourselves about that. As individuals we can do little, but we can live the agony of suspense of every European each hour that passes. We shall truly pray that Hitler's enormous egotism may feel a check in the world disapproval of his militant methods & empirical aims.

In the meantime we go on living our lives of daily routine while we hang on the edge of the abyss of our civilization. Hens lay eggs, Hitler or no Hitler, crops must be harvested when ripe and the weather permits; little pigs eat & grow; children must go to our democratic schools, etc. So we cut our corn, shuck it; cut hay and stack it; grade our eggs & market them; kill a fine beef for our own table & put it in frozen storage for use during the coming year, and all the time we draw nearer to the brink.

Questions for Discussion

1. How have conditions in pre-war Europe affected the Benitts?
2. Do they expect war to come?

21.
Charles Kikuchi
Diary from a Japanese-American Detention Camp, 1941–1942

Charles Kikuchi, born in the United States of Japanese parents, was a twenty-six-year-old graduate student at the University of California, Berkeley, when Japan bombed Pearl Harbor. In April 1941, he was imprisoned at Tanforan, a former racetrack in San Bruno, California, where 8,000 Japanese (American citizens and alien immigrants) were housed. Four months later Tanforan was evacuated and Kikuchi was transferred to a "relocation center" in Arizona. In 1943 he was permitted work leave outside the center, and was drafted into the military shortly before the end of the war.

Kikuchi's diary is the record of an assimilated American who is torn between his loyalty to the United States and his indignation over the country's policy of internment. The diary is also a record of the effects of that policy.

December 7 1941, Berkeley, California   Pearl Harbor. We are at war! Jesus Christ, the Japs bombed Hawaii and the entire fleet has been sunk. I just can't believe it. I don't know what in the hell is going to happen to us. . . .

Charles Kikuchi. *The Kikuchi Diary: Chronicle from an American Concentration Camp. The Tanforan Journals of Charles Kikuchi.* John Modell, ed. Urbana: University of Illinois Press, 1973. Reprinted by permission.

If we are ever going to prove our Americanism, this is the time. The Anti-Jap feeling is bound to rise to hysterical heights, and it is most likely that the Nisei [*those born of Japanese immigrants*] will be included as Japs. . . .

December 8, 1941, Berkeley I should have confidence in the democratic procedures, but I'm worried that we might take a page from Hitler's methods and do something drastic towards the Issei [*Japanese immigrants to the U.S. and Canada*]. I hope not. I don't give a damn what happens to me, but I would be very disillusioned if the democratic process broke down. . . .

December 9, 1941, Berkeley Holy Christ! San Francisco last night was like nothing I ever saw before and everybody was saying that the Japs are going to get it in the ass. . . .

I told Alice to tell Mom to have Pop's [*United States*] Navy discharge framed and put on the wall next to the barber license and take that Buddha statue the hell out of there. Alice says the Army should put me in charge of patriotism because I am suspicious of my own father. I did not mean it that way; but it is true, I don't trust the Issei. If just one of them sabotaged something, what hell there would be to pay. . . .

/////

April 30, 1942, Berkeley Today is the day that we are going to get kicked out of Berkeley. It certainly is degrading. I am down here in the control station [*evacuation center*] and I have nothing to do so I am jotting down these notes! The Army Lieutenant over there doesn't want any of the photographers to take pictures of these miserable people waiting for the Greyhound bus because he thinks that the American public might get a sympathetic attitude towards them.

I understand that we are going to live in the horse stalls. I hope that the Army has the courtesy to remove the manure first.

"The Japs are leaving, hurrah, hurrah!" some little kids are yelling down the street but everybody ignores them. Well, I have to go up to the campus and get the results of my last exam and will barely be able to make it back here in time for the last bus.

May 3, 1942, Sunday [*Tanforan*] I saw a soldier in a tall guardhouse near the barbed wire fence and did not like it because it reminds me of a concentration camp. . . .

May 4, 1942, Monday Down by the stables there is an old restroom which says "Gents" on one side and "Colored Gents" on the other! I suppose it was for the use of the stable-boys. To think that such a thing is possible in California is surprising. I guess class lines and the eternal striving for status and prestige exist wherever you go, and we are still in need of a great deal of enlightenment. . . .

Gila River Relocation Center, to which the Kikuchis moved after Tanforan, had barracks rather than horse stalls, but the lines for the messhall remained the same. *(Courtesy, National Archives)*

May 5, 1942, Tuesday   We got approval to go ahead with the [*camp news*] paper and the boys are working hard in order to get the first issue out by Saturday; I'm supposed to write up the section on the employment situation in camp. The whole setup needs centralizing. There are too many conflicting orders about who is supposed to do the hiring, etc. . . .

It gripes me no end to think of being confined in the same place with these Japanists. If they could only realize that in spite of all their past mistreatments, they have not done so bad in America because of the democratic traditions—with its faults.

/////

May 7, 1942, Thursday   A new menace has entered our lives to make the pioneer conditions more uncomfortable. We are infested with tiny fleas that bite like hell. They must be horse fleas or something that come from the old stables. Gods, they certainly make life miserable. . . .

May 8, 1942, Friday   The question came up as to what were we fighting for. All of us were agreed that Fascism was not the answer, but there was a difference of opinions on whether an Allied victory would be any solution to the whole mess. . . . Would the solution include only the white races . . . ?

May 10, 1942, Sunday   I don't like the reasons why we were put here, but I am finding it interesting so far. I don't know how I will feel a month from now though. . . . All this still doesn't compensate for my liberty and freedom of movement from place to place. . . .

May 11, 1942 I've been here only a week yet I can catch myself getting extremely anti-Japanese again. I'm being forced to live by Japanese ways and I rebel inwardly and outwardly. And I'm not the only one. I have noticed this same reaction among several of my progressive friends—one symptom of this is that they refuse to talk Japanese among themselves and they use the term "Japs" more often when they feel disgusted with the people. I hope this camp doesn't make us conform to the standard Japanese ways. . . .

About half of the Japanese have already been evacuated from the restricted areas in this state [*California*]. Manzanar, Santa Anita, and Tanforan will be the biggest centers. Now that S.F. has been almost cleared the American Legion, the Native Sons of the Golden West, and the California Joint Immigration Committee are filing charges that the Nisei should be disfranchised because we have obtained citizenship under false pretenses and that "we are loyal subjects of Japan" and therefore never should have been allowed to obtain citizenship. This sort of thing will gain momentum and we are not in a very advantageous position to combat it. . . .

/////

May 14, 1942, Thursday News of the wage scale for evacuees in the Assembly, reception and relocation centers was announced today by the government. The scale announced is even lower than what was expected. Unskilled workers will get $8.00 a month; semi-skilled workers will have $12.00 a month; and the professional and technical workers will receive $16.00 a month. The reaction to this news was varied. Many took the view that they would not have much use for money anyway since there would be little to spend it on around here. Skilled workers took it better. . . . Some have already quit their jobs, feeling that it was not worth it. . . .

May 15, 1942 The thing that I have feared is going to happen. The WCCA and WRA announced today that thousands of Japanese would be granted special furloughs to help bring in America's food crop. . . . Once signed up, it will be very difficult to do anything else but work as a farm laborer for the duration.

/////

June 3, 1942, Wednesday During lunch it was announced that the rest of California would be evacuated and a curfew had been set for this area. . . . B.I. hopes that they take those bastard disloyal Italians and

Germans next, and the hell with the Japs who are too old to be of any harm. . . .

/////

June 8, 1942, Monday 11:00 P.M. Cast my absentee ballot today for the S.F. special elections. Voted yes on both measures to increase the bond debt for no special reason. The only reason I voted today was to protect my voting privileges for the important elections which will come up in the fall. The man elected at that time will shape the post war policies for the world. A special deputy came in and notarized our ballots. . . .

June 9, 1942, Tuesday 11:30 Already Tom and Miyako are getting much too sassy. It probably is our fault since we have practically taken all responsibilities away from Mom. She is fighting for her position although she does it in a quiet way. Pop bears the brunt of her suppressed feelings. This morning Mom told him to shut up and went out and slammed the door. . . .

All of this indicates that all of us are a little uncertain about things and very touchy. Arguments result over little things. . . . Pop feels he is getting neglected by the family and sort of pushed aside. . . .

June 10, 1942 The daily count will go into effect shortly under order from General De Witt. The house managers are responsible for counting us in the morning and at night. It's practically a curfew. Don't see the necessity for it here, but there must be a reason. . . .

/////

June 14, 1942, Sunday The latest Army rule is that the guards at the gate can't even speak to us except on business. . . .

/////

June 17, 1942, Wednesday Physical facilities are sad and the teachers are not so good. They sit in the messhall tables for a class and these classes are strung side by side right down the length of the grandstand. The teachers have to yell to get attention and compete with their neighboring teachers. On top of that the classes have to be chiefly lecture due to the lack of textbooks. The Hi School students are much more noisy than the others. . . .

/////

June 19, 1942, Friday 11:05 Yesterday another statement was made against the "Japs" in the U.S. Day by day these native fascists are getting louder and louder. So far, few liberal groups have rallied together to stop them. Dr. Willis H. Miller of the California State Planning

Board addressed the American Association for the Advancement of Science in Salt Lake: "There must be no negotiated peace in this war, nor no armistice. This is a total war. The Axis nations must be crushed and divided into little units. The U.S. must maintain a military force capable of enforcing world policies. At home all citizens of Japanese ancestry must be expelled from the U.S. No longer need we regard our country as an asylum for all who wish to enter. . . ."

Pop and Mom went to English classes for the first time today. Pop is the oldest one to sign up (67) among the 250 in the class. . . .

/////

June 21, 1942, Sunday Lots of visitors as usual. Many of them probably came out of curiosity to look at us and the camp. Makes one feel like being either in a zoo or a prison. The person who owns the property across the highway in front of the main gate has opened up a very profitable enterprise. He has a 15 cent parking lot! . . .

June 22, 1942, Monday The Army photographers disrupted our day by taking a moving picture of our [*camp newspaper*] pressroom in action. These official documentary films will probably be used to show the "bigwigs" how well off we are and they will also be kept for the record of the "greatest mass migration in American history." We can't write about it in the *Totalizer*, the sergeant says. Anyway, we were excited about being in the movies. . . .

June 23, 1942, Tuesday No visitors were allowed in today because of Army orders to search all barracks for contraband. Rushed home to hide all the knives and tools. Went to Chief Easterbrooks to ask for a clarification of the order and he said that the search was necessitated by the fact that the luggage was not gone through at the time of our arrival. He had a whole pile of saws, hatchets, knives, and Japanese literature in his office. He said that the tools were . . . "potentially dangerous weapons." Who in the hell would we attack anyway . . . ? The poor Issei have nothing left to read, except their bibles and religious books. They even collected anti-fascist literature translated into Japanese. . . .

June 24, 1942, Wednesday The Army has definitely clamped down on Japanese even here. All of the Japanese signs were torn down today by the interior police. . . .

/////

June 29, 1942, Monday Heard over the radio this morning that 100 of the former restricted areas around power plants, etc. have now been reopened to the Germans and Italians under orders from [*General*] De Witt. Implying that the danger of sabotage is now gone with the

Japanese evacuated. The liberals around camp are disgusted as hell. They said that this action proves that evacuation was only on a racial basis. . . .

/////

July 1, 1942, Wednesday 1:45 Two months here and I'm not feeling so rebellious this week. . . .

Outside I can hear the swish of the cars as they go by down the highway. The barbed wire fence way below us reminds us that we are on the inside. On the other side of the highway there is a huge glass hothouse where they raise chrysanthemums and dahlias. The tiny men working hard way in the distance look like ants, but they are free men. The armed soldier, some lonely boy from the middle west, paces back and forth up by the main gate. In the sentry boxes, the soldiers look bored. . . .

The police chief has ordered that all Negro visitors be checked closely and their slips be kept in a separate file. Evidently they think that there is a great danger of the Japanese stirring up the Negroes. (They call it race hatred.) . . .

Draft registration for the 18–20 years olds took place during the past few days, and 271 signed up from here. I asked the member of the . . . draft board just what our status would be but he would not commit himself. . . . Right now most of the Nisei have been placed in 4-C: aliens ineligible to citizenship.

July 2, 1942, Thursday Another censorship note: McQuuen put "seeming" in front of "injustice" in the editorial Taro wrote for the 4th. . . .

/////

July 8, 1942, 12:00 The chief topic of conversation these days is our next move. People are getting uneasy about it. A rush is being made to spend all the scrip books at the canteen because they won't be any good in the relocation centers. . . .

I keep saying to myself that I must view everything intellectually and rationally, but sometimes I feel sentiments compounded of blind feelings and irrationality. Here all my life I have identified my every act with America but when the war broke out I suddenly find that I won't be allowed to become an integral part of the whole in these times of national danger. I find I am put aside and viewed suspiciously. . . .

/////

July 27, 1942, Monday 11:15 p.m. The Japanese phonograph records were confiscated today and already 2000 have been brought into the police department. The innocent ones will be returned but Japanese military music will be stored away and returned after the war. The chief has to play and listen to all of these records. I feel sorry for him because Japanese music is hard on the ears. . . .

/////

July 31, 1942, Friday 12:30 Three months in a concentration camp! Life goes smoothly on. I should be more dissatisfied and rebellious, but much against my will I'm forced to admit that I'm getting adjusted to this restricted life and falling into a smooth and regular rut. There still is something within me that makes me feel uneasy but these momentary lapses are getting more infrequent, or else I am feeling better tonight than usual. . . .

Our Grant Avenue is no longer a mud hole. It has been leveled off and a gravel walk has been put in. Roads have also been built in the infield. . . . Gardens have sprung up all over the place and vegetables are now ready to eat. . . .

The attitudes of the people have settled down in many respects. From fearing and hating everything about the place, many of them have arrived at the point where they like it here and would not mind if they stayed on indefinitely without moving on to a relocation area. . . .

/////

August 8, 1942, Saturday I knew what the new visitors' setup would be, but when I actually saw the benches all lined up with visitors on one side and the residents on the other, it got me so damn mad! "What in hell do they think we are, a bunch of prisoners?" I thought. And I was not the only one. I stood by the receptionist's desk and three out of four first reactions were the same. . . .

/////

August 31, 1942, Monday In reviewing the four months here, the chief value I got out of this forced evacuation was the strengthening of the family bonds. I never knew my family before this and this was the first chance that I have had to get acquainted. . . . It sort of binds strength to an individual thrown into a completely strange group. . . .

I wonder what will happen if we all suddenly rebelled against this kind of living? The postwar period is going to be trying no matter which way we look at it. . . .

Questions for Discussion

1. What were Kikuchi's attitudes about being Japanese-American? About internment?
2. On June 9, 1942, Kikuchi records what is frequently described as a breakdown in the family due to internment. Why do you think that breakdown occurred? What, on the other hand, does Kikuchi tell us about family unity?
3. What were the reasons the U.S. chose to intern Japanese-Americans? Why didn't the country also intern German-Americans with whom it was also at war? Does Kikuchi provide a response to this question? What are your thoughts about internment?

22.
Dorothy Blake

Home Front Diary: World War II, 1942

Spanning the period from December 7, 1941, until December 1, 1942, is the diary of a woman faced with responsibilities and challenges as a result of the war. Her husband, Jim, was in Washington, D.C.; her son, Art, was in the Air Force; and her two daughters, whose husbands were in military service and shipped abroad, returned home with their infants.

The following excerpts reflect her patriotism and activities for the war effort, her fears and hopes for America and the safety of her family. They also provide a profile of life in New York during the early years of World War II.

February 4, 1942 Came back from the First Aid Class today to be met halfway up the road by Artie who was shouting and waving both arms. . . .

"My teeth are O.K.—they're going to take me! Isn't that swell?" . . . I'm proud . . . and happy for him, but it's going to take a lot of pantry cleaning and digging into war work to keep my chin where it belongs as the mother of a flier.

/////

February 24, 1942 If I had a dollar for every confidential, right-off-the-boat piece of information that comes my way these days I'd be

Dorothy Blake, pseud. for Dorothy Atkinson Robinson. *It's All in the Family: A Diary of an American Housewife, Dec. 7, 1941–Dec. 1, 1942.* New York: William Morrow, 1943.

a rich woman. The latest is that there is going to be a terrible shortage of toilet paper! Women were down at the market this morning buying every roll they could lay their hands on—some beautiful friendships went to pieces before my eyes. . . .

/////

March 2, 1942 I saw Art off on the train this morning and had the strangest experience. Some way, how I'll never know, I managed to smile and wave and keep the tears down deep inside my heart. As the last car finally went around the bend my eyes simply spilled over and I stood there in the crowd too blinded to see anything. . . .

/////

March 24, 1942 Planes droning overhead tonight, as they have every night since war began, back and forth at regular intervals. I got up and looked out of the window and the sky was criss-crossed with beams of light. Every once in awhile the beams would catch the plane and I knew that on the records of the practice flight a score would be marked up. How long will it be practice for those boys and how soon reality? Down the hill and across the bay a few bright windows in homes—the rest in darkness; a dog barked on our hillside and the sound echoed, everything was so quiet. It's hard to realize the war here in spite of the fact that Art is on his way into the middle of it, sons and husbands of other neighbors have gone, our whole lives are rearranged and different, our point of view changed, our plans for the future put aside for the duration. . . .

March 27, 1942 Mrs. Ralph Waldo Emerson is coming into her own. She has been quoted over and over, in various uplifting essays and articles, for her thrifty rules of "Eat it up, wear it out, make it do," and nobody paid any attention. Now it's fashionable and patriotic to be thrifty and I saw this same quotation, in letters half an inch high, on a poster down in the village.

/////

April 4, 1942 . . . The general public seems to be divided into two classes—those who say it is ridiculous to even imagine the Germans will try to bomb us and those who are convinced they will. I belong to the "It's coming, sure as fate" group. I can't for the life of me see why they wouldn't attempt to at least give us a nuisance raid to see how well we scare. But I don't believe we'd scare worth a darn. Nothing makes the average, everyday American madder than to have some big bully try to push him around. . . .

Women on the home front do their part to help the war effort. *(Courtesy, National Archives)*

June 20, 1942 Canned currant juice this morning, without benefit of sugar, and I'll make the jelly gradually as I can save up for it. I couldn't see any sense in going down to the rationing board to ask for extra sugar for canning. From all the grapevine information I get there is going to be an extra supply later on anyway. . . .

/////

July 15, 1942 Took down my first can of fat for salvage today and was paid twelve cents for the three pounds. A ten cent War stamp and two cents for the penny jar toward another. I hope I'll get more expert at collecting the fat when I have more practice—certainly made a mess of it this time with two strainers, one table, a patch of floor, and the front of a brand clean apron as the casualties. . . .

It was really funny to see and hear the women at the meat counter. Some of them had brought scrap fat in bags, some in glass jars, and one bride had hers neatly stored in an old perfume bottle. She showed it to me with great pride. . . .

/////

July 24, 1942 Letter from Art. It is full of Fighters, Divers, Scouts, and Interceptors. Full, too, of a pride that is fine. "Our bunch is swell! The Air Force is the most important branch of the service and the winning of the war depends on how we carry on. Went up at sunrise this morning and I felt as though I owned the world. Don't worry—I'm having the time of my life!" I tell myself I won't worry—but I can't help thinking. . . .

July 26, 1942 The authorities are still at it! The latest instructions [*for handling incendiary bombs*] are, "Use direct jet of water, not a fine spray, on incendiary bombs. Use sand only where water is not available and when the bomb falls far from any inflammable material." Hope the ones that land here are that considerate. The report goes on to say, "With the new method we will save more lives and more property in the event of a raid. That is the only criterion for judging the matter." . . .

/////

August 7, 1942 . . . The water heater wouldn't work because I had forgotten to order oil! The tank was completely empty. Learning to be the man of the house is going to take some intensive study on my part. I really felt terrible at being such a nit-wit but, for years and years, Jim has always attended to these things and you can't make yourself over in a few months. Somebody once said, "Only the adaptable will survive"—so I guess this old dog will have to learn some new tricks. Stoking a furnace may be one of them, because the oil shortage is getting worse and worse. . . .

/////

August 26, 1942 Saw in the paper that there is a new organization—the Unknitters Club. They ravel out the pairs of sox that are made up of a size eight and a size ten. They undo the sweaters that have an Army neck on a Navy sweater and ones that are suitable only for a man who has one arm six inches longer than the other. I just wonder if my one and only pair of Sea Boots landed in their laps? Goodness knows they looked queer enough to be worn by a penguin but I followed directions and trusted to fate. Ever since then I've knitted scarfs—you can't go far wrong on those. Jim insists mine are made for giraffes but I measure them on the floor and, according to the book, they are the specified length. Straight garter stitch, for an hour before bedtime, is better than counting sheep—far more soothing and monotonous.

/////

October 12, 1942 If we ever have a real air raid I am sure that it will come when I am right in the middle of doing something. Tonight I was boiling eggs for tomorrow's lunch and baking prune-filled cookies which are a tricky bit—but good. I heard sirens blowing but paid no attention because we have fire alarms nearly every day when somebody's oil burner decides to go on the rampage. I finally came to and decided it was a surprise blackout. Called upstairs to Sally and dutifully put out all the lights on the first floor. Then I sat in the quiet and waited. It was unusually still and I could hear the Wardens' whistles clear across the bay. A voice shouted, close at hand, "Put out that light!" Queer, I thought, how long it takes some people to catch on. The shout came again. Then a banging on the door. Hosky gave a low growl and Jonesy wandered in and out between my feet as I groped my way to the front of the house. The Air Warden stood, as stern as a Justice of the Supreme Court.

"Put out your lights—there's a glow from your kitchen windows."

Those blamed eggs were boiling merrily away and the gas flame shining like a mild beacon. Funny how long it takes some people to catch on!

/////

October 19, 1942 A card from Art this morning—I could hear Milton shouting up the hill before I could see the top of his hat—"Your boy's landed safe and sound!"

"Where?" I shouted back and ran down the road toward him.

At last I had the card in my hand and could barely read it for the tears of relief that filled my eyes. It was mailed from this side but the message was, "Arrived safely. Love, Art."

That was all, but it was enough—for now.

/////

October 26, 1942 . . . Coffee is to be rationed to one cup a day for all persons over fifteen, or rather who were fifteen or over when registering for sugar rationing on May fourth and fifth last—which certainly includes me and Sally—and how we do love coffee! . . .

/////

November 5, 1942 Our oil registration form, which I had mailed so carefully and according to instructions by my lord and master to the local Ration Board, came back by mail today with a letter saying it should be taken to the school where we registered for sugar. . . .

/////

November 11, 1942 Armistice Day and Sally and I sat reading the paper, with its encouraging news from the battle in Egypt, and listening to the speeches and ceremonies being held in so many places. There is renewed hope but little exultation or over-confidence. I believe all of us have, at last, realized that there is a long, hard road ahead through darkness and difficulty and each one, in his own way, must help. The whole pattern of our lives is changing and we have gradually learned to accept it from day to day and hour to hour until it is sometimes strange to try to think back to nine short months ago. Even so small a thing as watching the trains go over the trestle at night—the shades tightly drawn on every window and only a dim bar of light showing between the coaches. The signs in the cars read—"U.S. Army requires shades drawn sunset to sunrise." And I have yet to see a single shade raised or to hear one passenger complaining about it. It is only some of our nervous congressmen who fear for the breakdown of the morale of the people if more restrictions are imposed. The people themselves will take anything necessary. When you've given up your menfolks for the duration, and perhaps forever, nothing else seems of very great importance except doing your job to the best of your ability and clinging to an undying faith that kindness and decency and fairness to one another will and can and must be the law of life to survive. Otherwise, life itself is of no value.

/////

November 15, 1942 Too much happening, and too fast, to keep track of time or events. War has its tragedies and its comedies. Perhaps tragedy is too strong a word to use for the passing and signing of the new draft bill for the eighteen- and nineteen-year-olds, but it is going to bring the war very close to so many families who have hoped and prayed for a little more time for their boys to grow up—or for the war to end before they were needed. . . .

/////

November 22, 1942 Gas ration to be cut to three gallons a week—coffee sales to be stopped for one week, starting next Sunday, and then rationed to one pound every five weeks—further cut in oil for heating is likely on Eastern seaboard—heavy cream to be taken off the market soon and butter rationed—meat rationing to start early in new year—few vegetables to be shipped and fewer still to be canned—no raisins or chocolate or olive oil or bacon—less of everything including trains and buses and cars and telephones. But more of neighborliness and family loyalties and appreciation for the beauty and freedom and worth of the country we have so long taken for granted. We're all in it together and we'll all come out of it with colors flying—no matter how hard and long the way. This I do know with my heart and mind and faith.

Questions for Discussion

1. What responsibilities and problems did Blake, and other women, face as a result of the war?
2. How did Blake respond to her new role? Where in her diary does she express her attitudes about the war and its effects on the wives and children of soldiers?

23.
Augusta H. Clawson
Shipyard Diary of a Woman Welder, 1943

In 1943, Augusta Clawson held the position of Special Agent for the Vocational Division of the U.S. Office of Education. Her department (Training Women for War Production), which subsidized the nation's vocational schools, discovered that many women were leaving their shipyard jobs soon after employment. With its costly program, the Division wanted to know why. Clawson agreed covertly to go through application, training and employment as a shipyard welder in order to answer that question. She was hired, accepted into the Union, trained for eight days at a vocational school and worked as a welder during April and May 1943 at an Oregon shipyard.

What Clawson discovered was that the training at the vocational school was "giving women skill in welding without preparing them for the environment in which that skill would be used." Her diary provides a vivid picture of women in nontraditional wartime industry.

Wednesday, April 7 [*1943*]   Well, I've done it! I've joined the ranks of war workers—I'm going to be a welder in The Shipyard. . . .

I started off at the United States Employment Service. A big sign read "INDUSTRIAL WOMEN: Shipyard Women." I stepped up to a

Augusta H. Clawson. *Shipyard Diary of a Woman Welder*. Illustrated by Boris Givotovsky. New York: Penguin Books, 1944. Used by permission of Viking Penguin, a division of Penguin Books USA Inc.

window (like a bank teller's) under the sign and said: "I want to get a job as a welder." . . . [*The clerk*] filled out what I found later was a "War Manpower Certificate of Availability" (Form WMC-10). . . . I was told to take the slip over to the Counselor who sat at a desk behind a railing.

I found the Counselor pleasant and efficient. She got right to the point. "So you're going to be a welder? Well, the training will take you from forty to sixty hours. You'll need overalls and high shoes; or oxfords will do. You'll have to have goggles and helmet, too. And you'll need to buy leathers [*leather trousers*]. . . .

. . . off to a chain store I went, and found not only work shoes, but overalls and jacket, bandana, socks, and shirt. . . . I would walk up to a counter in the men's department and say with great dignity, "I'd like a man's work shirt for a welder." With equal dignity, the clerk would ask, "What size is his neck?" Then I had to say, "It isn't 'his' neck—it's mine." . . .

At last I was equipped with enough clothing to live in comfortably at the North Pole for a month. . . .

My conclusion after my first day is this: . . . I've been pigeonholed and instructed and fingerprinted and photographed and warned and counseled and signed and sealed. I feel as if this shipyard job were as inevitable as taxes and as if any attempt to escape would bring dire penalties. Maybe that's how you feel when you join the Army: as if you'd voluntarily signed away your own will, and now you're cornered no matter what. Oh, well, it's in a good cause—so let's go!

Thursday evening [*April 8, 1943*]: . . . "My Day" started when the alarm clock made nasty remarks to me at four minutes of five. . . .

I caught the 6:00 A.M. Shipyard bus. . . . The trip was probably four or five miles and I stood and looked down at a sea of metal and plastic hats and wondered what kind of people lived inside those hard shells. It looked like a turtle convention.

. . . went to Booth 15 where I was to work [*in training*]. These booths are covered overhead but are otherwise open to the outside. It is strange to sit and weld all shut into a world by yourself inside of that helmet, and then push up the helmet and see trees and sunshine and out-doors. . . .

[*Mr. Dunn, the instructor*] put a piece of iron about six inches square and about 3/4 of an inch thick on my work bench. He sat down on my stool (the cross section of a log of wood, still complete with bark and roughness). "Pull down your helmet now and watch me. *Never* look at an arc with your bare eyes. If you do, you'll get a flash burn, and it's no fun. A burn from an arc is like a very severe sunburn."

We pulled down our hoods. He had already pushed the "on" button of the machine and the motor had roared into life. He struck the rod on

Women welders in the Navy Yard (1944). *(Courtesy, National Archives)*

the iron plate and the arc leaped into brilliance. A tiny pool of molten metal flowed from the rod. He moved the rod steadily across the plate in slow, gentle scallops, and the molten pool followed his rod. When we raised our hoods again the completed weld lay straight across the plate and its surface had a dainty feathered pattern. He gave me the stinger and let me try. My arc went out twice because I held the rod too far from the plate and broke the circuit. My finished weld looked as bumpy as the Rocky Mountains. . . .

We welded for four hours and a half, with an interim of only about thirty-five or forty minutes for a safety lecture. This covered Lifting, Carrying, Piling Material, Use of Gloves, Falling, Climbing, Air Raids, etc. About seventy-five trainees, men and women, attended the lecture. At 11:30 we were given thirty minutes for lunch. . . .

Back to work and more welding. I "dis-improved" as rapidly after lunch as I had improved during the morning. . . .

My conclusions on this day are: It was very exhilarating being part of the gang, especially this morning. But I'm glad I didn't have to come back tonight to a husband and four children all waiting for me to cook dinner. I'm glad I didn't have to do a family laundry. . . . Tonight my only wonder is "How long will it be before 5:00 A.M.?" . . .

/////

Wednesday [*April 14, 1943*]: I have completed six days of training, and tonight am the proud owner of two things: one—a black metal lunchbox complete with thermos; two—a firm conviction that I shall become a welder. I've had a few doubts about the latter, wondered sometimes if I could take it. . . . Tonight I'm sure, because I'm getting such a kick out of it, and because I can see progress. . . . When I started, my beads looked like a very irregular mountain range. As I went on they did assume some order, and now they look more like a cable stitch in knitting. Sometimes I'd get the "feel" of welding—and then it would leave me. . . . Tonight I "got the feel" and for some reason I'm confident I won't lose it again. . . .

Thursday [*April 15, 1943*]: I crowed too soon. Today was horrible. I went in expecting to conquer the world, and was thrown by a vertical weld. I'd get it smooth about eight inches up—and then let a huge bubble roll down and spoil it. I don't understand it. Usually when you learn a thing, you retain it. But that isn't so with welding. You think you have the hang of it beautifully, and then you do welds that are inferior to day-before-yesterday's. And tonight I'm so much more tired than before.

. . . My arm aches and every muscle in my hand is yelping. . . . .

We were called to another safety lecture—good sound advice on Eye Safety. Pontocaine 1/2 sol. is the best treatment. Potato juice or juice from tea-leaves is good. Report to First Aid immediately in case of arc flash. . . .

The lecturer brought up the rumor that arc welding causes sterility among women. He said that this was untrue, and quoted an authoritative source to prove its falsity. In the Girls' Room afterwards, this question was the topic of conversation. Two of the women had completely misunderstood him. One said: "I'm not going to stay in welding if you can't have babies. . . ." Another agreed. . . .

Friday [*April 16, 1943*]: . . . I'm becoming so used to this life that when I come back, clean up, and dress for dinner I feel as if I were masquerading as a lady. Back in leathers again, I am myself. None of it was too hard to get used to. The high shoes raised a few welts the first few days (from the heavy tongue which folds back under the laces). And until today my temples were sore from the helmet; they're scarcely sore at all now. The leathers seemed heavy the first day, and goggles over glasses weighed a ton on the bridge of my nose, but it all seems quite natural now.

. . . I feel as though I'd been a shipyarder for ages. The only time it seems unreal is when I go out in the early morning. It is still dark as night, street lamps are on, and cars send out glimmers here and there. As I go through Pine Street I pass between two old brick warehouses. It is so dark I can't even see the doors until I am in front of them. (What holy horror would have been voiced a few years ago at a female parading through such streets alone! As a matter of fact, I'm quite a formidable character, armed as I am with my chipping hammer.) . . .

Saturday [*April 17, 1943*]: . . . after eight days of training, I am a welder. Honesty makes me qualify that last remark. . . . But we are called welders here, and I'm so bursting with pride that I won't cross out that exaggeraton—in fact, I shall glory in it! . . .

I got my assignment to Ways 4 [*ship's passageway*] and am to report tomorrow at 7:00 A.M. . . .

. . . My only regret right at the moment is that I had a full Sunday planned—sleep, laundry, mending, letters homes, etc. But the Shipyard didn't consult me. It just told me:

> "Hers not to reason why,
>> Hers but to weld or quit;
> Into the old shipyard
>> She goes to do her bit."

Sunday [*April 18, 1943*]: I am back from my first day on the Ways, and I feel as if I had seen some giant phenomenon. It's incredible! It's inhuman! It's horrible! And it's marvelous! I don't believe a blitz could be noisier—I didn't dream that there could be so much noise, anywhere. My ears are still ringing like high-tension wires, and my head buzzes. . . .

I, who hate heights, climbed stair after stair after stair till I thought I must be close to the sun. I stopped on the top deck. I, who hate confined spaces, went through narrow corridors, stumbling my way over rubber-coated leads—dozens of them, scores of them, even hundreds of them. . . . I welded in the poop deck lying on the floor while another welder spattered sparks from the ceiling and chippers like giant woodpeckers shattered our eardrums. I, who've . . . sat at a bench welding flat and vertical plates, was told to weld braces along a baseboard below a door opening. . . . I did overhead welding, horizontal, flat, vertical. I welded around curved hinges which were placed so close to the side wall that I had to bend my rod in a curve to get it in. I made some good welds and some frightful ones. But now a door in the poop deck of an oil tanker is hanging, four feet by six of solid steel by *my* welds. Pretty exciting. . . .

. . . I realize now what Oscar Wilde meant when he wrote of "that little tent of blue which prisoners call the sky."

I do know one thing from just today. There is nothing in the training to prepare you for the excruciating noise you get down in the ship. . . . Once . . . I screamed loud and lustily, and couldn't even hear myself. It was weird. So then I proceeded to sing at the top of my lungs . . . and I couldn't hear the smallest peep. . . .

. . . after all this racket stops, you can't hear anything for a short space of time. Then your hearing flows slowly back and you find you're still sane and normal. And people wonder whether it involves "adjustment" when a housewife takes up ship welding. . . .

/////

Thursday [*April 22, 1943*]: . . . The men know their muscles are strong enough to pull them up if they get a firm grip on a bar above. But we women do not yet trust our strength, and some of us do not like heights. But one does what one has to. And it's surprising what one *can* do when it's necessary. . . .

/////

Saturday [*April 24, 1943*]: . . . Almost none of the women I talk with complain of too much housework after work. They seemed to have turned it over to daughters or mothers or they eat out a lot. Many do their shopping on the way home, dirt and all. One grimy mother was to meet her children in town to buy their Easter clothes. That must have been a picture. . . .

Easter Sunday [*April 25, 1943*]: . . . I don't believe I have ever in my life spent a more vigorous day. Talk about physical exertion. I even had to abandon my greenhorn trick of counting the stairs I climbed, for I went first to the fo'c'sle deck to set my machine, down to the main deck to get a lead, pulled it up to the fo'c'sle deck (it weighs *plenty*), attached it to my machine, and then was called down again to the main deck by Pete to be given a job down in the hold. I chased up another lead, attached that for extra length, climbed down a ladder that seemed endless, squeezing past cross scaffolding that didn't leave squeezing room, crawling over some, under others, and finally landing where the job was. It consisted of horizontal tacking at about three feet from the floor and in another place at about five feet. The latter was just too high for me to reach and maintain any steadiness with my arms at that in-between angle; so I pulled myself up the side wall by means of various beams, and stood precariously on one while I hung on with my left hand and tacked with my right. . . .

. . . Margaret from Wisconsin . . . told me all about herself and her husband, how he helped with all the housework, said it was only fair when she worked as hard as he. They both want youngsters and are so disappointed not to have any. I suggested that modern medicine had made great strides in this field, but she said, "Harry says to wait till after the war. He'd feel bad leaving me with a baby to look after. Men don't ever know how women feel. They think babies are a burden. They don't see that we want them more than ever if our men don't come back." . . .

Monday [*April 26, 1943*]:   I have completed seven days of work in the Shipyard, and something has happened. I don't quite know what it is, but after work today I suddenly realized that I had no dread or fear any more in connection with this job. I feel like an emancipated welder. . . .

/////

Friday [*May 7, 1943*]:   I earned my $9.60 today, every penny of it. And what's more, I earned it working for two green [*novice*] "female" shipfitters. As Lil put it, "Lord help us when we have to work for wimmin; especially wimmin who don't know what they're doing." . . .

/////

Tuesday [*May 11, 1943*]:   . . . I went to the beauty parlor for a haircut and heard this conversation between a patron and the operator.
Patron: My dear, you know it's simply frightful—this shipyard business. Why, women are flocking out there! I'm just sick about it. It's gotten so almost every woman has to work. It takes two to make one salary.
Operator: I guess they're just there for the duration, don't you think?
Patron: I wish I did. But they've got to get out. They ought to be *made* to get out after the war. . . .
Operator: Maybe they're working out of patriotism, to help in the war.
Patron: Patriotism nothing! It's the wages they get. It's sickening. They're getting all out of adjustment. And my dear (in a hushed voice creating a climax), they're *losing their looks*. They're developing those awful muscles.
I wonder if she thinks that ships build themselves, or that looks will win the war. . . .

Wednesday [*May 12, 1943*]:   . . . I am beginning to think that here is one of the biggest differences that women must become accustomed to on this job. On the whole, women are likely, I think, to commend work well done. Apparently men aren't. You realize after a bit that it doesn't mean lack of appreciation, any more than some of their other tricks mean lack of manners. It's just the way they are, and one must accept it. The same treatment from (say) professional men would be definitely rude. . . . I don't really believe discourtesy is meant. It's just that courtesy isn't thought of. They probably feel it has no place in the day's work. . . .

/////

Friday [*May 21, 1943*]:   . . . I'm thinking now about how soon I must leave. I shall miss these women. I've learned a lot from them. . . .

And don't talk to me about the pettiness of women. I've seen too much of the courage, endurance, and bigness of women in this Yard to listen to talk of pettiness. . . .

/////

Tuesday [*May 25, 1943*]: . . . At 3:30 came the launching of No. 15. Admiral Land of the Maritime Commission presented the Maritime "M" for efficiency in production, and I am now the proud possessor of a maritime pin. It is an inexpensive little thing, but I take great pride in it, and am interested to see that every worker has made a point of getting one, so that the pins are appearing on overalls, caps, jackets, etc. How small a thing will boost morale! A representative of the employees accepted the banner, and his wife christened the "S.S. *River Raisin*" and dedicated it "To the men and women of The Yard who have built her." Each one of us swelled with pride, but we merely glanced at each other in a knowing way as if to say, "That's as it should be."

Questions for Discussion

1. What are Clawson's views of the women and men employed in the shipyards?
2. What are some of the facts that made it especially difficult for female welders?

24.
Richard O. McIntire
Combat Diary, 1944–1945

Richard McIntire, of Warren, Indiana, served with the 54th Armored Field Artillery Battallion in France, Belgium, and Germany. The diary he kept during the nearly two years that he was in combat has the sense of urgency that the battlefield reflects: he reports his position, sketches the highlights of the battles, records the occasional misfiring by American planes onto his battallion, and relates the names of those men who died and were wounded in combat. His notes—for they are more notations than detailed descriptions—provide, nonetheless, a vivid picture of war.

June [*1944*]
20. Boarded L.S.T. at Weymouth [*Massachusetts*]
24. Landed in France.
25. First firing.
29. Fired on regiment of German infantry
30. Battle continues.
July
7. More engagements with the enemy.
8. Crossed the Vire River. [*Normandy*]
9. First casuality. Batteries ran out of ammo no ground lost.
   11. P47's saved the day by knocking out tanks that tried to break-through and split the first army German tankers looked like roast turkey. Forty one tanks knocked out.

Richard O. McIntire Diary. Third Armored Division Association Archives, Box 49, University of Illinois Archives, Record Series 26/20/76.

24. Today push was supposed to start, it rained and was called off.

25. Push starts. Thousands of heavy bombers bomb enemy front lines in St. Lo. The ground shook. McNair was killed here.

28. A Battery captures first prisoners.

29. We took Coutances.

31. Caught hell from 88's and small arms. Planes dropped flares all around us, while on the road 88's dropped all around us. Many vehicles hit. Pull into position Germans in next field.

August

2. Caught hell again from 88's and 75's. We were almost bombed by [*American*] P38's who bomb short of target. Hamilton hit.

3. Shelled at night, big stuff.

4. Mortain. Worst shelling we ever got. Novak killed. Macneil, Alderman and Ware hurt. German planes bombed all night.

14. Our objective at this time is to close the Falaise Gap which will trap a great portion of the German seventh army. Keeler killed. Huttin killed.

15. Many hit in all batteries.

19&20. We were pulled out for a 24 hour rest. Plenty of wine, calvados, cognac and eggs.

22. We push 93 miles.

24. We push 75 miles. Crossed Seine River, near St. Leu and Cesson. One Battery captured truck of Champagne, cognac, candy, and coffee.

28. B battery knocked out train load of tiger tank

September

1. Shelled again. One killed and seven wounded in C battery

2. Arrived in Mons, Belgium. Kissed by men and women and children.

4. Shelled again.

5. City of Mons, lots of dead Germans lying all over the ground.

12. Still dashing through Belgium. Shelled and bombed again at [?] a city on the Belgium and German border. Forward elements entered Rotogen first city in Germany. Shelled with A.P. A.A. track hit no one hurt.

14. C battery ran into a German position got 50 prisoners. Young killed.

15. Start hitting Seigfreid line using plenty of ammo.

18. Still firing fast and furious.

19. German bombers over at night. R.A.F. [*Royal Air Force*] over Cologne, heavy flak.

October

2&3. Maintenance of vehicles.

10. Germans shell positions, big stuff. R.R. gun.

13. Germans bomb position. Steady rain since reaching Germany.

15. Still raining bombers around at night. About this time Gartsite Williams and Sherrard were killed many hurt. Direct hit on the shop.

26. Shelled at night.

28. Shelled again this time bad.

29. Hurtegen forrest. Germans adjusted by air bursts. Two killed in firing batteries.

31. Got some beer from freshly taken Aachen. 5 Marks for five gallons. No kick to it.

November

11. Snow falls.

15. Men leave for [*U.S. savings*] bond tour in the states.

16. Preparation for new push. Shot a lot of ammo. P38's bomb batteries by mistake. No one hurt.

17. Still firing like hell.

18. Our P47's gave them hell today, still firing lots of ammo. . . . Krauts drop anti personal on us they missed again. Strauss killed, Sweet wounded.

23. Thanksgiving Day. Germans shell us. German dead stacked like cord wood being hauled away in trucks.

24. Germans counter attack we set four of their tanks on fire. Later we fire on the retrievers that came to pick the tanks up.

December

1. Move to new position. Artillery and bomb craters every ten feet. A Battery fired 840 rounds in less than two hours.

3. German planes strafed to our rear. A.A. knocked down three. Moved to Musbach.

4–8. Shacked up in our foxholes, cold snow.

9. Moved again.

10. Shot up lots of ammo. Lt. Willis wounded.

11. "A" battery fired 30,000 rounds at a cost of a million and a half dollars. We fired across the Roer.

13. On the alert for German paratroopers. Plenty of jerry planes overhead. Ack Ack all over the place. One knocked down. Colten wounded, Lt. Willis died.

17. Saw a dogfight, ME109 went down in flames. Same as the last four nights many German planes bombing. [*They're*] softening for the Ardennes breakthrough.

18. Prepare to move to the bulge.

19. A German plane came so low we could see the pilot. Drove to Bulge. Bad night for driving. Buzz bombs over every few minutes.

21. In position at the bulge. Very cold. Stayed at Barveaux.

22. Plenty of snow and cold. Many buzzbombs over.

23. Germans all around us. P38's bomb and strafed one of our batteries, mistook them for the enemy.

24. We were awaken and told that the Germans had broken through. We leave Manhay and go back to Barveaux. All quiet there. Solomon wounded.

25. Christmas day. "C" battery comes out of the trap all but one man "Walker" a medic who stayed to care for the wounded. Saw B17 go down in flames.

26. Lt. Valis is killed by sniper.

27. Firing in support of the 75th Div. And they need it. It is their first action.

28. Firing batteries have everything thrown at them one dead a few hurt, Ammo sections help to hold lines with the [?] troops. Gennette killed. . . .

29. Tankers count 800 dead krauts. Germans tried to wipe out our firing batteries but failed. They were hurting instead. The place [*is*] Marche.

30. A clear day many of our bombers over.

31. The batteries came back for a rest.

January 1945

1. Went to an assembly area.

2. Moved up with the 83rd Division.

3. Firing for the 83rd

4. Same

5. Moved again. Dead G.I.s all over the place, many more Krauts.

6. Moved again.

7. Snow knee deep and still snowing.

8. Still snowing and still firing.

11. Move in house and go to bed. Half hour later the house burnt down. The boys lost equipment but no one hurt. Slept in snow.

12. Very cold.

13. New position and we are shelled.

14. P47's bomb and strafe the batteries. 3 hurt.

21. We go back to Petit-Han for rest and regrouping.

February

7. Back to Brenieg Germany

25. Start push across Roor River. Shelled on roads and positions.

26. Our bombers dropped bombs very close to us. Bomb hit a house and buried eight boys alive.

27. A lot of firing, attacks repulsed.

March

1. Saw M109 go down in flames, lots of firing at night. German bombers bombed all night very close. Berrendolf.

2. Crossed [?] canal.

3. 2 "C" Battery used direct fire in new position. Lt. Pratt killed.

5. We fired on Cologne.

20. We have spent the last few days in rest area 1000 yds from the Rhine. Bruhl is the city. Crossed the Rhine at Hollinsdeck on pontoon bridge over three hundred yards long.

22. Move into assembly area.

24. Move today to prepare for drive tomorrow.

26. Firing batteries got shelled bad.

28. We are Spearheading again going like hell.

29. Still going.

30. Hit the objective Paderborn. General Rose killed.

31. Paderborn taken.

April

4. Reached the outskirts of Dessau which is our last stand in Europe.

12. President Roosevelt dies.

16. We fired a 21 gun salute for Roosevelt. We fired on Dessau from here.

25. Moved back to Brucken for rest.

May

7. V.E. day

Questions for Discussion

1. What do you learn about the battlefield from McIntire's brief accounting of his combat experiences?

2. What is the effect of this rather slim record? How might the circumstances of combat restrict reflection?

3. Compare McIntire's diary with the World War I diary of Guy Emerson Bowerman (p. 89).

25.
Phyllis Fisher

Letters from Los Alamos, 1944–1945

In 1939 the physicist Albert Einstein, by then a refugee from Germany living in the United States, wrote a letter to President Franklin D. Roosevelt pointing out German advances in nuclear physics and describing the potential military uses of such research. When the United States entered World War II, the production of an American atomic bomb became a military priority.

Research was conducted at several sites in the United States, but increasingly centered on the isolated New Mexico community of Los Alamos. There, under the leadership of the charismatic physicist J. Robert Oppenheimer, scientists produced the first atomic weapon and successfully tested it on July 16, 1945, in a nearby desert location known as the "Trinity Site." Soon after, on August 6 and August 9, atomic bombs were dropped on the Japanese cities of Hiroshima and Nagasaki.

Research at Los Alamos was conducted under conditions of great secrecy. When scientists and their families left their former positions to go to Los Alamos, they were unable to tell other family members where they were going or what they would be doing. Even spouses living at Los Alamos were kept in the dark as much as possible until the test.

One of the scientists recruited to work on the atomic bomb was Leon Fisher. With his wife Phyllis and their son Bobby, he

Phyllis Fisher. *The Los Alamos Experience*. Tokyo: Japan Publications Inc., 1985.

moved to Los Alamos in October 1944. Phyllis Fisher wrote often to her parents, telling them what she could within the limits of government censorship.

The letters below, all written to Phyllis Fisher's parents, fall into two parts. Before August 6, 1945, she describes life in the highly unusual community of Los Alamos, while never mentioning it by name. After Hiroshima, she is free to discuss her feelings about the bomb, and to describe the reactions of some of the scientists to it.

October 4, 1944

We're moving! Believe me, you're not any more surprised than I am! You'd like to know where we're going? So would we! And it isn't that Lee won't tell me. It's hard to believe, but he doesn't know either. The only encouraging thing he could say was that we'll know where we are when we get there. Great!

Lee came home from the university early this afternoon, tossed his briefcase on the couch and said, "Sit down, Phyllis, we've really got to talk." He was so serious that he ignored Bobby, who had toddled across the floor to greet him. He told me of an important phone call that he had made earlier in the afternoon, which really leaves us no choice and which will result in our making this sudden move.

Here's what I can tell you. We'll be going "there" next week (less than a day's trip from Albuquerque) to select our living quarters, and we will move "there" sometime between the 26th and 30th of this month. We have been directed to drive to a certain city and report to an inconspicuous address where we will be given further instructions. It's alright with me, so long as we're not met by a bearded mystic, given a piece of thread and instructed to follow it to its end. At this point, nothing would surprise me. . . .

For the time being, let's call the place Shangri-La or Sh-La for short. I'm tired of writing "there" and "the place," and I don't know what to call it. I couldn't tell you its real name if I knew it. Please don't say anything to anyone yet, at least until I tell you what you can or should say. I'll write all I can about Sh-La. Please understand that if I don't answer your questions, there is a reason. I have been told that our mail, both incoming and outgoing, will be censored. If my letters have less coherence than usual, please blame it on the rules and regulations of our future home.

Well, here we go, two so-called adults, one baby and one fox-terrier, heading off to play "hide and seek" for the duration. I'm pretty excited about it, but I'm frightened too. It's very much like stepping off into space and I just hope we land on our feet.

[*October 1944*]

Authoritative books on child-rearing warn me that when Bobby is three (or is it four?) he'll ask countless questions, many of them unanswerable. Well, it will take him a full year to ask as many questions as you did in your last letter. The worst of it is, I can't answer anything! I don't know the answers and I couldn't tell you if I did! No, we can never give you the size of the project. They take precautions that this information not be known. For example, we have been told not to transfer what they flatteringly term our "entire bank account" to a bank nearer the project. And, "What kind of work will Leon do?" and "Is it dangerous?" Mom! How can I answer you? Then you ask, "Can you assure us you will stay in New Mexico or, at least in continental U.S.A.?" I can tell you're both worried. I don't know what to say to you.

October 11, 1944

I'm breathless! We've been "there"! Shangri-La is super! We drove up yesterday and stayed just long enough to tour the place, pick out our house and learn some of the rules, regulations and by-laws of this Never-Never-Land. Naturally, the day was not uneventful. In fact, Lee and I are still blushing over our latest butch.

I wrote you that we were given an address in Santa Fe from which we were to receive further instructions. We dutifully followed our little map, found the address alright and stared at it in amazement. The place was a bakery! Once in, we didn't know what to do. A girl behind the counter asked if she could help us and we boobs were tongue-tied. Lee finally stated that we were "told to come here." Silence reigned. More silence. Believe me, I fully expected the girl to break open a loaf of bread, surreptitiously extract from it a message written in code and slyly slip it to us. Instead, a bored voice from the other side of the room said, "You must be looking for the office down the way; people are going in and out of there all the time." We felt like four cents, said our thanks and meekly ambled out. Fine beginning! The office down the way was presided over by Dorothy, a genial, relaxed woman from whom we learned that we were expected and were given our directions to Sh-La. Then we stared out on a most spectacularly beautiful drive.

Shangri-La is a streamlined, alpine settlement, size unmentionable, location unmentionable, altitude unmentionable. But it's very complete. We found theater, sports field, playground, and a school. There is even a radio station that picks up programs and adds music. Apparently, we will live in a spot where ordinary radio reception is extremely poor.

The main gate at Los Alamos. *(Courtesy, National Archives)*

Anyway, the inmates assure us that there is plenty here to compensate for the very extreme isolation. We saw notices of picnics, dances, bridge parties, etc. If we get tired of my cooking, and that's entirely possible, we can eat out at the mess hall. We are entitled to use the Army commissary and PX, and they seem quite adequate.

Lee and I were lectured briefly on the importance of developing an anti-social outlook. We're not to be friendly with residents of nearby towns. (I hadn't noticed any nearby towns.) If we go to Santa Fe (which isn't my idea of nearby) we are to keep to ourselves and not talk to outsiders unless it is necessary in the transaction of business, etc. However, we are allowed a half-smile and a slight nod to persons we already know there. "Only this and nothing more.". . .

October 27, 1944

. . . You can tear up the floor plan I sent you. Any resemblance between it and the place we're living in is purely coincidental. Our belongings were unceremoniously dumped in the wrong house, a smaller place (classification: garage style) at about six o'clock this evening. Our chosen home, we were told by a WAC [*Women's Army Corps member*] in the housing office, had been assigned by mistake to someone else. Instead, after a great deal of scurrying around, we were deposited here to remain until another batch of houses can be built. The WAC tried to be comforting, assuring us in her most languid southern accent, that it would be but a week or so before these next prefabs would be tossed together, and we could move.

November, 1944

Now, listen to this very carefully and try to understand. I can't. We have a gate here that isn't a gate at all. It consists of a guardhouse and an unfriendly signpost surrounded by sentries. Regulations governing passage of said "gate" top any screwy regulation of any Army post anywhere. It seems that you can drive past it in an automobile without showing a pass, but you can't walk past it. Pedestrians must show passes. No exceptions.

I drove past the gate (to the vet's) with Fawn and, naturally, wasn't stopped. The veterinary hospital is only about 100 yards beyond and is visible from the gate. After our visit to the vet, I rushed out with my shivering dog, climbed into the car to start back, and—you guessed it—the car wouldn't start. By this time, it was snowing. I began to run as best I could, with Fawn held securely inside my coat. Of course, I was promptly stopped at the gate. I had no pass! In my rush to get Fawn to the vet's and back, I had neglected to take it. I explained to the sentries that my car wouldn't start. I had to get back. My husband had to get to work. My baby would be alone! My dog was dying! None of which made any difference. Only one word seemed to have meaning, the word "regulations." There were, it seemed, no provisions for someone who drove out the gate and had to walk back through it. Too bad. By then the snow was slanting and spinning angrily, and I wasn't getting any warmer. Fawn wasn't getting any lighter. They could see my car standing there, but that didn't make any difference. One MP suggested that I phone someone who could come out and identify me. Fine help! No one I knew had a phone. Lee couldn't be reached by phone until he left Bobby and went to work. And he wouldn't do that (I certainly hope he wouldn't do that) until I was safely home. What to do?

Then through the gloom and the swirling snow, there appeared a jeep, with driver, of course. Through chattering teeth, and right in front of the MPs, I asked the stranger for a lift. He agreed. I climbed into the jeep and in we went with full permission of the guards at the gate!

[November 1944]

. . . Our guests were two completely balmy SEDs [*Special Engineering Detachment members*], Bob and Norman. Bob, an attractive fellow with a nice smile, was in high spirits. He told us that next Wednesday he is going to fall madly in love with a girl named Shirley. A whirlwind romance will follow, culminating in marriage sometime in December. I was most impressed, but a little baffled by it all. But there is an explanation. Military regulations here forbid the wife of an enlisted man to come to live in Sh-La. If Bob goes home to marry his Shirley, he'll have to leave her and return to our little exile alone. However, if Shirley qualifies for a position here, meets Bob here, falls in love here, marries here, why then, she can stay. In fact, she has to stay! Hence the plotted romance. See? And Shirley has already been hired by the project and will arrive next Wednesday.

[November 1944]

This evening we were invited to dinner with friends. It was the sort of evening one learns to expect around these parts. Dinner is eaten in a mad rush. The men dash back to work. The wives do the dishes and chat a while. At ten o'clock the men return jabbering a strange language most nearly identified as "scientese." Tonight it was particularly pleasant. We discovered we had many interests in common. In other words, we all are very fond of Mozart and heartily dislike Dewey [*Republican presidential candidate*].

This afternoon a group of Leon's co-workers dropped in. Apparently, they are very charming and comical as well as very bright and interesting. You'll have to take Lee's word for it. You see, they, too, speak little English, but mostly "scientese." The only conversation directed my way was "Hello" and "Goodbye" and oft-repeated moanings about dreading Thanksgiving dinner at the mess hall. Hint, hint.

Monday, August 6, 1945

Please note ———————— LOS ALAMOS, NEW MEXICO

Well, today's news makes everything else seem pretty unimportant! You can't possibly imagine how strange it is to turn on the radio and hear the outside world talking about us today! After all the extreme secrecy, it seems positively unreal to hear stories about the bomb, the site, and everything.

The "gadget" worked better (!) than anyone dared to expect, and Hiroshima, a city we have never heard of, and its population of 350,000 has been wiped out. The radio announcers could hardly control their voices. They told the whole story. How had they gotten the information so quickly? They named names! Who had told them? They described our hill, our hill. They located us on a barren plateau in the mountains north and west of Santa Fe.

They identified us as LOS ALAMOS!

We couldn't believe what we heard! 'Over one hundred thousand Japs killed by one bomb,' the announcers bragged. They ticked off the figures as though they were reporting scores at a sporting event. But, hey, those are people! A radius of one mile vaporized, they cheered as I shuddered. They are talking about a populated target, a city. And part of me keeps saying, "This can't be real." It's also actually unreal to hear names connected with the project, names like Oppenheimer, Segre, Fermi, Bohr and others. After months of caution and secrecy, it's too much.

Kaltenborn [*a news commentator*] somehow seemed more detached and more objective than the others. He took time, in spite of the hysteria, to consider the bomb's potential for good or evil. Then he described the first test atomic explosion in the southern "arid part of the state" in New Mexico and named the date, the place, and even the code name, "Trinity."

After "Trinity," days went by while we waited to hear how and when the gadget (maybe I'd better get used to writing the word "bomb") would be used. Which brings us up to today. By comparison the excitement on the hill today has put that of July 16th far down the scale of insane rejoicing. You can't imagine it. I can't describe it. I'm certain that it will take time for the emotional bits in all of us that were triggered by "Trinity" and that blew up with the bomb to settle down into place.

August 10, 1945

Now I am upset! Yesterday's bombing of Nagasaki was shocking! I cannot understand the necessity of a second bomb. The Japanese were known to be suing for peace and trying to negotiate terms that they could accept. Why destroy another city and its inhabitants? Why couldn't both bombs have been dropped over some unimportant unpopulated island as a demonstration of what could happen to Japan?

[August 1945]
I almost fainted when a traveling salesman knocked at my door. There has never been one here before. He had gotten a temporary pass. Amazing! I was so busy questioning him that he had trouble telling me what he had for sale.

> *[The following paragraphs describe varying reactions to the success of the project. Some were on the verge of hysteria; others took it more calmly.]*

... for instance, yesterday, Scotty [*who works in the tech area and*] who lives across the street, called to me at around 9:00 A.M. I went over to his house, found him in bed sobbing convulsively into his pillow. He had turned on his heater, which had exploded and burned about a square inch on his arm and spread soot around the living room. It was just too much and the poor guy was nauseated, dizzy, and completely hysterical. I got him quieted down somewhat, notified his wife, who [*also*] works in the tech area, and called a doctor.

Lee goes around with a "Cheshire Cat" grin that won't wipe off. He is very tired and has gotten little sleep. He gets up and wanders around at night when he should be sleeping. And I've lost four pounds in all the excitement.

> *[In October, J. Robert Oppenheimer spoke to the scientists and their families.]*

[October 1945]
... And what he [*Oppenheimer*] said was so exactly what I've been feeling but have been unable to express. His talk was short, even faltering. He told us that the whole world must unite or perish. He felt that unless there is a way to prevent wars, the pride we are feeling today will give way to concern and fear for the future. He said that the day may come when "mankind will curse the names of Los Alamos and Hiroshima."

> *[After the war Phyllis Fisher became a clinical social worker while Leon resumed his academic career. From 1979 to 1982*

they lived in Japan while Leon was a senior scientist in the Office of Naval Research at the United States Embassy in Tokyo.]

Questions for Discussion

1. What was life like at Los Alamos?
2. What was the reaction of the scientists and their families to the dropping of the bomb? What do you think of their reactions?

Part 4

Contemporary America

Prosperity returned in the years after World War II, but the nation remained troubled by foreign tensions and internal divisions. The Cold War with the Soviet Union, conducted in the shadow of the nuclear cloud, had repercussions at home as well as abroad. As the Soviet Union developed its own atomic and hydrogen bombs and Communism came to dominate China and much of Eastern Europe, some Americans began to argue that traitors at home had helped the Communist cause. Senator Joseph McCarthy was the most prominent of those searching for domestic treason. The diary of Martin Merson provides an insight into McCarthy's methods and their effects.

If the prevailing tone of the 1950s was conservative, however, that of the 1960s and early 1970s tolerated political dissent. African Americans such as Martin Luther King, Jr. led the way, demanding first an end to disfranchisement of blacks and the removal of legalized segregation. The lack of progress in removing the economic and social effects of racism led some African Americans to question the wisdom of integration as a goal and non-violence as a method. The letters from civil rights workers in Mississippi capture the movement at a time of triumph but also of increasing doubt.

By the late 1960s and 1970s other non-white minorities began to seek more equal treatment and a greater degree of self-determination. An important arena for Mexican-Americans in this struggle was the

165

campaign for more rights for migrant farm workers. The diary of
Johanna Von Gottfried describes one such protest in California.

Women, too, demanded an equal place in American society. During
the 1950s most women devoted their lives to home and family. Under
the surface, however, there was growing discontent, as shown in the
letters women wrote to Betty Friedan after the publication of her
ground-breaking book, *The Feminine Mystique*. Such concerns would
soon arise within the contemporary women's rights movement and the
effort to achieve an Equal Rights Amendment.

American involvement in Vietnam was a product of the Cold War
that went back to the 1940s. President Lyndon Johnson dramatically
escalated the war in 1965, leading both to an increased military presence
in Vietnam and the development of a growing and vocal protest movement at home. The letters from soldiers in Vietnam reflect some of the
experience of those who fought in the war, while Susan Stern's diary
describes the anti-war protest at the Chicago Democratic Convention in
1968.

The cynicism of many Americans about their government was
deepened in the 1970s by the Watergate scandal and the resignation of
President Richard Nixon under threat of impeachment. The diary of
journalist Elizabeth Drew describes part of that long and traumatic
process. The 1970s also saw the rise of an increasingly influential
environmental movement. Among the most dramatic illustrations of the
threat of environmental pollution was the crisis at the Three Mile Island
nuclear power plant. The diary of Nancy Austin reflects the experience
of an area resident during that crisis.

The last selection in this volume returns to the theme of the first
selection in Volume I—immigration. In the 1980s and 1990s immigration again became a controversial political subject in the United States.
As economic prospects dimmed, particularly for workers in traditional
blue-collar jobs, the resentment of immigrants by the native-born grew.
An old pattern was being repeated: when times are good, immigrants
are usually viewed in a positive light; when economic conditions are
poor or uncertain, they are often regarded as a threat. New considera-
tions of overpopulation and stressing of natural resources in crowded
areas such as southern California were being argued over. The letters
of undocumented workers illustrate the experience of the most recent
wave of immigrants seeking a better life in the United States.

26.
Martin Merson

Joseph McCarthy and the Search for Communists in the United States, 1953

Martin Merson was educated in the law at Harvard University; he served in World War II and then resumed a career in his profession and in community service. In February 1953, he was drafted as executive officer to Dr. Robert Livingston Johnson, head of the International Information Administration (now the United States Information Agency, USIA). His diary, written during the five-and-one-half months he served in that position, describes what he calls "the hysterical days of 1953 when one minor Senator and a few fanatical aides intimidated even the President of the United States. . . ."

Merson is referring to Senator Joseph McCarthy, who accused that agency, and its Voice of America arm, of Communist sympathies. McCarthy's search for subversives, stimulated in part by a growing Cold-War concern among Americans of a Communist threat, stretched beyond government service. As a result of his crusade, thousands of people were accused and officially censured. Though jobs were lost and reputations smeared, McCarthy was unable to uncover evidence leading even to the conviction of one subversive in the government.

Martin Merson. *The Private Diary of a Public Servant*. Reprinted with the permission of Simon & Schuster. Copyright 1955 by Martin Merson, renewed 1983 by Martin Merson.

In the following diary entries, Merson describes McCarthy's attack on his agency and reflects upon the kind of misdirected power that can destroy innocent lives.

Washington, 23 February, 1953 . . . Together we [*Johnson and Merson*] wrote out the conditions under which Johnson would take on the job with myself as his chief assistant. These were:

1. Sixty to ninety days to study the operation.
2. No operational responsibility during that time.
3. Assurance of Administration backing for separation of the information agency from the State Department.

Johnson went to the White House that night to clear the conditions with the President.

The President, who had been playing golf that afternoon at the Burning Tree Golf Club, readily agreed with the reasonableness of Johnson's conditions.

While Johnson was there, the President telephoned Robert Cutler, his appointee as secretary of the National Security Council, regarding the separation of the agency. Cutler confirmed that there was some sentiment among the Council members for taking the information agency out of [*the*] State [*Department*].

Well, everything was settled, we thought. We had a big job ahead. We both were anxious to get started.

/////

Philadelphia, 26 February, 1953 . . . After our meeting, Johnson was besieged by reporters who wanted to know, among other things, what he thought of McCarthy. Johnson said he was ready to give the Senator the benefit of the doubt in his investigation of the agency he, Johnson, was about to take over.

"I think he is trying to be helpful, and maybe he'll dig up stuff that will help us," Johnson said. He pleaded ignorance of the Voice of America or of its personnel, on which McCarthy then was concentrating. As to McCarthy personally, Johnson said: "I think he is a good American who wants to see that the Voice works properly." So do I. . . . That the Eisenhower Administration wanted a vigorous, persuasive information program, I had no doubt. . . .

Congress had . . . appropriat[*ed*] $70,000,000 for the program for fiscal 1951 and had appropriated $50,000,000 more for the construction of a world ring of short-wave transmitters to reach every corner of the world and penetrate the Iron Curtain.

Senator Joseph McCarthy and Counsel Roy Cohn of the Senate
Investigations subcommittee. *(Courtesy, National Archives)*

*[With Senator Joseph McCarthy at the helm, public hearings
began on February 16, 1953, charging Communist literature
had infiltrated the Voice of America libraries. His claim was
based on the presence of books critical of American policy.
Merson notes that "the purge of books was on" and that books
were even burned at some of the libraries.]*

Washington, 3 March, 1953 Following the swearing-in ceremony
in Mr. Dulles's office, a group assembled in Undersecretary Lourie's
office. . . .

. . . Up to this time I had been thinking of "security risks" as applying
to Communists—205 in the State Department alone, McCarthy had
charged. . . .

"Security," as defined by McCarthy, [*Senator*] Bridges, [*Scott*]
McLeod, [*Assistant Secretary of State*] McCardle, and others, I began to
see, was being used to cover a lot of things that I had always thought

were a man's personal affair—something between himself and his own conscience and having little to do with his value to the Government. I wasn't sure that the God I looked to for guidance had endowed anyone on earth with the power and wisdom to judge these things. I could see I had a lot to learn. . . .

As Bob Johnson and I arrived back at our offices . . . the questions arose: Whom can we trust? Are our own telephones tapped? . . .

/////

Washington, 5 March, 1953 . . . Johnson and I wrote and sent to Dulles a memorandum urging prompt action on a new policy for book selection, especially clarification on the use or mention of Communist material. . . .

The memorandum urged that whatever modification in previous directives was agreed on should "be comprehensive and final." We did not want a directive that would be canceled the next day, or the day after, if McCarthy or someone else didn't like it. . . .

. . . McCarthy had just [*in February 1953*] opened his investigation with the now well-wearisome charges of espionage, sabotage and Communist infiltration of the agency—charges which had not been proved to the satisfaction of anyone who had studied the record. . . .

/////

New York, 20 March, 1953 . . . Not having met McCarthy or [*Roy*] Cohn [*McCarthy's chief legal counsel*], I could only wonder as to the motives for their actions. . . .

I couldn't help asking myself: If McCarthy and Cohn were themselves Communists, could they be doing a more skillful job of sabotage? Or if not themselves subversives, were they unwitting tools in the hands of fiendishly more clever minds?

. . . If McCarthy and Cohn had substantial evidence of subversion in the Voice [of America], and deliberate sabotage, wouldn't they *quietly* arrange to communicate the facts to Eisenhower? To Dulles? To Johnson? . . .

/////

Washington, 19 May 1953 Senator McCarthy finally condescended to see Johnson and me to discuss the information program, which he had been busy trying to wreck for three and one-half months. . . .

Johnson reserved the Presidential Suite at the Statler for our dinner meeting with McCarthy. . . .

I cannot recall that Joe—and he was soon that to all of us—even had a drink. Certainly he did not smoke.

Many of us have formed an impression of McCarthy from the now familiar Herblock caricatures. He is by no means grotesque. Herblock's sensitive fingers convey the vision of an ogre. McCarthy, the relaxed dinner guest, is a charming man with the friendliest of smiles. He has the appearance of strength and virility. The contrast is great between McCarthy and most of the garden variety of flabby, paunchy politicians. This strength stood him in good stead as he battled his way up from a simple beginning as the fifth son of an immigrant farmer, Timothy McCarthy, of Outagamie County, Wisconsin.

. . . His mood was genial and he seemed to be pressing for nothing in particular.

Afterward we were joined by Robert Morris, Counsel to the Jenner Committee, and Julius Cahn, Counsel to the Senate Committee on Foreign Relations. The conversation dealt with the hunt for subversion in government and some of the interesting experiences of these professionals.

At one point Cohn raised a question about the composer Aaron Copland. His music was used, I believe, in some of our overseas information centers. This produced the only real argument of the evening. Sokolsky, who was present, of course, was an admirer of Copland's music. He took the view that Copland should not be blacklisted. Cohn, who may or may not be musically inclined, felt equally strongly that he should.

As I sat quietly listening to the Copland colloquy, I was suddenly struck by the ludicrousness of the whole evening's performance. Cohn, Schine, McCarthy, Sokolsky, and for that matter the rest of us, meeting to discuss the manners and morals of our times. By whose appointment? By what right? What qualification did any of us have?

Just a bare century and a half ago, the Founding Fathers were meeting in Convention Hall in Philadelphia to create one of the most memorable documents of all times. While it hadn't insured "domestic tranquility," certainly it wasn't for lack of stature of the delegates, men who had made a revolution and gone on to build a great nation.

Where were men like these giants of an earlier day—the Washingtons, Franklins, Jays, Madisons, and Hamiltons? A resentment which had been smoldering deep inside me for days flared up. I controlled it, but I resolved to find a way out of this morass of chicanery and pettifoggery which was due principally to the timidity and ineptness of our leadership.

Who were these men to whom we felt we had to toady?

McCarthy is too well known to require much biographical material from me—a small-town judge who, it has been alleged, falsified his war record and courted Communist votes to get elected to the United States Senate. As a Senator, his financial activities came under investigation by a Senate election subcommittee. . . .

As I left the dinner I remembered a point made by De Tocqueville in his great book on the American experiment in democracy. He wrote, over a century ago:

"What is to be feared is not so much the immorality of the great as the fact that immorality may lead to greatness. . . ."

It seemed to me to apply to the spring of 1953 in Washington.

/////

Washington, 9 June, 1953   A special table always was reserved in the grill room of the Carroll Arms Hotel for the convenience of Senator McCarthy, his staff, and any guests. I joined the circle today. . . .

I always felt uneasy when with McCarthy. I had the sensation that if he were not a charlatan, as some have described him, he certainly was easy prey for a reasonably sophisticated espionage agent.

The atmosphere in which he lived made him ripe for such maneuvers. He had many people around him at all times. . . .

During the conversation at the table Schine, who was always somewhat subdued in McCarthy's presence, suggested a certain person to take Connors' place as head of policy. McCarthy and Cohn enthusiastically supported the suggestion.

I had not been back at my desk more than an hour when the phone rang. The F.B.I. was calling. They had heard of the recommendation made to me at lunch and were calling to suggest that I ought not to touch the man with a ten-foot pole.

Long before this experience I had concluded that what the McCarthy group did not know about fighting Communism effectively would fill all the books in my favorite library room at Harvard.

/////

Washington, 23 July, 1953   . . . Now I could see, more clearly than ever before, why McCarthy had got away with murder. Even at the risk of lowering United States prestige throughout the world, the Republican Party line was to give the hatchetman a free hand in his public appearances. Even at the risk of creating chaos in the executive branch, he was not to be impeded. Even when the man deliberately lied, the truth was not to be told. . . .

Washington, 24 July, 1953   Despite the ban imposed by the White House (which I assumed also applied to me) on Johnson's appearing at the Senate Appropriations hearing, I went anyway. Before I left the office I wrote out my resignation. Consultants, as a rule, do not resign; they just fade away. I decided to set a precedent.

I went to room F-39, where the hearings were to have been held. I learned that a shift had been made to the Senate Caucus Room. . . .

[*This room was the one in which the McCarthy censure hearings would take place. The room was large and well lighted, McCarthy encouraging public attendance.*]

From the outset it was a Roman holiday for McCarthy. His questions, his domination of the committee, and his aides scurrying in and out were what impressed themselves on one's mind.

Was this democracy in action? Was this the raw stuff out of which reasonable men would compound reasonable decisions? I had heard a lot about one-man hearings and how essential it was to prohibit them. But I fail to see what earthly difference it can make to have other members of a committee on hand unless they take an active and intelligent part.

I was struck by the fact that aside from Ellender and Robertson's inquiries about the klieg lights and the change of room, *the Democrats contributed very little.* Were they too in fear of McCarthy?

The list of witnesses was impressive: Undersecretary of State Walter Bedell Smith, Senator H. Alexander Smith, Senator Bourke B. Hickenlooper, Senator Ralph E. Flanders, Senator J. William Fullbright.

At times Ferguson would get into the act. But he asked much the same questions as McCarthy. No witness every really was given a chance to answer the question directly.

Most of the McCarthy-Ferguson questions, as might be supposed, dealt with the alleged Communist infiltration of the information agency. . . .

I sat far to the rear. I longed to get up and shout, "Cowards! Why don't you put this demagogue in his place?"

Sadly enough, not a single representative of the executive branch, including Eisenhower's close friend Bedell Smith, defended the President's literary judgment. Nor did any Senator.

/////

[*President Eisenhower did not comply with McCarthy's wishes to incorporate the agency into the State Department; on July 30, 1953 he appointed Theodore Streibert as the agency's director.*]

Washington, 31 July, 1953 . . . I believe that Americans still can dream the big dream; that they instinctively understand, even if they are not articulate about it, what a great heritage they have, which is that here on this Continent was founded a government of the people, by the people, and for the people; and that ultimately they turn to the men who they believe are best fitted to make that dream a reality of their own time.

We have had our McCarthys before. We shall have them again. In time, they pass on. . . .

Questions for Discussion

1. What were the conditions that permitted Joseph McCarthy to carry on his quest for Communists among American citizens? What reasons does Merson give for McCarthy's reign?

2. Can you think of other people who have (or had) the effect on government leaders or the public that McCarthy had? What is the solution for what Merson calls demagoguery?

27.
Civil Rights Workers
Letters from Mississippi, 1964

In the summer of 1964 almost one thousand white students from the North joined black civil rights workers in a voter registration and education campaign that became known as Mississippi Freedom Summer.

Organized by the Student Non-Violent Coordinating Committee (SNCC), the most daring and idealistic of the civil rights organizations, the summer was a mixed success. The threat of violence was always present, and sometimes became a reality. A number of civil rights workers died that summer, and SNCC workers soon became disillusioned with the efforts of federal authorities to prevent or punish attacks by white Mississippians. While seventeen thousand black Mississippians filled out registration forms at courthouses throughout the state, only 1,600 were allowed to register. Tensions between white student volunteers and African-American veterans of the civil rights struggle emerged during the orientation sessions and never disappeared. SNCC leaders debated the value of Martin Luther King, Jr.'s credo of nonviolence and passive resistance.

The following letters reflect the experience of that summer as seen by the student volunteers.

[Orientation for those going to Mississippi was held on the campus of Western College for Women in Oxford, Ohio in

Elizabeth Sutherland, ed. *Letters from Mississippi.* New York: McGraw-Hill Book Company, 1965.

mid-June. It was not always a comfortable experience, as the following letters reflect.]

Oxford, Ohio, June 14

Dear Mom and Jo,

The reception at Western College was not warm. I was surprised at how unfriendly and unextending people were. Small groups formed and people seemed concerned with "fitting in." I went to bed. Later that day (today) I went to register. I still felt uncomfortable but attempted to shake a few hands. (It wasn't too bad.) Some people were friendly and helpful. Tremendous enthusiasm was generated when we all began singing after dinner. It was the spiritual revival type singing and you know how I love that. We all must have sung for about 2 hours, and the previous in-grouping of Negroes and reservedness of whites seemed to disappear—but not really. . . . Maybe we'll be able to at the end of the summer, but right now we don't know what it is to be a Negro and even if we did, the Negroes here would not accept us.

It's the old case of having to prove ourselves. In their eyes we're rich middle or upper-class whites who've taken off a summer to help the Negro.

Intellectually, I think many of us whites can understand the Negroes' resentment but emotionally we want to be "accepted" at face value. We want this acceptance because this is part of our reason for going down south, i.e., the basic worth of the individual. . . .

June 15.

. . . Us white kids here are in a position we've never been in before. The direction of the whole program is under Negro leadership—almost entirely. And a large part of that leadership is young people from the South—Negroes who've had experience just because they're Negroes and because they've been active in the movement. And here "we" are, for the most part never experiencing any injustice other than "No, I won't let you see your exam paper. . . ."

Dear Mom and Dad,

A lot of the meetings have been run by a Negro Mennonite minister from Georgia, a member of the National Council of Churches. (The NCC is paying for this orientation, and has some excellent staff people here.) His name is Vincent Harding, plump, bespectacled, a brilliant moderator in discussions because he reacts so honestly and humorously to every question. Yesterday he gave a long talk about people using each other

Robert Moses (far right) and other SNCC workers recruiting black Mississippians to register to vote. *(Courtesy, Danny Lyon, Magnum Photos)*

and where to watch out for this within the movement itself (Negro man accuses white girl of being a racist if she won't go to bed with him, or vice versa; or white girl looking for "my summer Negro"; or Negroes in the community using volunteers as the only available victims of their suppressed hostility to whites in general, etc., etc.) These are examples of the kind of honesty that characterizes the whole training session. His main point was that people within the movement must not use each other because it is that very exploitation of someone else, which turns him from a human being into an object, that the movement is fighting against.

Love,
Susan

Dear Folks:

Yesterday was non-violence day here. In the morning we heard Jim Lawson of Nashville, who gave us the word on non-violence as a way of life. Lawson speaks of a moral confrontation with one's enemies, catching the other guy's eye, speaking to him with love, if possible, and so on. . . . "Violence always brings more harm to the people who use it; economic and political forces have no place in the Movement . . . etc." These are the things Lawson came up with . . . I feel very strongly that he does NOT represent the Movement.

Stokely Carmichael of SNCC rebutted him in the afternoon session: Nonviolence used to work because (1) it was new; (2) the newspapers gave it top coverage week after week, and most important (3) the demands were minor and the resistance to change was not hard-core. Now the North is tired of demonstrations, a very vigorous backlash has emerged, and the papers will only report major violence. Now we are responsible for what we do, and have to explain the stall-in instead of having it welcomed on the front pages of the press. Again most important, the movement has grown up, and is now aiming at the places where the white society really feels threatened—at jobs and at voting.

There comes a point when you get tired of being beaten and going back the next day for your beating for 5 days in a row. You get tired of being asked whether you are a Negro or a nigger, and ending up on the floor of the police station screaming at the top of your lungs that yes, you are a nigger, boss. You get tired of seeing young women smashed in the face right in front of your eyes. Stokely does not advocate violence. No SNCC workers are armed, nor are there guns in any SNCC office. What he is saying is that love and moral confrontations have no place in front of a brute who beats you till you cry nigger. . . .

[The rest of the letters are from Mississippi.]

June 21

Dear Stark . . .

Hi. As you said, no picture postcards to be had, or at least not anywhere I've been, so this'll have to do.

They said that Meridian was an easy town. Comparatively speaking, of course, meaning that the police aren't altogether that terrible, and they try to hold down the vigilante types. Right now, tho, we're all sitting here in the office being quietly nervous as hell. This morning Mickey, who's the project director, and Chaney, a local staff member and Andy, who's a volunteer, all went out to one of the rougher rural counties to see about a church that was burned down a few days ago. They said they'd be back by four, and now it's coming on to ten. We've been calling the Jackson office all day, and have checked all the jails around, and they're not in any of them. No word from them of any kind. We've had people out looking for them and they haven't found anything. We've been in touch with the FBI and DJ [*Department of Justice*] but I don't quite know if they're doing much of anything.[1]

Canton, July 10

Dear John and Cleo,

Our hostesses [*the black families with which the volunteers lived*] are brave women. And their fear is not at all mixed with resentment of us, but that makes it none the easier for them. The other morning a local newscaster said that someone was reported to have offered someone else $400 to bomb all the houses where volunteers are staying. I'm not convinced that that particular story has any basis, but it touched off the terror that must lie latent always in our sisters' hearts. I overhead one of them on the telephone: "My guhls probly think I'm out of mah head; I been singin' all mornin, every song I knows—I just has to." And she had been moaning, "Lord have musee" in between the songs. I talked with her a little bit. She told me she knows people have suffered and died too long and that we must take risks now so it won't go on forever. But that doesn't make the risk any less painful to bear. She sleeps with a hatchet under her bed. She told me she used to have a gun under her pillow until one night when she almost accidentally shot a neighbor boy. . . .

> [*The voter registration drive faced serious obstacles, though in some cases it met with notable success.*]

Holly Springs

Dear Mom,

When we walk up to a house there are always children out front. They look up and see white men in the car, and fear and caution cover their expressions. Those terrified eyes are never quite out of my mind; they drive me as little else could. The children run to their parents, hide behind them. We walk up, smile, say howdy, and hold out our hands. As we shake hands I tell them my name. They tell me their names and I say Mr.—, how do you do. It is likely the first time in the life of this

---

[1]The reference is to James Chaney, a black Mississippian, Michael Schwerner, a white CORE [Congress on Racial Equality] worker from New York, and Andrew Goodman, a white volunteer from Queens College who had been in Mississippi for one day. On August 4 their bullet-ridden bodies were found buried in an earthen dam near Philadelphia, Mississippi.

farmer or housewife that a white man has shaken hands with them like that. This does not necessarily bode well to them. They think, if Mr. Charlie knew. . . . Many are sharecroppers, who must turn over a third to a half of the year's harvest to a man who does no work at all, but who owns the land they till. They may be evicted, and have often been for far less serious offenses. Nearly everyone black in Mississippi is at least a year in debt. The threat of suspended credit and foreclosure is a tremendous burden. . . .

Love,
Bob

Batesville, August 1

We're all a little nervous. Four . . . rightsworkers—including me—are staying with the Robert Miles' on their farm just outside of Batesville. Mrs. Miles' 25 yr. old son Robert Jr. is stationed out in the yard with a gun. (Yes, the Movement is still non-violent; but every farmer—white and black—in the Delta has a gun. Mr. Miles has seven, all loaded.)

Things are getting very tense around here. Last night, while I was eating a peanut butter sandwich in the kitchen and talking to the other white girl staying here, two shots whizzed right by the kitchen window—I could even see a flash of light from the gun. Since last Saturday night when the Miles' house was bombed with a tear gas grenade, several other Negroes in town have received bomb threats. . . .

We think that the heightened tension is pretty much a testimonial to the success of our voter registration drive. About 500 Negroes have registered since the summer volunteers arrived in Batesville—this in a county where until recently only two Negroes had been able to register in seventy years. . . .

[The "Freedom Schools" were an important part of the Mississippi project.]

Monday, July 20. The first day of school—14 students, ages 12 to 47. A student was assigned to report on civil rights news for the next few days. . . . We gathered on benches under the trees. I asked one of the students to read an excerpt from a speech by Frederick Douglass. Asked three others to read aloud poems by Langston Hughes. When we finished, Arthur asked if he could take the Langston Hughes book home overnight. . . .

Friday, July 24. 'Lectured' on the Reconstruction period. Discussed the Civil Rights Act of 1875. The big hit of the week was the poetry of Langston Hughes. There was hardly a time during the day when some one wasn't reading our one copy of Selected Poems.

Sunday, July 26. At church today the congregation agreed to have the library. Everyone seemed pleased at the idea because there has never been any library available to the Negroes here. . . .

Tuesday, August 11. Gluckstadt Freedom School burned to the ground late last night. There is little doubt of the cause of the fire. There have been too many others like it in Mississippi. We start tomorrow to raise money to rebuild the building.

[Violence was an ever-present danger.]

Moss Point, Monday, July 6

Tonight the sickness struck. At our mass meeting as we were singing "We Shall Overcome" a girl was shot in the side and in the chest. We fell to the floor in deathly fear; but soon we recovered and began moving out of the hall to see what had happened. . . . When I went out I saw a woman lying on the ground clutching her stomach. She was so still and looked like a statue with a tranquil smile on her face. I ran to call an ambulance and police. . . .

Hattiesburg, July 10

. . . They [*two black and three white civil rights workers*] were walking along the railroad tracks. A white pickup truck stopped and two white men in it began shouting insults and profanities; the team walked on. Then the men got out and ran up the incline to the tracks in front of the five workers.

[One of the victims takes up the story.]

. . . The younger man with the iron rod started beating me about the head and shoulders . . . he struck me, pushing me over the tracks and down the embankment on the other side into a little ravine. He followed and kicked me with his work boots and beat me with his fists. He was swearing at me, calling me such things as "nigger lover," "white nigger" and "Commie," "Jew" and different combinations of these. . . . At one point he grabbed up a handful of canvassing papers which had fallen down with me to the bottom of the ravine and tried to force them in my mouth. He then continued to kick me and beat me with his fists but as

I had assumed the position I was able to ward off and soften the blows he gave me. When he had finished beating me he said, "Run, nigger.". . .

[The following letter describes the trial of the assailant.]

Hattiesburg, August 7
    . . . I was called, took the oath, and sat down. It was a long room dominated by a table and surrounded by a dozen red-faced men in open shirts and weathered necks and hands. I was asked the address of my family in Hattiesburg. At this time I asked if I could see counsel before answering that question and the interrogating District Attorney screamed, "NO!" He said, "Boy, you realize that you may be liable for contempt of these proceedings? Do you refuse to answer that question?" I replied politely that I would rather see counsel before I answered. Half standing he screamed, "Get outa this room,". . . his finger trembling. I left.
    . . . Since the hearing before the Grand Jury, we have found out that a semi-secret trial was held for Mr. Estus [*the accused*]. He pleaded "no defense" in order to avoid having a public trial and our participation as witnesses. He was fined $500 and 90 days at hard labor—suspended. There was no newspaper coverage of the trial, the plea of no defense, or the decision.

Ruleville
    It's night. It's hot. No lights because there aren't any curtains—meaning they can see you and you can't see them. They, the word they, takes on its full meaning here. You slap at a dozen or so mosquitoes that are buzzing in. You doze off and the phone rings again, about the fifth time, and the other end stays mum. By now you know that somebody, someone on the other side, knows where you are. They know who you're staying with. . . .
    Violence hangs overhead like dead air—it hangs there and maybe it'll fall and maybe it won't. Sometimes it's directed at people in the movement, sometimes it's indiscriminate. Cars have been roaming around; seven or eight vigilante trucks with their gun racks and no license plates have been seen meeting at the city dump. What will they do? When? Something is in the air, something is going to happen, somewhere, sometime, to someone. . . . A few nights ago cars roamed the streets, empty bottles flew from their hands, striking cars and homes. They were empty that night—the next night the bottles were loaded—exploding as they hit the church and setting it afire.

[At the memorial service for James Chaney, an African-American civil rights leader drove home a lesson of the young man's death.]

Laurel, August 11

Dear Folks,

. . . The memorial service began around 7:30 with over 120 people filling the small, wooden-pew lined church. David Dennis, the Assistant Director for the Mississippi Summer Project, spoke. . . . It was a speech to move people, to end the lethargy, to make people stand up. It went something like this:

"I am not here to memorialize James Chaney, I am not here to pay tribute—I am too sick and tired. Do YOU hear me, I am S–I–C–K and T–I–R–E–D. I have attended too many memorials, too many funerals. This has got to stop. Mack Parker, Medgar Evers, Herbert Lee, Lewis Allen, Emmett Till, four little girls in Birmingham, a 13-year old boy in Birmingham, and the list goes on and on. I have attended these funerals and memorials and I am SICK and TIRED. But the trouble is that YOU are NOT sick and tired and for that reason YOU, yes YOU, are to blame, Everyone of your damn souls. And if you are going to let this continue now then you are to blame, yes YOU. Just as much as the monsters of hate who pulled the trigger or brought down the club; just as much to blame as the sheriff and the chief of police, as the governor in Jackson who said that he 'did not have time' for Mrs. Schwerner when she went to see him, and just as much to blame as the President and Attorney General in Washington who wouldn't provide protection for Chaney, Goodman and Schwerner when we told them that protection was necessary in Neshoba County. . . . Yes, I am angry, I AM. And it's high time that you got angry too, angry enough to go up to the courthouse Monday and register—everyone of you. Angry enough to take five and ten other people with you. Then and only then can these brutal killings be stopped. Remember it is your sons and your daughters who have been killed all these years and you have done nothing about it, and if you don't do nothing NOW baby, I say God Damn Your Souls. . . ."

[Twenty white men were arrested for the murders by federal authorities. Among them was the deputy sheriff of Neshoba County, where the murders had taken place. Since a state court was unlikely to convict on the crime of murder, the men were charged in federal court with the federal crime of depriving the victims of their civil rights. Seven of the accused eventually went to prison.]

SNCC, disillusioned by the experience of the summer and by the rejection of much of the civil rights organizations' challenge to the all-white Mississippi delegation to the Democratic Convention in August, turned in a more radical direction. In 1966 Stokely Carmichael, newly elected chair of SNCC, popularized the slogan "black power," rejecting both the integrationist goals and the nonviolent philosophy of Martin Luther King, Jr.]

Questions for Discussion

1. What was the experience of the volunteers in Mississippi in 1964?
2. What position would you take in the debate over nonviolence and passive resistance?

28.
Anonymous

Questioning the Domestic Ideology: Letters to Betty Friedan on *The Feminine Mystique*, 1963–1964

In 1963, Betty Friedan, a graduate of Smith College, wife and mother, published The Feminine Mystique, a critique of the domestic ideology of the postwar period. In an insecure world, home and family became identified with security and fulfillment, and women were defined almost exclusively as wives and mothers, whose place in the home came to symbolize social stability. In her book, Friedan gave this domestic containment policy a name—"the feminine mystique"—and questioned the notion that women should find their fulfillment solely in the domestic arena rather than in public roles or careers. She urged women to break out of their confined roles by going back to school and finding meaningful work outside the home, rather than making careers out of their children.

The book inspired hundreds of discontented women across the country to write to Friedan, telling their stories and thanking her for putting a name to their malaise. While some scholars have recently taken issue with Friedan's analysis, many of the letters reveal a widespread discontent among women who had struggled to conform to the postwar domestic ideal.

The Friedan Manuscript Collection. Schlesinger Library Manuscript Collections. Radcliffe College. Cambridge, Massachusetts.

21 January 1963
New York City

. . . Since scientific findings reveal the strong effect of the child's environment upon the child, the poor mother has been made to replace God in her omnipotence. It is the terror of this misinterpreted omnipotence that in many cases is keeping women home. I still remember the tear-stained face of a brilliant young woman economist who had earned a Ph.D. in her field when she had to give up a newly discovered exciting job because her pediatrician convinced her that her six- and three-year-old children would become social menaces without her presence 24 hours a day. . . . [*Quoting a school official*] "Show me a delinquent child and I'll show you a working mother."

13 March 1963
Ridgewood, N.J.

. . . [*I am*] the mother of five and the wife of a successful partner in an investment banking firm. In seeking that something "more" out of life, I have tried large doses of everything from alcohol to religion, from a frenzy of sports activities to PTA . . . to every phase of church work. . . . Each served its purpose at the time, but I suddenly realized that none had any real future. Our children are all in school except for the baby. . . . However, I felt that if I waited until she's in school I'll be too close to forty to learn any new tricks. I've seen too many women say they would "do something" when the last child went to school. The something has usually been bridge, bowling or drinking.

23 April 1963
Leicester, Mass.

For the last few years, I have been on the "old housekeeping merry-go-round.". . . I cleaned and I cleaned . . . and then I cleaned some more! All day—every day. My mother had returned to teaching school when I was twelve, and I had resented it, and consequently vowed that when I married and had children I would make it my vocation. I was quite convinced that I was very happy with my role in life as we had our own home and my husband is a good husband and father and a very sufficient provider. However, one night last November, all Hell broke loose in my psyche. I was sitting calmly reading when I became overwhelmed with waves of anxiety. I couldn't imagine what was happening. . . . I visited my family doctor. He put me on tranquilizers and diagnosed it as a mild state of anxiety. However there was no explanation. . . . I see now . . . I chose security over everything else. . . . I felt I had something more to offer the world and wanted to do something about it. . . . I now have a goal and no longer feel like a vegetable.

14 May 1963
Brookline, Mass.

My life spans the two eras—the ebb tide of feminism and the rise of the "mystique." My parents were products of the early twentieth century Liberalism and believed firmly that everyone—poor, Negroes, and women too—had a right to have a 'rendezvous with Destiny.' . . . My feeling of betrayal is not directed against society so much as at the women who beat the drums for the 'passionate journey' into darkness. . . . My undiluted wrath is expended on those of us who were educated, and therefore privileged, who put on our black organza nightgowns and went willingly, joyful, without so much as a backward look at the hard-won freedoms handed down to us by the feminists (men and women). The men in my experience, were interested by-standers, bewildered, amused, and maybe a bit joyful at having two mommies at home—one for the children and one for themselves. . . . My children grew up in the mystique jungle but somehow escaped it.

24 August, 1963
Pittsburgh, PA

. . . I entered graduate school at Yale, met a man, left school, and married in 1951. I have since then moved thirteen times, lived in eight states, had four miscarriages and produced two children. . . . Finally, when I fill out the income tax now, it is occupation: Painter, not housewife. . . . My one advantage over the rest of my generation is, I suppose, the fact that I was raised in a family of feminists. . . . I still tend, belatedly and belligerently, to champion women's rights. The cloying and sentimental public effort of the last decade to raise the prestige of the home and represent it as demanding all that we have to give has more than once precipitated me into incoherent outrage. . . .

Rockaway New York

. . . What is wrong with the women trapped in the Feminine Mystique is what's wrong with men trapped in the Rat Race. . . . Isn't it true, that one of the problems, the biggest really, of our present day society is that there isn't enough meaningful creative work for *anyone* these days? Isn't that one of the reasons fathers are taking their parental role with the seriousness of a career?

[The following writers take issue with Friedan and describe the hardships of working wives and mothers.]

29 May, 1964
Folcroft, Pa.

Believe me, a modern woman of today would have to be *four* women to be everything that is expected of her. . . . My husband wants me to work not for the satisfaction I might get out of working, but for the extra money *he* will have for himself. . . . *But*, how about the extra burden it would put on me? I would go out to work if possible, but I cannot do that and come home to a house full of screaming kids, dishes piled in the sink, and mountains of laundry to do. It is no fun to come home and see the sweet, dear, lazy bum asleep on the couch after being on my feet all day. He still likes his home-made pies, cakes, and appetizing meals. . . . I have worked in stores; the post-office; given dinners for a pot and pan outfit; minded children; and sold things door-to-door. At present, I take in sewing and ironing. . . . If I work, then my housework suffers and I get told about that. I would like nothing better than to just do my own work, have some time to myself once in a while so I could just go down-town once in a while without having someone else's work staring at me. I get very tired of reading about women working outside the home. . . . I cannot divide myself into more than one person. . . . I have plenty to occupy my time and I happen to enjoy being a house-wife. . . . My husband . . . thinks it's great for women to work, but until men get some of their Victorian ideas out of their heads then I am staying home. Unless he would be willing to help with the housework then I cannot go to work. He thinks he would lose some of his masculinity if anyone saw him hanging out the wash, or washing dishes. And if he had to give up any of his fishing or hunting or running around visiting his buddies to keep an eye on the kids, well, I'm not killing myself for the almighty dollar.

4 August 1964
Glen Ridge, N.J.

Most of us would be delighted to chuck the wage earning back in our husbands' laps and devote ourselves exclusively to homemaking and community projects. We worry about the children while we're at work. We don't really like to throw the last load of clothes in the washer at

11:30 P.M., and set the alarm for 6:00 so we can iron a blouse for a school age daughter, fix breakfast and school lunches all at the same time, do as much housework as possible before bolting for the office, and face the rest of it, and the grocery shopping and preparing dinner when we get home. This isn't our idea of fulfillment. It doesn't make us more interesting people or more stimulating companions for our husbands. It just makes us very, very tired.

[This writer disagrees with Friedan from the perspective of her emigrant family of the 1930s.]

23 October 1963
Queens Village, N.Y.

. . . the emigrant mother often had to work not only in her home, but outside as well, under the most harrowing conditions. . . . For the son, it was important and necessary to obtain an education, so he could escape the sweatshop labor of his father. For the daughter, however, the most precious legacy was an escape from the hard work and drudgery of her mother and the attainment of leisure—the very leisure this emigrant mother never knew herself, and which she so desperately needed. . . . To this emigrant mother, education was only necessary for her son to get a better job, and the daughter, with nothing else besides her femininity, would, with luck, marry well and thereby achieve the leisure her mother never knew.

Questions for Discussion

1. What tensions surrounding domestic life and roles for men and women are evident in these letters?
2. What kinds of complaints about the then current domestic ideal do these writers express? What seem to be its negative features?
3. What arguments are raised to explain or defend the status quo?

29.
Susan Stern

Diary of a Protester at the Chicago Democratic Convention, 1968

The year 1968 was one of the most traumatic in American history, marked by assassination, political upheaval, and violence in the streets. In April, Martin Luther King, Jr. was assassinated, and in the aftermath, riots shook many northern cities.

At the same time the war in Vietnam was becoming increasingly controversial. The February Tet offensive launched by the Vietcong and North Vietnamese convinced many Americans that President Lyndon Johnson's Vietnam policy was a failure. Johnson, challenged within his own party on the Vietnam issue by Senators Eugene McCarthy and Robert Kennedy, announced in March that he would not seek reelection. In June, Robert Kennedy was assassinated, and by August it was clear that the nomination would go to Johnson's Vice President, Hubert Humphrey, a reluctant but loyal supporter of Johnson's policies. The war seemed no nearer an end than it had been before Johnson's withdrawal.

As the Humphrey forces triumphed in the convention hall in Chicago, riots broke out in the streets. Antiwar forces, including the "Yippies" (Youth International Party) organized by Abbie Hoffman and Jerry Rubin, had converged on the city,

Susan Stern. *With the Weathermen: The Personal Journal of a Revolutionary Woman.* New York: Doubleday & Company, Inc., 1975.

and television viewers throughout the nation witnessed the battles between them and the Chicago police. Some Americans were appalled by the clubbings and tear gassings they saw; others believed the police were only doing what was necessary. The violence in Chicago not only fractured the Democratic Party, making Humphrey's election unlikely, but also increased the political and social divisions within the country as a whole.

Susan Stern was a participant in the antiwar protest in Chicago. She was a member of Students for a Democratic Society (SDS), a New Left political organization, and later of the more radical Weathermen. Stern rewrote her journal in narrative form for publication.

[Saturday, August 24th]   The demonstration to which I was flying had been billed by the Yippies as a Festival of Life versus the Convention of Death. It was to be a head-on collision between the old way of life and the new, between young and old, left and right. Jerry Rubin and Abbie Hoffman, Yippie leaders said, "The mission is to freakout the Democrats so much that they disrupt their own convention."

The National Mobilization Committee (Mobe) declared the week of demonstrations to be largely anti-war, and were very serious about disruptive, nonviolent protest. Initially SDS hadn't supported the demonstrations, but in July, it became apparent that it was going to be a big event. Klonsky [*a friend of Stern's*] began to encourage SDS organizers from around the country to go to Chicago, with the sole purpose of reaching the McCarthy kids. . . .

That night in Chicago, before the action began, there were already more than two or three thousand people milling around Lincoln Park . . . blowing joints down by the lake, talking quietly in groups or couples. There were hundreds of young couples with long hair and beautiful bangles, representatives of the hippie counterculture. Mixed in with them were the clean-cut, collegiate-looking McCarthy supporters. These young students would learn the most from the week of demonstrations. . . .

Hundreds of people were hungry and I stood laughing and smiling and dishing out spoonfuls of stew-type glop and rice and loaves of bread, and everyone smiled back at me through the filmy night. I felt part of a great whole, a feeling that would grow on me as the days of the demonstration passed. I felt at home and serene among the smiling youth that had come to Chicago to protest the war, to dance the sundance of freedom. A feeling of tenderness for my nightfriends surged up in me and beaming, I attracted a huge crowd of people who helped

Police attack antiwar demonstrators during the Chicago convention.
(Courtesy, Jack Barnard)

me ladle out the stew and eat it. It never occurred to me to worry about where I would spend the night, I never felt alone there, although I knew no one in Chicago but Klonsky, and he was nowhere to be found. I felt very strong and at ease, I was happy and at peace with myself. . . .

   [Sunday, August 25th]   It was about eight o'clock, but it was still light outside. We walked in a small group swiftly to Lincoln Park. . . .

   This was my first street action and I was nervous. The speed had me quivering, and as Klonsky and I threaded our way through the crowded park, every noise every motion made me jump. But I felt good. I could feel my body supple and strong and slim, and ready to run miles, and my legs moving sure and swift under me, and the hot sun growing pale as night came on cooling my sweat and fanning my perfume into my nose. I was ready to riot. And my feeling was buzzing through thousands of other young, strong people, who, laughing and singing, were building up momentum for the kinetic stomp through the Chicago Loop.

   There were several speeches, one brief one by Bobby Seale of the Black Panthers. He ended his speech by wishing "power to the people."

About an hour later we began to move. From all directions the stoned and smiling flower children, the crew-cut and Oxford-shirted McCarthy students, the tie-and-jacketed Humphrey supporters, the stockinged and high-heeled sorority girls, the leather-jacketed greasers, helmeted bikers, springy walking, hotly dressed black dudes, ragamuffin hippies, baubled love children, and tense, urgent radicals streamed in spectacular color and rhythm out into the streets of Chicago chanting, "Take the streets," "The streets belong to the people," "Ho, Ho, Ho Chi Minh, Vietnam is gonna win," "Freedom now," "End the war in Vietnam"; screaming, laughing, jeering spectators, giving the peace sign, the finger sign, the fist sign, in glorious profusion the Yippie action romped and glittered on toward the downtown section of Chi-town, the Loop. After the first ten minutes everyone was on the streets and the traffic was stalled honking and groaning as the colorful youth threaded its way between the cars, and finally a huge crowd began to run down the streets of the August night.

All I could see were oceans and waves of running, chanting people around me, and glowing lights and neon signs flashing hotly, and the street lights flipping by above me, and the restaurants, movies, stores, and bars zipping by, and couples walking, looking dazed and terrified as we surged upon them. It was muggy-hot, and I was dripping sweat, but the breezes coming from Lake Michigan cooled me continuously. I began screaming chants with the crowd, until I couldn't scream any more. My arms were flung out in fists above my head and I pumped the air with them; I was boiling, singing, dancing, erupting with the spontaneous surge of freedom, of having the streets. Yes, I felt it, I knew it—crash—a gigantic rock hurled past my nose and a big bank window fell like billions of icicles. "End the war in Vietnam," "Power to the people;" smash—a spectator who tried to stop a man from throwing a rock was jammed up against a wall and bashed with a fist and he fell like a sack of potatoes. More rocks. The sound of shattering glass everywhere. Destroy the capitalists' property or else take it for the people. We gobbled up the night in a singing roar, violent and wild, saying clearly that we were on the side of the Vietnamese, on the side of freedom—and then the pigs were on us.

They closed in from all directions; from every street they came running, with their clubs stretched out before them . . . and they came smashing; heads, not windows; noses and teeth, not windshields; flesh and blood, not steel and glass. Blood streamed and splattered on me and I could hear the sickening thud of the club followed immediately by the crunch of breaking bones. In front of me, almost in slow motion, I saw a burly pig swing with all his might across the face of a pretty young man, and I saw the nose cave in and I saw the teeth spill out of his mouth, and I felt the sickness rolling in me, and I stopped and puked. . . .

The fighting went on not more than ten minutes, although it seemed like hours, and little by little the crowd thinned. I split down a side street, and hiding in an alley, tried to clean off my face with spit. As I sat there I could hear sirens and screams in the distance. A light breeze was still blowing, and I leaned my head against the building and listened to my heart pump. . . .

/////

[Wednesday, August 28th] . . . The day of the big march to the amphitheater dawned hot and breezeless. I drove from the Sedgwick Center to Grant Park with J.J. and his brother. We parked several blocks from the park under a railroad trestle. We were rather quiet and tense. On the way downtown, we had driven past the amphitheater, and it looked like a scene from a war movie. There were a tank and several gigantic guns that may have been cannon; there were at least a dozen large army trucks and a militia of jeeps; rows of soldiers stood surrounding the building itself, and dozens were stationed at the periphery. All stood at attention and all were armed. It was frightening and we shivered as we passed by. There was no doubt in our minds that if the march ever got to the amphitheater there would be a tremendous bloodbath.

There were already thousands of people in Grant Park when we arrived. Hundreds of park benches had been set up in front of an outdoor amphitheater, where march officials would be speaking later. The usual mellowness of previous park scenes had vanished. Although the suited and high-heeled McCarthy kids could still be seen, the hippies and Yippies and other commie-type freaks were not quite as bedecked and bedangled and baubled as they had been three days ago. Dozens of people limped and leaned on canes or crutches; many more were bandaged in one place or another. Hundreds nursed cuts and gashes. People looked tired and serious.

Surrounding the immediate area around the amphitheater were rows of helmeted, riot-geared pigs, standing in formation, with their clubs gripped in front of them with both hands. Behind the pigs were troops with gas masks on, their rifles slung over their shoulders. There were jeeps with barbed wire strung around the top of them, so that nobody could attack the driver. There were army trucks and all kinds of military equipment. There were also small deployments of National Guardsmen in groups of twenty or thirty, standing in formation or marching.

I lay down shuddering on a piece of blanket, and looked at the clouds gauzy in the blue sky. I thought about bullets ripping through flesh, about napalmed babies. I thought about Malcolm X and lynching and American Indians. Lying there, sweating from doses of speed and terror,

I thought about Auschwitz, and mountains of corpses piled high in the deep pits dug by German Nazis. I closed my eyes tightly, but tears oozed from under my lids and rolled off my face.

A new feeling was struggling to be born in me. It had no name, but it made me want to reach beyond myself to others who were suffering. I felt real, as if suddenly I had found out something true about myself; that I was not helpless, that life meant enough to me to struggle for it, to take chances with it, to thrust out and wrestle with it. I thought about all the years I had been strangling my misery as I turned my cheek. Now it would be different; now I would fight. . . .

About one o'clock we began to leave the park in a line that stretched for several blocks. Suddenly the line stopped. A half hour passed, and people began to sit down in their places. Whispers—the pigs are coming; no—they are arguing about the parade permit. Rennie Davis was talking to the Chief of Pigs. To march or not to march—that was the question. Finally we started moving, but those of us at the end of the line never knew if we had obtained permission to march or not. It didn't really matter anyway. . . .

We must have run for several blocks before the people in the front ran smack into a line of pigs. J.J. and I ran holding hands so that we wouldn't be torn away from each other in the chaos. But as the front ran against the rows of pigs, the people behind them turned around and began running back the way we had just come. They were terrified, screaming, whitefaced, eyes glazed; I had never seen such wild fear. They catapulted into J.J. and me, and our hands were torn apart. He was pulled with the crowd who was still heading toward the pigs, and I was pulled back by the part of the crowd running from them. That was the most frightening thing; being pulled along helplessly by the terrified, out of control mob, right into another army of pigs.

And they were smashing. Up and down with methodical persistence went those clubs, and blood began to spill, and the shrieks and moans of terror filled the air.

The police encircled about fifty of us, pressing us together in a smaller and smaller circle. The people around me began to kick and struggle like wild horses; I was punched and battered as they threw themselves about. I saw a bus drive near us, and to my horror, more police came out. I looked from the bus into the wild eyes of a pig. He was holding his club like a baseball bat and his lips were pulled back over his teeth, and he was giggling like a maniac. He was as scared as I was. I stared at him for a moment, and then he swung his club across my chest. The blow wasn't hard, but it was enough to knock me down.

I crawled among the falling and screaming people and right between the legs of a pig who was twisting the arms of a young girl and under the pig bus to the other side where, to my complete amazement, there was absolutely nobody to be seen. Limping, I began to run in the direction of the amphitheater until, a block away, I saw more fighting. . . .

For a couple of hours there were minor skirmishes. But mostly everybody stood waiting for night to fall and give protection to our activities.

While we waited, the march of the poor people . . . passed by. The poor people wound their way down Michigan Avenue, walking quietly beside covered wagons pulled by swayback mules. They walked with solemn dignity, their heads held high, looking in wonder at us dirty, cheering radicals who lined the sidewalks and jammed the park to greet them as they passed. Tired, old, young, exhausted, eager, smiling, crying they came, fulfilling the dream of Martin Luther King. The whole group had an air about them of pilgrims going to the Holy Land. . . .[1]

. . . Up Michigan Avenue, searing up to the top floor of the Hilton, to the dignified, benign and honeysuckle-rosed McCarthy, to the fat-paunched, heaving, pasty-faced Humphrey, to their compatriots and campaign supporters, to the youth who believed in them. The cries rose and fell, waking up the night, waking up the blood, waking up the hearts of youth who had grown depressed and fallow in the great universities, and with a vibrating scream, the children of America exploded and the streets were filled with streaming bodies, and once again we were fighting. Cars were stalled everywhere, honking, their petrified drivers and occupants gagging and crying from the tear gas. And up on the top floor of the Hilton, the air conditioner carried into Humphrey and McCarthy the noxious fumes until those two venerable candidates were puking and gagging like the rest of us. And out on the streets more of their children were getting their heads cracked open. . . .

Questions for Discussion

1. What do you think of Susan Stern's political views, the cause she believed in, and the actions she took?
2. What is your reaction to the violence in the streets of Chicago in 1968?

---

[1]The Poor People's Campaign had been begun by Martin Luther King, Jr. and was carried on by his successor Ralph Abernathy. At the time of the incident described above, Abernathy was on his way to address the Democratic Convention.

30.
Richard Marks, Daniel Bailey, Marion Kempner, George Williams, John Hagmann, Alan Bourne, Jim Simmen, George Olsen, and Lynda Van Devanter
Letters from Vietnam, 1965–1969

The Vietnam War is the longest war the United States has been involved in. It began with an advisory role to South Vietnam in its struggle against the Communist North and escalated sharply in the mid-1960s under President Lyndon Johnson. Its result was a war lost on the battlefield, with U.S. casualties reaching 57,685 killed, over 153,000 wounded, and a nation still coming to grips with its lack of recognition and respect for those who served. The following letters reflect that episode in the American experience.

Bernard Edelman, ed. *Dear America: Letters Home from Vietnam.* New York: Pocket Books, 1985.

The Richard E. Marks letter is from *The Letters of PFC Richard E. Marks, USMC.* Copyright 1967 by Gloria D. Kramer, executrix of the Estate of Richard E. Marks. Reprinted by permission of HarperCollins Publishers, Inc.

Last Will & Testament
of PFC Richard E. Marks
December 12, 1965

Dear Mom,

I am writing this in the event that I am killed during my remaining tour of duty in Vietnam.

First of all I want to say that I am here as a result of my own desire—I was offered the chance to go to 2nd Marine Division when I was first assigned to the 4th Marines, but turned it down. I am here because I have always wanted to be a Marine and because I always wanted to see combat.

I don't like being over here, but I am doing a job that must be done—I am fighting an *inevitable* enemy that must be fought—now or later.

I am fighting to protect and maintain what I believe in and what I want to live in—a democratic society. If I am killed while carrying out this mission, I want no one to cry or mourn for me. I want people to hold their heads high and be proud of me for the job I did.

There are some details I want taken care of. First of all, any money that you receive as a result of my death I want distributed in the following fashion.

If you are single, I want you and Sue to split it down the middle. But if you are married and your husband can support you, I want Sue and Lennie to get 75% of the money, and I want you to keep only 25%—I feel Sue and Lennie will need the money a lot more.

I also want to be buried in my Marine Corps uniform with all the decorations, medals, and badges I rate. I also want Rabbi Hirschberg to officiate, and I want to be buried in the same cemetery as Dad and Gramps, but I do not want to be buried in the plot next to Dad that I bought in mind of you.

That is about all, except I hope I never have to use this letter—

I love you, Mom, and Sue, and Nan, and I want you all to carry on and be very happy, and above all be proud—

Love & much more love,
Rick

[Richard Marks was killed in action on February 14, 1966.]

Tuesday, Sept. 6, 1966

Dear Mom,

. . . You'll probably be hearing about us again. Yesterday my platoon had six injured and one killed. We had a fire fight that lasted nine hours.

A soldier in Vietnam.
(Courtesy, National Archives)

We killed a lot of VC on this operation we're on now, but we also have had a lot killed. . . .

Well, Mom, I don't have much time, and I just wanted you to know I'm all right.

When you go to church, I want you to give all the people you see this address and tell them to send anything they can, like old clothes and anything.

I went down to this orphanage the other day, and these little kids are pitiful. They sleep on plain floors and don't get hardly anything to eat.

The reason I want you to tell everyone to help them is because I feel I may have killed some of their parents and it makes me feel sick to know they have to go on with nothing. Address: Mang-Lang Orphanage, Le-Loi Street, Tuy Hoa, Vietnam.

Love, Your son,
Dan

[PFC Daniel Bailey served from May 1966 through June 1967. He returned to Clarington, Pennsylvania and received treatment for post-traumatic stress disorder.]

October 20, 1966

Dear Aunt Fannie,

This morning, my platoon and I were finishing up a three-day patrol. Struggling over steep hills covered with hedgerows [*sic*], trees, and generally impenetrable jungle, one of my men turned to me and pointed a hand, filled with cuts and scratches, at a rather distinguished-looking plant with soft red flowers waving gaily in the downpour (which had been going on ever since the patrol began) and said, "This is the first plant I have seen today which didn't have thorns on it." I immediately thought of you.

The plant, and the hill upon which it grew, was also representative of Vietnam. It is a country of thorns and cuts, of guns and marauding, of little hope and of great failure. Yet in the midst of it all, a beautiful thought, gesture, and even person can arise among it waving bravely at the death that pours down upon it. Some day this hill will be burned by napalm, and the red flower will crackle up and die among the thorns. . . .

The flower will always live in the memory of a tired, wet Marine, and has thus achieved a sort of immortality. . . .

Love,
Sandy

[Twenty-four-year-old Marion Lee Kempner, 2Lt. from Galvaston, Texas was killed by a mine explosion on November 11, 1966.]

[April 1967]

Dear Ma,

How are things back in the World? I hope all is well! Things are pretty much the same. Vietnam has my feelings on a seesaw.

This country is so beautiful, when the sun is shining on the mountains, farmers in their rice paddies, with their water buffalo, palm trees, monkeys, birds and even the strange insects. For a fleeting moment I wasn't in a war zone at all, just on vacation, but still missing you and the family.

There are a few kids who hang around, some with no parents. I feel so sorry for them. I do things to make them laugh. And they call me "dinky dow" (crazy). But it makes me feel good. I hope that's one reason why we're here, to secure a future for them. It seems to be the only justification I can think of for the things that I have done!

Love to all.

Your son,
George

[George Williams served in the Infantry from February 1967 to February 1968; he became a firefighter in Brooklyn, New York.]

24 May 67
Di An

Dear Mom & Dad,

. . . It sure is going to be different being around clean things again. I hope I can take it. It's going to take a while to get used to stateside living. Guess I have to watch my manners.

You know, when you get over here all you think about is getting back to the World. But when your time gets near, it sort of scares you because you know in your heart that you're not like the people back home. There are a lot of mixed emotions—worrying about hurting the people close to you, or maybe your dreams about the States will shatter when you get home. And then there's always the way you regret leaving your buddies in this hell hole. We all joke about "Put your time in," but in our hearts we wish we could all go home together. . . .

All my love,
Butch

[Sgt. John Hagmann served in Vietnam from February to October 1965 and July 1966 to July 1967. He returned to Ballson Lake, New York, where he worked for the telephone company.]

Jan 31, 1968

Chris:

I guess letters are going to be a long time writing over here . . . there is so much going on.

Yesterday afternoon we were given an emergency mission to move about 10 miles to a new position. We got there about 6:30 and deployed the men. About midnight all hell broke loose. We were sitting right in the middle of the boondocks [*when*] rockets, flares, machine guns, and planes started shooting. The VC got Bien Hoa airport and Long Binh province about 24 hours after I got out! Chris, someone said a prayer for me. . . .

We just had a Vietnamese man come into our position with a terrible cut on his leg. "Doc" took a look at it and said that "gang green" had set in. We called in a helicopter and had him lifted to a hospital. One minute we're killing them, the next we're saving their lives.

I miss you.

Love,
Alan

[1Lt. Alan Bourne served from January 1968 to January 1969 and during the Tet Offensive. He worked in real estate in New York City upon his return. This letter was written to his girl-friend.]

13 March [*1968*]

Hi Vern,

The shit has been hitting the fan, but I've managed to miss the spray.

One guy was shooting at my ambush last night. I reported it as heavy contact and got eight barrels of artillery to shoot white phosphorous and high explosives in the wood line. We found a body this morning so the colonel was happy.

A company ambushed my platoon, and I only lost one man. A rocket ricocheted off my truck, and the VC charged it. Your prayers must have been talking up a storm to God then. No kidding. I believe!

You'd be surprised how similar killing is to hunting. I know I'm after souls, but I get all excited when I see a VC, just like when I see a deer. I go ape firing at him. It isn't that I'm so crazy. I think a man who freezes killing a man would freeze killing a deer. I'm not perverted, crazy, or anything else. Civilians think such thinking is crazy, but it's no big deal. He runs, you fire. You hunt so I think you'd feel the same way. It isn't all that horrifying.

. . . Of course, revenge has a part in wanting him, just like you want a deer for a trophy and meat. I know I'm not nuts. If I killed a man in the U.S. everyone would stare. Last night I killed and everyone has been patting me on the back, including the battalion commander. What do you think?

A friend got killed on an ambush last week. [*The colonel*] told him to move in the middle of the night. As he drew in all his claymores [*mines*], Charlie hit. Last night they told me to move twice. It'll be a cold day in hell when I move. Thirty minutes later I reported "Moved." The colonel isn't about to come out to see where I am. I'm chicken but not stupid!

It isn't all that horrifying. It's rough living in the field, but big deal. They sell mohair tailored sports coats for $35 here and sharkskin suits for $60. I'll buy a few before I leave. What a deal! . . .

Hi Vern,

Got your letters today. It was great hearing from you. Actually, I can't summarize my feelings of my trip to Australia [for R&R]. . . . Getting back to a completely English-looking and -speaking country made me feel kind of ashamed of the way I've thought and acted over here. I realize that I've actually enjoyed some of the things I've done which would be repulsive to a healthy mind. This place does make you sick in the head. When one starts to enjoy the sickness of war, he is sick. . . .

Your brother,
Jim

[1Lt. Jim Simmen served in the Infantry from January to December 1968, and returned to work as a carpenter in Alaska. These letters were written to his brother, a pastor in Martinez, California.]

31 Aug '69

Dear Red,

Last Monday I went on my first hunter-killer operation. . . .

The frightening thing about it all is that it is so very easy to kill in war. There's no remorse, no theatrical "washing of the hands" to get rid of nonexistent blood, not even any regrets. When it happens, you are more afraid [than] you've ever been in your life—my hands shook so much I had trouble reloading and it took visible effort to perform each motion and control what would normally be called panic but which, somehow, isn't. You're scared, really scared, and there's no thinking about it. You kill because that little SOB is doing his best to kill you and you desperately want to live, to go home, to get drunk or walk down the street on a date again. And suddenly the grenades aren't going off any more, the weapons stop and, unbelievably fast it seems, it's all over and you're alive because someone else is either dead or so anxious to stay alive that he's run away and you are the victor—if there is such a thing in war. You don't think about it.

I have truly come to envy the honest pacifist who honestly believes that no killing is permissible and can, with a clear conscience, stay home and not take part in these conflicts. I wish I could do the same, but I can't see letting another take my place and my risks over here, and the pacifist ideal cannot drive one burning objection to it from my mind: the fact that the only reason pacifists such as the Amish can even live in an orderly society is because someone—be they police or soldiers—is taking risks to keep the wolves away. To be a sheep in a world of sheep is one thing; to be a sheep in a world of predators is something else, and if someone hides behind the label of sheep due to cowardice while another has to take his place, holding the predators at bay . . . somehow I just can't see it, or do it. . . . I guess that's why I'm over here, why I fought so hard to come here, and why, even though I'm scared most of the time, I'm content to be here. At least I'm doing my part according to what I believe. The only thing keeping the wolves from the flock are the hounds. But I tell you that, allegorically speaking, it is a hard and scary task to be a wolfhound. . . .

George

[Sp/4 George Olsen served in the Infantry from August 1969 to March 3, 1970 when he was killed in action. This letter was written to his girlfriend.]

29 December 1969

Hi all,

. . . I don't know where to start except to say I'm tired. It seems that's all I ever say anymore. Thank you both for your tapes and all the little goodies in the Christmas packages. Christmas came and went, marked only by tragedy. I've been working nights for a couple of weeks and have been spending a great deal of time in post-op. They've been unbelievably busy. I got wrapped up in several patients, one of whom I scrubbed on when we repaired an artery in his leg. It eventually clotted, and we did another procedure on him to clear out the artery—all this to save his leg. Well, in my free time I had been working in post-op and took care of him. I came in for duty Christmas Eve and was handed an OR slip—above-knee amputation. He had developed gas gangrene. The sad thing was that the artery was pumping away beautifully. Merry Christmas, kid, we have to cut your leg off to save your life. We also had three other GIs die that night. Kids, every one. The war disgusts me. I hate it! I'm beginning to feel like it's all a mistake.

Christmas morning I got off duty and opened all my packages alone. I missed you all so much, I cried myself to sleep. I'm starting to cry again. It's ridiculous. I seem to be crying all the time lately. I hate this place. This is now the seventh month of death, destruction and misery. I'm tired of going to sleep listening to outgoing and incoming rockets, mortars, and artillery. I'm sick of facing, every day, a new bunch of children ripped to pieces. They're just kids—eighteen, nineteen years old! It stinks! Whole lives ahead of them—cut off. I'm sick to death of it. I've got to get out of here. . . .

Peace,
Lynda

[Lynda Van Devanter served as an Army nurse from June 1969 until June 1970. She returned to teach in Washington, D.C. and wrote Home Before Morning *about her experiences in Vietnam.]*

Questions for Discussion

1. What do the letters tell you about the attitudes and experiences of those who served and those on the home front?
2. How might you compare and contrast these letters with the diaries and letters of Americans who fought in previous wars? In what ways were their attitudes and experiences the same or different?

31.
Johanna Von Gottfried
Diary from the California Farm Workers Movement, 1973

During the 1960s and 1970s, César Chávez, founder of the United Farm Workers Union, and his followers drew attention to the farmworkers' struggle for better conditions by leading huelgas *or strikes against the growers. In August 1973, ninety-nine women were arrested outside Parlier, California, for picketing in support of striking union members, an activity forbidden by a local court order. The picketers were joined by Chávez, folksinger Joan Baez, and cofounder of the Catholic Worker Movement Dorothy Day, together with a large delegation of Roman Catholic sisters and priests. The following diary was kept by a woman who admits that she had just "come to march," but found herself becoming involved and standing in moral solidarity with the farmworkers. The excerpts describe the picketers' arrest and incarceration at the Fresno County Industrial Farm.*

August 2, 1973 We arrived at Parlier Park a little before dawn. The crowd was fairly quiet, gathering slowly. . . . As the sun rose, the east end of the park filled with sisters, Jesuits, strikers and *las mujeres*, wives and sisters of strikers, many of them pickers themselves. . . . The "visitors" were all asked to introduce themselves and state their religious orders, their home states. There were Sisters of the Holy Child from

Johanna Von Gottfried. "Diary from the Fresno County Farm," *America* (October 13, 1973): 262–66.

César Chávez, speaking at
a farm workers rally.
*(Courtesy, National
Archives)*

Rosemont College, Pennsylvania, Maryknollers from a Stockton parish,
a Sister of St. Joseph of Kansas working for UFWV in a nursing capacity
at the Sanger Clinic outside Fresno. . . . To my dismay, almost everyone
was signing the list of people who, if it came to that, would stay on the
picket line unless ordered to prison by law officers. I had come to march,
not to get arrested.

After prayer and singing, there was a sudden movement toward
the street: César Chávez had arrived. An island of calm in the middle
of a rush of loving faces, he spoke earnestly, stressing the peaceful aim
of the picketing; *la paz* was the most frequent recognizable word to
English-speaking hearers. . . .

It took a while to get to Song's orchards where strike-breaking
workers were picking nectarines. The police were lined up, arms folded,
casual; lusty cries of *Viva la Huelga!* and *Si! se puede!* rang out. The scabs
were fairly far back in the field; growers, growers' sons and cops lined
the road. Many of those marching cupped their hands over their mouths
and called to those back among the trees, pleading with them to come
out. Most just chanted *Huelga!*

A Maryknoll priest explained to me why the 75 dollars a week which the AFL-CIO contribution to the union had made possible to striking members was not enough. The workers in the fields and orchards were making three times that much while the pick was on; later, there would be no work at all for anyone.

We had been marching for twenty minutes to half an hour when the county buses started to cordon off the area, a sign to all those who did not wish to be arrested to leave. Evidently there was an order to disperse given; everyone started to move the cars out of the area. I felt just awful standing on the "other side," watching strikers and supporters pile into those buses in orderly lines. I knew that there were many people longing to go to jail but unable to do so because of responsibilities—housewives with children, organizers on the outside with paper work and more picket lines to organize. . . .

I knew in my cowardly soul that I was relatively free of responsibilities—that I didn't belong among the wistful watchers. . . . And so I ran back to the buses—just in time, really. I who had never marched in a peace march or attended a rally more political than a football team's, I who had never placed so much as a sticker anywhere.

August 3, 1973   Everyone was taken to the Fresno County Industrial Farm, but not everyone was incarcerated here. After the booking procedure, most of the men were taken to the County Jail and the overflow to the County Fairgrounds. . . . The information-gathering in the booking process was fairly thorough. . . . I was told that if I had been arrested on a felony charge, "mug" shots of my face and prints of all my fingers would have been taken. It all seemed very unreal. Here was someone talking about the different levels of criminal charges, and I had just taken part in the most peaceable of assemblies.

Down here on the farm they are treating us very well. We are offered three meals a day and the use of an exercise yard. Inspection, after the first "frisk," has not been too insulting. We have been put in semi-air-conditioned barracks and given clean linen. . . .

August 3, Late Evening   . . . Dorothy [*Day*] came to California specifically to go to jail with *las huelgistas*. Sitting in her straw hat on the tripod folding stool, with the New Testament in Spanish on her lap and Sister Felicia holding the UFWU flag over her, she had formed a quiet center of our marching line in front of Song's nectarine orchards. She was here to declare her solidarity with the strikers, to go to jail with them and, as the representative of the Catholic Worker Movement to be a historical link with the nonviolent Christian labor effort in this country. . . .

August 4   Yesterday we were taken into Fresno to be arraigned. The county bus broke down, and there was some mad skirmishing to find us a means of transportation (we had to be arraigned within twenty-four hours). I don't think they made the deadline. . . . In the end, they got a Fresno city bus to come out and get us. The driver informed us that the local bus-driver union, which has 60 members, had noted to contribute $200 to the UFWU.

At the county courthouse, we were divided into groups of ten. . . . I found the number of sheriffs present very amusing. Perhaps I am an unconscious victim of a TV stereotype, the cowboy sheriff who passes on his star when he quits. I sort of thought there was only one per town. They were lining the walls and embarrassed by the sisters. They spoke politely and blushed. . . .

August 5 Last night Maria Hernandez had to be taken to the county hospital. She was having coronary trouble, caused mainly by her worries about her children. She knows who is taking care of them, but not where. She does not speak English, nor does she seem to have any close friends in this group. It seems that she has been trying to get in touch with her children by phone, without success. In fact, she wasn't allowed to make her phone call during the proper hours, so Sr. Felicia stepped in and got the guards to let her get in touch with her brother. . . .

We have two nurses among us who found her short breathing and the pain in her chest alarming. . . . Several sisters were pleading with the office voice to contact a union doctor . . . so that there would be someone who would care nearby, someone who could make sure, for instance, that she would not be taken to the county jail if she improved. By now we had heard about the awful conditions of the Fresno County Jail, its locker-sized, airless solitary confinement cells, its windowless tanks. . . . These women are under a strain more personal than might be imagined. . . . They all know some horrible experience of injustice, their own or a relative's. They are also very anxious for their children. One has a five-year-old in surgery; many have eleven or twelve-year-olds taking care of the house and younger children. Some have husbands in the county jail, and are relying on other relatives to see to the children.

Yesterday night the union legal aids came. We were asked to vote for two witnesses as representatives who would testify to our good character. We then chose Emma Hernandez our 20-year-old bilingual "captain," who has been in jail four times for picketing in spite of the injunction, and Terry Salazar, who looks like a carefree teenager but, at nineteen, has two children and has also been in jail before. The other women's barracks will probably pick a sister or two, since there are more sisters on that side. (There are 14 sisters among 45 women here.) . . .

It is impossible to eat and watch these nuns fast. More people join them every day. They do daily yoga and eat protein pills when available. They also drink horrid grape Kool-Aid and awful coffee in the mess hall.

Today I joined them but, like St. Paul's hypocrite, I get cross when I fast. I'll probably quit tomorrow. There was roast beef for dinner tonight, wouldn't you know!

August 7 Besides the sketches of one another that hang on our walls, our barracks are decorated with telegrams of enthusiastic support and mobiles of paper flowers. . . . The vigil last night was for a dismissal of the injunction, which has been modified to allow five pickets every 100 feet. "No feet," demands Maria solemnly. . . .

The new policy is not to arrest anyone. The county can't jail everyone here, it seems; also, the more people the county incarcerates under bad conditions, the greater the scandal. . . .

August 8 . . . This afternoon Joan Baez came and sang to us, and Daniel Ellsberg[1] expressed his solidarity with "the victims of violations of the same Amendment" that had been violated by his persecutors. Joan described our place of incarceration as a "summer camp," which was descriptively accurate. She sang De Colores, the beautiful cursillo movement song, and announced that she will sing it on the next record she cuts. Several small growers and their wives have come to speak with Dorothy Day about their predicament. Like the field workers, they have labored all their lives, but unlike those they employ for such meager wages, they have had no joy. . . . Some of them have wept before her because they see their security, their hold on the land, slipping away. Ownership as a source of happiness is not something Dorothy encourages. Even so, do these people realize that the threat to their security is from above rather than from below, from the large grower whose hiring policies they are pressured into following and who, sooner or later, will take over their land?

Emma Hernandez was asked to make a statement to the FBI telling of her mistreatment during her last arrest on July 20. Because they are "captains," picket leaders whom the older women obey, she and her sister Gloria had been asked to come out of their barracks to make phone calls and were instead handcuffed, insulted, shoved around and taken to the county jail. The effect of the presence of the religious on our keepers has been incalculable; the incidents are few, the products more of the bigotry of a few individual guards than a general policy set by those who run this Farm.

---

[1] In 1971, Daniel Ellsberg released to the press the classified Pentagon Papers, documents which seemed to question U.S. policies in Southeast Asia as well as the government's role in representing itself to the American people. The administration attempted to stop publication of the papers, but was overruled by the Supreme Court, which cited the first Amendment.

August 9 After a long day we have finally heard our fate over the evening news. The judge has not granted us "release on our own recognizance."

August 11 Despite the vicious flies and mosquitoes, we are fairly comfortable physically. . . . Today, after hearing vague talk about writs of *habeas corpus*, we heard that Superior Court Judge Peckinpah has waived the denial of O.R. [*on Own Recognizance*]. . . . We hope to trickle out of here this weekend. . . .

August 12 There are *huelga* flags passing around like autograph books at graduation. . . . When the news comes on we howl at the little lies, the report of murder on the picket line and the high tension in Delano. Watergate gets very little attention around here.

August 14 . . . I was in the last group of women freed, at 2:00 A.M. this morning, and all day we have been waiting for the men in the county jail to be freed. . . . I recall . . . Mickey, the girl with the baby afraid of his shadow, saying: "I keep wondering what comes after this. We are all so nervous in here, it's so long—but afterwards, will we be happier?" . . .

Questions for Discussion

1. Compare the treatment of these women in the County Farm to that of the IWW workers in Part 2 (p. 53). To what extent do you think that the Catholic sisters' presence may have affected the treatment of the picketers? What techniques of nonviolent protest were used by the sisters? In your opinion, are such techniques effective?
2. Why do you think the diarist felt a responsibility to be arrested?
3. What do you know about conditions for migrant farmworkers or pickers today? What are the issues debated between growers and workers?

32.
Elizabeth Drew
A Watergate Diary, 1973

Elizabeth Drew was the Atlantic's *Washington correspondent when, on June 17, 1972, the offices of the Democratic National Committee at the Watergate complex in Washington, D.C. were burglarized, an incident foiled by a security guard. The investigation uncovered wiretapping and a complex network of espionage and cover-up that implicated White House officials, including the President's Counsel, John Dean; Chief of Staff, H. R. Haldeman; Special Assistant on Domestic Affairs, John Ehrlichman; Attorney General, John Mitchell, and President Richard Nixon. The political upheaval scandalized the nation and led, on August 9, 1974, to the first resignation of a U.S. President. One month later, President Gerald Ford pardoned Nixon, giving him immunity from federal prosecution.*

The following excerpts from Drew's diary record the events in 1973 as they came to the public's attention.

May 1. . . . The Watergate story feeds on itself. The news and the events it is about are often part of the same process in Washington—the news is an event, affecting the next event, which is then in the news—but never, in memory, to this degree. Skills at reading between the lines of the newspapers to determine who is leaking, and doing, what to whom are put to the test as never before. Some stories are both leaked and denied by the same person, or his allies.

Elizabeth Drew. "A Watergate Diary: Notes of a Washington Correspondent During the Month of May, 1973." *Atlantic Monthly* 232 (1973): 60–70.

Following the President's speech last night, there is a pause now, a sort of collective catching of breath, to assess the situation. We have developed a habit of looking toward presidential speeches to define situations. Even when the definitions the President offers are very controversial, they let us know where things stand. But this one is elusive.

May 2. . . . Through all of the details there is a stark simplicity. It comes down to two themes that have been shadows on Richard Nixon's political career: aggression against the opposition, and money. . . .

/////

May 5. . . . Every once in a while, there is a shift in the way that the Watergate affair is perceived. Its proportions seem larger, and so do its implications. Suddenly, now there are conversations about the procedures for impeachment, and resignation. There is no precise reason for this shift; the atmospherics of Washington often defy rational explanation. But there is a sense that more is coming, and that no one knows where it will end. The concepts of "impeachment" or "resignation" suggest a resolution, a definition of what has happened. We seem to find it hard to live without definitions or resolutions.

/////

May 7. . . . The way the networks handle it shows how much things have changed. At first, White House denials about the Watergate affair—a "third-rate burglary"—were taken pretty much at face value. When the President said last August that an investigation by John Dean had shown that "no one in the White House staff, no one in the Administration presently employed was involved in this very bizarre incident," some time elapsed before questions were asked about the qualifying phrase, "presently employed." . . .

Some asked "Who did it?" as if we were still talking about a "third-rate burglary." We had no language to define precisely, and in fact we could not yet be sure, what "it" was. Some of the possibilities still sounded too dramatic, disturbing, hard to assimilate. A secret police force run out of the White House? The fixing of one party's nominating process by the other? Grand-scale selling of government decisions in exchange for campaign contributions? There was also, in talking about "it," the problem of drawing lines. Spying on the other party, trying to influence its primaries, arranging and gathering benefits for contributors, wiretapping and gathering information on journalists and other troublemakers—all were known to have gone on before. Where were the lines between the disagreeable and the unacceptable? Should we have drawn them sooner?

/////

May 10. The Washington *Post* reports that Frank Wills, the guard who discovered the break-in at the Watergate, has hired a lawyer and is charging "honorariums" for interviews. A record company has agreed to pay Wills $300 to put his picture on an album cover.

Why shouldn't Wills profit from this? Others will—especially the lawyers. Even the lawyers are getting lawyers.

John Mitchell, the former Attorney General, and Maurice Stans, the former Secretary of Commerce and Nixon fund-raiser, are indicted, along with financier Robert Vesco, for conspiracy to defraud the U.S. government and obstruction of justice. This may be just the first in a series of indictments for Mitchell. We had heard it was coming, but still there is shock, perhaps a healthy sign; we are not yet numb. . . .

. . . Through Haldeman and Ehrlichman the President had built a government within a government, and now that has collapsed. . . .

May 11. The question is being raised as to whether the President "can govern." It is being asked by many of the same people who were concerned, at the beginning of the year, that he was governing excessively. We are hooked, it seems, on the presidency. That wasn't the way it was supposed to work.

It is becoming fashionable to say that Congress is reasserting its powers. But its recent votes against the President have been less exercises in courage than instinctive reactions to his weakened position. The long-range effectiveness of the Congress is still in question. . . .

/////

May 13. The official confirmation that the telephones of reporters and White House aides have been tapped is more disturbing than might have been expected. For years, it had been assumed that reporters' and officials' wires were tapped, but the facts on this were never clear . . . the transfer from fantasy to reality is difficult. Abstract invasions of privacy are easier to live with than real ones. . . .

/////

May 16. Watergate is causing serious problems in the preparation of the next edition of the Green Book, Washington's social register.

At dinner, someone says that Washington needs a baseball team to take its mind off Watergate.

May 17. A lovely spring morning, exactly eleven months after the break-in at the Watergate. . . .

The Ervin hearings do not displace concurrent events concerning Watergate. "The Watergate bugging and the break-in into the office of Daniel Ellsberg's psychiatrist," Bernstein and Woodward write in this morning's *Post*, "were part of an elaborate, continuous campaign of illegal and quasi-legal undercover operations conducted by the Nixon administration since 1969, according to highly placed sources.". . .

May 18. James McCord, today's star witness, does not disappoint the audience. . . . Even the reporters are aping, as they struggle to take down McCord's words. . . . The press has a weakness for whistle-blowers. . . .

The politicians are nervous now that the spreading flood of Watergate will wash up over all of them. The taint of money in politics threatens the entire profession. The politicians fear a wave of anti-politics. Many Republicans are particularly eager to dissociate themselves from Watergate. . . .

May 20. No facts have yet linked the President with either Watergate or the cover-up, but it seems that a kind of web, not at all made of tightly knit evidence, is closing around the President. Therefore, it is a matter of whether one believes that he knew or that his highest aides spun a fantastic conspiracy, and it is as yet unanswered. Perhaps it never will be. The question floats above the facts. The facts are down there around calls from telephone booths, and missing files. A lot of people are waiting for some fact, or piece of testimony, that will topple the President. But that may never happen. It may end in ambiguity.

Will one of the people around the President, who have been turning on each other, turn on him? Do they have anything to turn on him with? Does it matter? . . .

Some people say that we mustn't lose perspective. Our politics, they argue, are still very honest compared to those of Latin America. This is an odd, and novel, standard.

/////

May 23. The President's astonishing 4000-word statement of explanation must have been issued in anticipation of further damage. (The Pentagon has a term for this sort of thing—"protective reaction.") . . . It is a fascinating document, worthy of lengthy study and exegesis. Now the President has confirmed that there were wiretaps; that an internal security plan—to include break-ins—had been drawn up by the White House but blocked by Hoover; that the White House had established its own "special investigations unit . . . to plug leaks of vital security information." He says that there may have been some covering up of Watergate by his aides, and that "unethical, as well as illegal activities"

August 9, 1974: President Nixon waves goodbye from the steps of the helicopter bound for Andrews Air Force Base and then to his estate in San Clemente, California. *(Courtesy, National Archives)*

took place in the campaign. The statement raises two important questions. One, to which we may never know the answer, is how much the President believes of what he says about the many threats to national security. The other, which will be answered in time, is how far he might seek to carry the "national security" issue.

The "national security" threat could be attached to all manner of real and imagined enemies. Candidates: bureaucrats who leak information and journalists who print it; doves; demonstrators. "Elitists"? The media? "Soft-headed judges"? If there is a witch-hunt, how many will go along?

May 24. . . . a number of practices which Watergate threw into focus have been accepted for a long time. It was not news that money buys access and government decisions; that there are enormous powers available to a chief executive who chooses to use them; that decisions that affect our fortunes and our freedom can be made in secrecy by people whom we cannot hold accountable.

/////

May 28. . . . Conversations now center on the question of who will be the Republican leaders to go to the President and tell him that he must resign. . . .

Questions for Discussion

1. What is the significance of the Watergate scandal?
2. How, if at all, has Watergate affected government or the people's perception of government?

33.
Nancy Austin

Nuclear Power and the Incident on Three Mile Island, 1979

In 1979, an accident occurred at the Three Mile Island nuclear power station near Harrisburg, Pennsylvania. It caused severe damage to the reactor's core and released radioactive gasses into the atmosphere, endangering the lives of thousands of people. While the accident was ultimately contained and official reports minimized the hazard, the people who lived nearby suffered psychologically during those fearful days of uncertainty. The following diary, written by a resident of the area, is a vivid and chilling record of the event and the concern it produced over the safety of nuclear energy.

Wednesday, March 28 Coming home from the grocery store I hear the news bulletin of a "minor" problem at reactor no. 2 on Three Mile Island. Having long felt uneasy with the concept of nuclear energy, I think, "Damn—here we go again!"

Thursday, March 29 Harrisburg made the news on all the major networks tonight, setting off a barrage of calls from relatives and friends. We quickly assure them that we are fine—and that there is no major problem.

Friday, March 30 Mid-morning we start hearing rumors about an evacuation. Whatever for? Four counties, did you say? Five miles? Ten miles? Twenty miles? Stay in all day with the windows shut? Don't run

Nancy Austin. "Diary of Three Mile Island Incident, 3/28/79–4/4/79." *Social Education* 43 (1979): 458–59. National Council for the Social Studies. Printed by permission.

fans? "Uncontrolled" bursts of radiation? What does it all mean—especially what does "uncontrolled" mean? What is fact—what is rumor—what is panic reaction? I have to run an errand on my lunch hour—so I go. People don't seem particularly frantic. As I drive I see women sweeping their sidewalks and working in their yards. The stores seem to have about the usual number of customers. Those reports that we heard about must have been exaggerated. I turn on the news. What is this about a hydrogen bubble in the reactor? I don't like the sound of that. For the first time I feel vaguely uneasy. I keep reminding myself not to be influenced by mob psychology and rumors, but to listen carefully and make up my own mind as to the seriousness of the situation. Back at work the atmosphere becomes increasingly calm as the afternoon routine takes over. I go to pick up the children after school. They have been kept inside all day because of those "uncontrolled" bursts of radiation. Gregg tells me that by the end of the day there were only five of 21 children left in his class. He says that all day long mothers were picking up their kids and going to Grandma's—in New York, Virginia, Florida—even California. Do they know something I don't? We are supposed to have guests for supper. I call them but, yes, they still want to come. . . . Supper brings with it a feeling of normalcy—guests, good food, and repartee. Only when we start to discuss the "what ifs" of a possible "meltdown" do we start to feel the tension. Bill and Dan go back to Bill's house to pick up some valuable papers "just in case." Two networks have special news programs on the problem and I begin to worry a bit—especially when Walter Cronkite closes his program with a reporter's view that this crisis will either pass safely and convince the general public that nuclear energy is safe and that the experts do indeed know how to handle crises, or . . . [*ellipses are diarist's*].

We go to bed and to an uneasy sleep with one ear cocked for sirens and dreams filled with hydrogen bubbles and traffic jams.

Saturday, March 31   The calls are still coming—and if there is any good thing about this whole series of events it is the love, concern, and caring that have poured out to us at this time. We have been offered homes in Philadelphia, Washington, D.C., and as far away as Arizona. . . . We make contingency plans for a "what if," and in case of an evacuation plan to meet in Washington, D.C. at the home of some good friends. My big concern is to keep all the children right here with me at all times in case we have to leave. . . . Dan returns by late afternoon and the fact that the situation seems to be about the same seems to give me a sense of security. We decide that things are probably not all that bad—and with that in mind we decide to go ahead with our previous plans to go to a dinner dance. . . . It is obvious that about one fourth to one third of the expected crowd is absent, however. Looking around, I spot the administrator of one of the major hospitals in the area at the party. Things must not be too bad, I reason, or he would be at the hospital. Reports must have been exaggerated.

Sunday, April 1   I am scheduled to work today, and do go. I am immediately told that there is a good chance of a "code green," which means to prepare patients to evacuate the hospital. . . . For the first time I feel a kind of knot in my stomach. Just what are we playing with? I understand that if the hydrogen bubble blows that even 100 miles away from here might not be enough. Ye Gods—what are they saying? Rumors? Truth? Are they exaggerating—or are they not telling the general public the truth because of the fear of panic? . . . I know one thing for sure—I want to get away from here—at least for a little while. After lunch we get into the car and drive to a lovely state park about an hour southwest of us. It is quiet, serene, a green refuge with a lovely clear stream. We take a walk on a nature trail and quiet seeps into my soul. I don't want to go back home, though. I want to eat dinner on the way home—to delay going home for awhile. Dan is worried about spending the money we do have in case we really need it, and I want the brief moments of respite offered by a relaxing meal. The meal is a disaster of tension. I am beginning to realize what this whole thing is doing to our entire family. We fill the car again "just in case." At home more morose news. I am sick of hearing the report that the situation is "stable." What the hell does that mean? I'm sick of the news but scared not to listen. The TV listings seem so prosaic and mundane against the drama being played out all around us. Many of our neighbors left today and more are leaving now. Many of our friends are gone. Are we making the right decision?

Monday, April 2   Governor Thornburgh says that it is business as usual for state workers. That is fine for him to say as he has the facts and we don't. We make sure that Dan has a car close at hand so he can get out separately—it's for sure in an evacuation, buses won't be running. Oh, who are we kidding? If that damn thing blows, none of us will get out. Let's face it, we are just gambling that it won't blow . . . the kids are driving me wild. I can't sit down for a second without them all over me with requests for "Mommy-love," a request from an earlier period of their lives. When they are not with me, they are fighting with each other. However, I am glad they closed the schools as I want them close beside me "just in case." The radio says that the bubble has been reduced in size. Praise the Lord. . . . Sick jokes are abounding. One disk jockey today dedicated a song to all those still in town and then played "I Will Survive." For supper we have sirloin steak with wine sauce and mushrooms with all the trimmings. After supper we go out for an ice cream treat—somehow we feel we deserve the special time after the mental anguish of the past few days. It is an eerie trip. There is a real "Hounds of the Baskerville" fog and the streets are by now nearly deserted. They estimate that 1/3 of the population has left. Is this a grade B movie? Is it real? It seems surrealistic. When we get home Dan and I talk, and I quietly shed a few tears—tears I needed to shed. We agonize together.

Tuesday, April 3   The news continues to be encouraging. The notorious bubble has all but disappeared. Schools will reopen tomorrow. Some of our friends who left the area have called to say that they are back. The banks and savings and loans are not being inundated with so many withdrawal requests today. The news does say that they have decided not to let any of the farmers within a five mile radius of the plant sell their cows for meat, and that traces of radioactive iodine are showing up in some of the milk. What about the apple and other fruit orchards and the vegetables grown in this fertile area? Will they be safe? Questions, questions, questions, questions. No answers—only questions.

Wednesday, April 4   At least a decent night's sleep. Still tired—but it is a more normal tiredness. The children are back in school, and the governor has declared that the "danger of an impending disaster" is over (nice of him to put it so clearly now that it is over). I only pray with all my being that it will be unnecessary for others to have to face a week like this past week ever again.

Questions for Discussion

1. What problems does this new technology—nuclear power—raise? What are Austin's reactions to the "incident"?
2. How would you compare and contrast this technology with that described by Martha Farnsworth and Hamlin Garland (p. 76) at the beginning of the twentieth century?

34.
Letitia Martinez Gonzales, Sylvia Martinez, Angela Gomez, Sergio Vega, Amparo Ramirez
Letters from Undocumented Immigrants, 1988–1990

That by the 1980s there were more immigrants from Mexico, Central America, and Asia than from Europe led some to proclaim that the United States was in the midst of another "new era" of immigration. Concerns of overcrowding and environmental stress were also considered "new" problems by many observers.

In many ways, however, the immigration picture of the 1980s and 1990s was a traditional one. Immigrants were driven by the same forces as always: economic need and, to a lesser extent, political persecution. The number of immigrants was also in line with past experience. One study in the late 1980s placed the number of immigrants, both documented and undocumented, at about 750,000 a year. This compared to about a million immigrants a year early in the century, when there was a smaller population base to absorb them. The number of undocumented immigrants, however, is hard to determine, and estimates vary widely. In 1995 the Immigration and Naturalization Service placed the number of undocumented immigrants in the country between 3.5 and 4 million.

Larry Siems. *Between the Lines: Letters Between Undocumented Mexican and Central American Immigrants and their Families and Friends.* Hopewell, N.J.: The Ecco Press, 1992.

The following letters are from undocumented immigrants in the Los Angeles area to family and friends in Mexico and Central America.

The Journey

[From Los Angeles, California to Oaxaca, Oaxaca, Mexico]

June 4, 1990

Argelia, Jaime, Nancy, Grandma,

What's up? How are you all? I hope all's well at the house because I'm feeling very sad here, since never in my life did I come to think that I'd have to go through so many, many things in order to be here. . . .

We arrived in Tijuana. The airport's ugly, we had the luck to pass through without them inspecting our bags or anything. On the way out we bought a ticket for the bus that would take us to the Alaska motel. When we arrived Gaby left me outside with the boy, Tijuana's horrible, it has nothing but pure slums at night. . . . When it struck 11 at night they directed us to a disguised diner, well in reality it was a cantina, from there we talked with the person who was going to take me across. [*The writer is referring to the person who would try to smuggle her across the border.*] But he told me to wait until the next day since everything was very rushed at that moment, from there we went back to the coffee shop and a dwarf arrived who told us to wait, but we didn't like his looks and so we went back to the hotel, passing all the while through the so-called "Zona Roja," everything is corrupt, and us making ourselves be brave, well there are many men in the street and women too, but you know which ones, don't you? We slept at the hotel and . . . the next day at 9 the man arrived, he took us and gave orders to his workers, we were waiting until 10 when the guys who would cross us over arrived, and they gave us orders that we all go out in pairs. I went with the dwarf, and Gaby with another guy who would cross with us. . . .

. . . We had to jump treetrunks, *aguas negras*, it was all very different from what I had seen, or what they had told me, Gaby says I was very brave, since she was going to die of nerves, well don't believe it. If I'm here it's because I believe in God and because in those moments I asked the Virgin of Guadalupe, Juguila and the Virgin of Solitude, and above all my son counted a lot to me. But now I'm here, with pains and scratches, bruises. . . . But I'm here. I arrived yesterday in the early morning at like 5 in the morning. Now by way of an anecdote, when we jumped into the gully the dwarf was grabbed by the migra [*the Border Patrol*], since when we fell he couldn't get up because of the shortness of his legs, and when we ran I would have liked to take him in my arms,

Undocumented immigrants being apprehended by Border Patrol. *(Courtesy, National Archives)*

well it drives you to despair that his little legs wouldn't give enough to run. Well though you won't believe this, I've never run so fast, now I laugh but in those moments I didn't feel my saliva, the blows, nothing, everything was worse than in the movies. I believe that we traveled like 7 to 10 kilometers, but in short I won't cross like this again. . . .

Kisses for my baby. Take care of him.

Warmly,

Lety [*Letitia Martinez Gonzales*]

The New Country

[From Los Angeles to Oaxaca, Oaxaca, Mexico]

March 1989

My very dear family,

I hope that on receiving this letter you find yourselves in good health and in God's good graces.

Mama, Lety and Nancy, I'll tell you all that things here are not as one imagines. . . .

. . . Ay, Mama, when you're imagining that things or people are in very good shape what a letdown you can have. Your brother has suffered very much and I believe that same suffering has made him very hard; you'll ask why these words, because I imagined that my uncle was in another position, that is to say materially. I thought he had at least for starters a beautiful house, a beautiful living-room, kitchen, bedroom, etc., there's none of that, your brother isn't working anymore in what his work was in billboards, because there's so much competition, or that is they're giving away his job I don't know if they are Egyptians or Chinese, Hindus, so his work was reduced, he has or had problems both of morale and illness. . . .

Mother, Lety, Nancy, I'm going to recount another point to you, although in these moments that I'm croaking out these letters I feel so sad, because reflecting on it I'm going to be sincere, one's worthless here without English, you'll ask why do you say that Sylvia, because even though the people who live with Gaby say that they suffered much more, they're given to saying that we were lucky to run into them because like me, in two days I already had work. That begins my big problem, even though I was accompanied by Tomi, both she and I feel so demoralized because if we hadn't asked for help I don't know what would have happened, I think that not being able to get in touch with our people and not having an orientation we would have failed because people here don't have an amiable expression because even though they speak Spanish, if they know English they communicate in that language, this is a very sad city here because, you see, the buses here don't even fill up halfway and it's pure blacks driving them and everyone speaks English, you can't even ask them anything, and even if they want to they don't understand us, not to communicate by telephone either because here you have to know how to use the phone because here in Los Angeles it's divided into three areas, 818, 714, 213, and if you want to communicate with 818, you should dial a 1 first because now it's long distance and vice versa. And so until I knew, that's why the phone didn't work for us for the places we wanted to communicate with, and even though we asked nobody understood us and I asked someone who spoke Spanish and it's not like Mexico where they give you the information, they make like they don't notice you and like you didn't say anything to them, and I asked another person how much the phone costs, he would have said a dime or a ten cents, none of that, nor do they offer you the dime like in Mexico nor a way to change the bill, another woman who saw us was observing us and she offered to change the bill, though somewhat suspicious I gave her a dollar, which they changed into 4 of 25 cents which they don't call by what they are here but by the name "coras" [*quarters*], Here in this city by what we've seen they aren't a united people; here the good gambler wins. . . .

. . . If you only knew, sincerely, what many people who have come to the United States have suffered, you'd be surprised the enormous things that have happened to them.

Warmly,
Sylvia Martinez

[From Los Angeles, California to Oaxaca, Oaxaca, Mexico]

July 2, 1989

My dear Mama,
. . . You ask me to do my bit from here until December, get this Mom, when I talked to you I had lost hope from not getting work and afterwards I got myself in as a seamstress without even knowing how to run a machine, and the first week I got 20 dollars, you'll say that just went for the bus alone without any extra, then the next week 50, but then they laid me off because production stopped and then I got in at another place where I again got 50 dollars a week, and even though I try hard to be quick I can't get more pieces out because for doing the hems they pay me from 5 to 8 cents, but rather than being in Gaby's house and not making anything I'm resigned to it for now, but it's making me despair because I have to pay 100 dollars in rent, food.

Warmly,
Sylvia Martinez

[From Fresno, California to Zapopan, Jalisco, Mexico]

March 5, 1988

Hello Mariana!
Receive this letter, wishing that it finds you very well. A little late, you know I'm a little lazy about writing, but here it is, one of the first letters I write.

Right now I'm studying English, it's a little hard to find work, but at least I'm not wasting time. I go to a school for adults where it's just about pure Chinese, Japanese and Iranians, almost pure Asian, in one of the groups I go to I'm the only Mexican woman, two other Mexicans go besides me, and like some 50 Chinese. . . .

There's a community radio station here in Fresno that's called Radio Bilingue, they give some courses for volunteers, they train you as an announcer, after the courses they give an exam and if you pass it they give you an announcer's credentials, all you have to do is program one day a week as a volunteer, you can program whatever you want (Canto Nuevo, etc.) I think I'm going to take these classes.

At the moment it's really boring here because it gets dark really early, and it's really dangerous to wander the streets, there are tons of crazies, a mountain of robberies, murders, rapes, and everything you can imagine, it's a really hostile environment, and more so for latinos. . . .

Greet me to those who remember me. Well, Mariana, I leave you now because I'm writing in the air.

Write.

I love you,
Angelita [*Angela Gomez*]

Family and Loved Ones

[From Los Angeles, California to Ciudad Netzahualcoyotl, Mexico City, Mexico]

October 30, 1988

Socorro,

I write these words in the hope that you find yourself well, together with my son and your folks; anyway, after the salutations I move on to the following, Butterball, if I haven't written it was because the truth is I wasn't working, and now blessed be God I don't work every day but there is some, I'm getting by. The first day when I arrived in Los Angeles I went to give thanks at the Church of the Mexicans, your brothers told me that as soon as there's work where they are they're going to take me on there, Coconut, I now acquired the card to be able to work and the social security one but it's crooked and it's dangerous to carry this card, but in whatever job they ask you for it, it cost me 50 dollars but I already paid them. Chubby take great care of yourself and don't think bad things, little darling. I'm sending you 100 dollars there, see what you can do with them, and I'm sending you photos of when I was in the church and where they give free meals, give my mom some 10 thousand pesos, tell her that if God wants it and all goes well for me I'll send her more, and say hello to her for me please, tell her that I'm well. Greetings to your mom and dad, to my Eri, tell him to behave himself well, if he doesn't I won't buy him what he asked for. My girl, now I'm going to start working with Mundo and every eight days God willing I'll send you money, with what's left over please go to the doctor and buy a couple smocks, the ones you liked. I'm going to work hard in order to go soon and to be together again, don't think that I'm forgetting you, I'm holding on though you don't believe me, I'm helping us out, and if you want to come tell me in some letter, and write me, I'm going to be writing to you every eight days, I don't say good-bye, only till soon, so writes one who doesn't forget you and loves you very much.

Sergio Vega

[From Los Angeles, California to Jurisdiccion Rosario La Paz, El Salvador]

[N.D.]

Rubidia,

Forgive me daughter, I didn't forget about you, you know, but it's that I didn't have money to send you anything, but I'll send you something any moment now.

How can you think I'm going to forget that moment, yes I remember all the time, and thanks for the cheese and chocolate and when you send me medicine, at any rate I'm grateful that you send me things. . . .

Ah Rubidia I don't say going to work is bad, but that I want you all to prepare yourselves so you don't suffer like me. Do you think it's beautiful to be like we are, me so far away and you all abandoned as though you were animals, because I didn't prepare myself, I didn't have the opportunity to prepare myself and nobody showed me the world farther away than what I was seeing every day, and on the other hand I tell you everything I've suffered, and that's why I want you to study, because a person with no preparation is worth nothing, she's like an animal or a plant.

Anyway I've already given you my reasons why I don't want you to stop studying and why I'm sick and in a little while you're going to be left so alone and the oldest ones are going to have to help the younger ones. That's why I don't want you wasting time, because I have little time and if you don't take advantage of it you're going to be left wishing.

Rubidia take care of everyone, for they're your children and they're going to serve you, and take care of my mama, and I'm sending you more money, don't you fail me, I trust you, because if you fail me your children will fail you.

Amparo [*Amparo Ramirez*]

Questions for Discussion

1. What is life like in the United States for these immigrants? What do they think about their experience?
2. How does the experience of these immigrants compare with that of the Jewish immigrants in the selections from "A Bintel Brief" (p. 60)?